Hub City
Nanaimo
1886–1920

Jan Peterson

Heritage
House

National Library of Canada Cataloguing in Publication Data

Peterson, Jan, 1937-
Hub City: Nanaimo, 1886–1920 / Jan Peterson.

Includes bibliographical references and index.
ISBN 1-894384-66-0

1. Nanaimo (B.C.)—History. I. Title.

FC3849.N35P472 2003   971.1'2   C2003-911145-8

First edition 2003

Heritage House acknowledges the financial support for our publishing program from the Government of Canada through the Book Publishing Industry Development Program (BPIDP), Canada Council for the Arts, and the British Columbia Arts Council.

Cover painting: *Harbour City*, acrylic, 24" x 36", 1984, by Paul Grignon.
Cover and book design by Darlene Nickull and Nancy St. Gelais
Edited by Terri Elderton and Ursula Vaira

HERITAGE HOUSE PUBLISHING COMPANY LTD.
Unit #108 – 17665 66A Ave., Surrey, BC V3S 2A7

Printed in Canada

BRITISH
COLUMBIA
ARTS COUNCIL
We acknowledge the support of the Province of British Columbia through the British Columbia Arts Council

The Canada Council | Le Conseil des Arts
for the Arts | du Canada

Contents

Acknowledgements

The resilience of the coal-mining community that was early Nanaimo continues to interest and amaze me. Mining tragedies, incidents at sea, explosions and fires, and deaths from the First World War and the Spanish influenza epidemic have all left an indelible mark on the community, yet despite these trials the community spirit has remained intact and strong.

Hub City: Nanaimo, 1886–1920 pieces together the stories that link the past with the present through early city council records, newspaper accounts, documents, letters, scrapbooks, and family-history files. The community is indeed fortunate to have all of these early documents available through the Nanaimo Community Archives. I gratefully acknowledge the continued assistance of the Nanaimo Community Archives Society manager, Christine Meutzner, and her assistants Dawn Arnot and Dorothy Young. I am indebted also to Christine and Daphne Paterson, who scrutinized this manuscript and offered suggestions for improvement. However, any mistakes are ultimately my own.

Thank you to librarian Gordon Miller at the Pacific Biological Station; Loraine Littlefield, First Nations Treaty Office research coordinator; and author and researcher Peggy Nicholls. Thanks also to the Archive volunteers, Anne Royle, Jill Stannard, Shirley Bateman, Ruth Tickley, Florence Williams, Natalie Catto, Barbara Cowling, Trudy Gilmour, and Marv Worden. The Nanaimo Historical Society, the Nanaimo District Museum, the Vancouver Island Military Museum, and the Vancouver Island Regional Library also gave valuable assistance.

Heritage House publishers Rodger and Pat Touchie have shown me what a class act they are. Darlene Nickull and Linda Martin reflect the same friendly and professional attitude of the company. Thanks also to Terri and Ursula, who helped turn the manuscript into a finished product. Through all my years of research, my husband Ray has been by my side, offering encouragement and support; without him this journey may not have been made. I thank him, and our children and their families, for their love.

Introduction

Hub City chronicles the history of Nanaimo from the arrival of the Esquimalt & Nanaimo Railway to the end of the First World War. Until the beginning of the twentieth century, Nanaimo had been a coal-mining community, but as transportation links by sea, rail, and road improved, the city became an important distribution centre for other developing parts of Vancouver Island and the Lower Mainland. The Vancouver Island Development League, the forerunner of the Chamber of Commerce, dubbed it "the Hub City," a name still used today.

The new face of the city was unmistakably multicultural. The Snuneymuxw were almost a forgotten people after they were removed to reservations. The Chinese established a Chinatown away from the white business district. The work force in the mines was no longer just British but now included Finns, Italians, Croatians, and others of different ethnic backgrounds. The Japanese joined the cultural mix when the herring fishery developed here.

Through the boom and bust of these years, businessmen and individuals represented the community on city council or as members of Parliament or members of the Legislative Assembly. The labour movement got its beginning here when James Hurst Hawthornthwaite and Parker Williams were elected. The First World War changed many families: It left some saddened, others victorious, and gave Nanaimo its first war hero, Raymond Collishaw. The number of deaths from mining accidents continued to accumulate, and added to these were those lost in the war and from the Spanish influenza epidemic. The city's war veterans were honoured when a British royal prince brought thanks from his grateful nation.

Nanaimo proved in the past it could move forward, putting tragedy behind. An exciting new era lay ahead, promising a bright and challenging future for another generation.

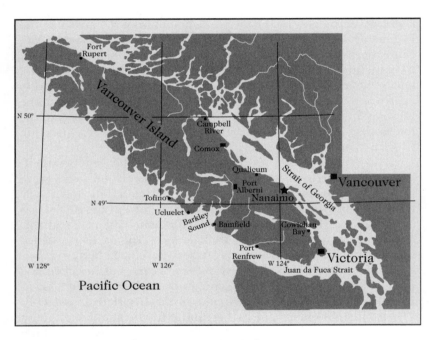

Directional map of Vancouver Island showing Nanaimo in relationship to Victoria and Vancouver.

CHAPTER ONE

Coal Industry—Tragedy, Renewal, and One Man's Legacy

*T*he Coal Industry of Vancouver Island brochure of 1898 predicted a bright future for the coal city.

> The coal city of Nanaimo has long been known as Black Diamond City and the Newcastle of the Pacific Coast and it aspires to be another Liverpool. As an industrial, commercial and distributing centre, Nanaimo yields to none, ...
> Of the established coal mining industries, the oldest now in operation is that of the New Vancouver Coal Mining and Land Company Limited, an English joint stock corporation, whose original charter dates from 1862. Its business has been conducted on so large a scale that during its existence of thirty-five years it is probable that the cash circulated by the company, for wages, services, machinery and supplies, will foot up to as many millions.[1]

In the beginning there was no rush by the Hudson's Bay Company to develop the coalfield at Nanaimo. But after the company's earlier exercise at Fort Rupert failed, Governor James Douglas wanted to prove that coal mining could be a success in Nanaimo. Coal was a valuable resource; there was a heightened demand for it as sailing vessels and industry turned to steam. The Hudson's Bay Company ended its trading-licence agreement with

Britain in 1859, and the Nanaimo enterprise was sold in 1862 to a British consortium: the Vancouver Coal Mining and Land Company, known locally as the Vancouver Coal Company. This company was underfinanced from the beginning, and it took many years before it could make improvements.

In 1884 a new superintendent arrived in Nanaimo to take over the Vancouver Coal Company operation. He would set the tone of development and labour relations for the next twenty years. Samuel Matthew Robins began "the immense works of construction and improvement that have lifted Nanaimo from the state of a small though happy and prosperous coal mining camp, into its present important and flourishing condition."[2]

Robins, who was born in 1834 in Cornwall, England, learned mining from his father. He was first appointed secretary of the company in 1868, but he remained in England until 1883 when he made a brief inspection visit to Nanaimo. He was impressed with the mines and, with his nephew F.W. Stead, returned the following year to take over management. Robins was determined to make the mines profitable. Mark Bate, who remained as his assistant, had worked for the coal interests since arriving in Nanaimo in 1857. As mayor since the city's incorporation in 1874, Bate had been involved in much of the city's growth during that time.

Meanwhile, Robert Dunsmuir had developed a mine almost at Nanaimo's back door. The Wellington Colliery became as large as the Vancouver Coal Mine operation. By 1886 Dunsmuir was a rich man, having built the Esquimalt & Nanaimo (E & N) Railway and received the first of his land grants that encompassed almost half of Vancouver Island. His younger son, Alex, managed the San Francisco sales office, while his older son, James, managed the Wellington Colliery.

In addition to the resources already owned by the Dunsmuir family through the E & N Land Grant, the company purchased more rights from the settlers who lived one mile south of the Vancouver Coal Company's Southfield Mine, close to the railway line.

By 1885 there were four companies mining coal in the Nanaimo region: The Vancouver Coal Company operated the Esplanade No. 1 Pit and the Southfield Mine; the Dunsmuirs had the Wellington Mine and No. 3, 4, 5, and 6 pits operating; R.D. Chandler of San Francisco owned and operated the East Wellington Colliery; and the E & N Railway Company owned and operated the Alexandra Colliery in the Cranberry District.

Mining Reports

Reports from the provincial minister of mines during the last part of the nineteenth century show growth in coal production at the expense of safety in the mines, resulting in an unprecedented loss of life. In 1884, the year Robins arrived, there were 31 fatalities from explosions on February 22 and June 30.

Provincial Inspector of Mines Edward G. Prior had said in 1878 that the Nanaimo mines had passed through a period of "unprecedented discouragements."[3] Prior had been mine inspector for only a year, but he knew the Nanaimo mines well from serving as assistant manager of the Vancouver Coal Company. Prices at San Francisco, the chief foreign market for the coal, had reached the lowest point ever; yet shipments continued to increase. There were three fatalities that year, two of them Chinese.

Another twelve men had lost their lives in 1879 in two separate accidents. On April 17, eleven men died in an explosion of firedamp in the Wellington Mine. Four were Chinese. Another Chinese miner, Ah Yung, died on July 8 in the same mine when a rock dislodged from the roof. That year there were also eighteen non-fatal accidents.

When Prior resigned in May 1880 to go into private business, Archibald Dick replaced him. Dick's mining reports document the years 1887 and 1888, which were especially tragic for Nanaimo and Wellington. He noted that the Vancouver Island Collieries had never been in better condition and that prospects looked good, but warned that competition from foreign suppliers was on the horizon. His mining reports continued to record the tons of coal produced each year, plus the deaths and injuries.

Esplanade Mine Explosion

Archibald Dick's report for 1887 is the most tragic of those available in the Nanaimo Community Archives:

> Everything about this mine (No. 1 Pit, Esplanade, owned by the Vancouver Coal Mining and Land Company, Limited) previous to the 3rd of May last, seemed to be in good order, no expense whatever being spared to make things safe. Ventilation was good, the motive power a large fan, as mentioned in my report, which fan, on 6th April last, was keeping in circulation 75,400 cubic feet of air per minute for the use of 142 men, or 530 cubic feet per minute for each person employed.

The main slope goes directly under the water of Nanaimo Harbour for about 1,100 yards; and the 'diagonal' slope branches off the main slope about fifty yards down from the head, and at an angle from the main slope of fifty-four degrees; this diagonal slope is down about 700 yards. Here the coal is from seven to fifteen feet thick. In this part of the mine a considerable quantity of gas was given off, but the ventilation was so good that there was no chance for it to collect; and at no time previous to the 3rd May did I see any gas there.

Sometimes I took a safety lamp (Clanny), and at other times I carried a naked light. I generally made my inspection when the mine was at work, so that I could see the general condition of the mine and hear if there were any complaints to be made. I went into the old works, as well as into the places where the miners were working. There were two shifts of men working in all the stalls, and in some of them three shifts worked, the one shift relieving the other. There was a fireman on each shift going through the workings and examining through all the places.

On 3rd May all the places had been examined by the firemen as usual, and everything appeared to be in good order. All the works went on apparently in safety, when a few minutes before six o'clock p.m., those on the surface were alarmed by a noise from both the hoisting and air shafts, accompanied by smoke and timber flying out of

Archibald and James Dick, Mine Inspector and Pioneer Miner

Archibald Dick was only eleven when he came with his family in 1850 from Kilmarnock, Ayrshire, Scotland, on the *Pekin*. His father, James Dick Sr., had signed on with the HBC to work at Fort Rupert and, like the other immigrant miners, was later transferred to Nanaimo. The family lived on Comox Road. Mark Bate described James as being "good natured, good humoured, and a jocular man. Inside his door he kept an Aneroid Barometer, which was not apparently a very sensitive instrument. There had been a wet day, and at night the barometer indicated Fair. Taking the aneroid outside, he hung it up, saying he 'would let it see it was raining.'"[1] Dick Junior could have used his father's good humour in his new job. History has recorded he was an irritant to the Dunsmuirs as he tried to enforce the Coal Mines Regulation Act.

both shafts. It was evident that a dreadful explosion had taken place in the mine. Shortly afterwards the No. 2 or air upcast shaft kept sending out smoke, which showed that the mine must be on fire. At the same time there were 154 men in the mine. The downcast was somewhat deranged, but the cage was got down as soon as possible, and when close to the landing it was seen that the cars, both loaded and empty, were piled up and twisted into every conceivable shape.

A party also went toward the bottom of the upcast shaft, where it was known there were some men working and about the engine-room. There, and on the other side of the shaft (where the foreman was found), seven persons in all were got out, who were all that were got out alive of the 154 that went down to work on the afternoon of the 3rd May. Everything was done to get in to the men that it was possible for men to do; and amongst the exploring party there was one man, Samuel Hudson, was overcome by afterdamp and died from its effects.

In the meantime the fire in the engine-room had got almost into the level, and this had to be mastered or no hope could be given for getting out any of the men alive, and nothing could have saved the mine but flooding it from the sea. Buckets with water kept the fire back until the fire engine from the city was got down, there being plenty of water close at hand. The engine was worked mostly by the seamen from the shipping in the harbour. The pumps were kept going for about two weeks before it could be said that the fire was extinguished. During all that time there were exploring parties in the mine looking for the lost, of whom none were got out alive excepting those already mentioned, and who were near to the bottom of the shaft; and there are still some bodies in the mine, viz: Jonathan Blundell, Robert Nicholson, George Biggs, Thomas Dawson, Thomas Hughes, and two Chinamen.

There had been a continuous search for the bodies up to the 27th July, when it was discovered that the debris in the workings of the diagonal slope was heating, and liable to burst out to an active fire at any minute. This part of the mine had to be filled with water, and that is how it stands at present, but the company intends soon to commence taking out the water. This operation will take a long time. Another engine has been erected at the head of the slope in place of that which was destroyed by the burning of the engine-room. The main slope is being cleared up, and it is expected to get into the face of No. 3 North Level in a week or two, when coal can be again taken out.

The No. 1 North Level has been put in order some months ago, and this is the only place from which the company have got out any coal since the explosion, and here there are only a few men working. Ventilation here is very good; there has been little or no gas seen in this division, and it is free from dust. After the public enquiry that has been made into the terrible accident of the 3rd May, conducted by Mr. Eberts for the Crown, at which enquiry the Vancouver Coal Company were represented by Mr. Drake, Q.C. Mr. James Young appeared for some of the widows and orphans. I do not think I can do better than refer you to the record of the inquisition filed in the office of the Hon. Attorney-General, in case you should desire to ascertain further details of the lamentable occurrence.

The Esplanade Mine explosion remains the worst mining accident in British Columbia's history. Nanaimo historian Lynne Bowen has written about the human tragedy of this and other mining accidents in her book *Three Dollar Dreams*. "On this day 150 men died, including one rescuer, Samuel Hudson, and 53 Chinese."[4] Victims ranged in age from 15 to 71, and they left 46 widows and 126 children without fathers. Only seven miners made it out alive. Nanaimo Mayor Richard Gibson was not at work that day, but was one of the many volunteers to go below to attempt to rescue the trapped miners. The bodies of the seven missing men were discovered twenty years later during a mining operation.

One of those men was George Biggs, son of John and Jane Biggs. He and the six others were believed buried under a fall of rock 40 feet deep. It was considered unwise to risk lives for a speedy recovery, so the area was sealed off.[5] Years later, George's nephew Herschel found the remains. The men's clothes fell apart when touched. Their bones were collected and buried. This was a tragic accident for the family, as George's sister, Louisa, who married Albert Meakin, also lost her brother-in-law Arthur, his father John Sr., and their brother-in-law William Hoy.[6]

Tuesday, May 3, 1887, began like any other working day. The mine was working two day shifts, and one shift went on duty at 2:00 p.m. Just before 6:00 p.m. a tremor shook Nanaimo, and a few minutes later black smoke poured from the No. 1 shaft.

Everyone in the city rushed to the pithead. It took an agonizing 24 hours to extinguish the flames near the main shaft so that it was possible to penetrate the mine. Over the next few days the community made preparations for the first of many funerals. Schools closed for two weeks. The Crace Street School was used as a temporary morgue. Most businesses closed and flags were lowered to half-staff. A special train with medical supplies and mining experts arrived from Victoria, and sailors from ships in the harbour offered assistance.

Each day an anxious and sometimes hysterical crowd surrounded the mine. The *Colonist* reported this scene:

> As each cage comes up, anxious hearts look for the glad tidings that never come. Women tear their hair in agony of their sorrow, and with babes to their bosoms continue to walk up and down mourning their loss. Many are determined that they should go into the cage to find their loved ones. The entrance to the main shaft is being fenced, to prevent a rush when the bodies are being brought up.[7]

Three days later, at 6:00 a.m., a group of prominent men entered the workings of the mine. Among them were John Bryden, Wellington Mine manager, Archibald Dick, inspector of mines, and Edward G. Prior, the former inspector of mines and now a member of Parliament for Victoria. The grim evidence of the disaster lay before them. The first man found was foreman Andrew Muir; behind him were 22 white men and 12 Chinese, all within yards of each other. Muir had obviously been guiding the men out. No one was burned; they had all died from afterdamp. Muir left his wife Mary and their six children.

Each day, more bodies were recovered. One young miner had written in white chalk on his shovel: "Thirteen hours after explosion, in deepest misery, John Stevens." Another counted down the hours by writing on the timbers. His final words were these: "William Bone, 5 o'clock."[8]

This was a tragic first day on the job at the Wellington Mines for a young doctor, Dr. Duncan William Ebert, who immediately placed his services at the disposal of the Vancouver Coal Company. Ebert, a graduate of McGill University, had been superintendent at Winnipeg General Hospital before being hired by the Dunsmuirs.[9]

A mass funeral was held at the cemetery. A fund that grew from donations across Canada and the United States administered relief money to the families; widows received twelve dollars per month, and allowances of four to six dollars were given for children up to the age of fourteen. The money lasted until the last widow died.[10] Some mothers took their fatherless children back to Britain. School classes were so small in St. Ann's Convent School that part of the school was converted into a hospital.[11]

There was no blame attached to the explosion, but miners lashed out at an easy target—the Chinese. Miners viewed the Chinese with suspicion and felt that working underground with them was dangerous. Petitions were signed in a public protest against Chinese working in the mines. There were 386 whites, 220 Chinese, and 2 Snuneymuxw working at the No. 1 Mine. Few families were untouched by the tragic event.

Dr. William Wymond Walkem opened the coroner's inquest on May 10, then adjourned it for two weeks to give time for experts to examine the mine. Most of the miners who testified said that the ventilation of the mine had been good. The jury blamed the explosion on the firing of an unprepared and badly planted charge that ignited accumulated gas fuelled by coal dust. The inquiry report commented that "in view of the fact of its being an acknowledged dry and dusty mine and that coal dust is a recognized factor in colliery explosions, we submit that necessary precautions have not been observed for minimizing the probabilities of a catastrophe." Nevertheless, "in rendering the above verdict we wish it to be distinctly understood that we do not wish to attribute any criminal negligence to anybody." The jury recommended that all firemen, or shotfirers, pass a qualifying examination.[12] Amendments were made to the Coal Mines Regulation Act a year after the explosion.

After the tragic event of May 3, city council did not meet for several weeks. The city clerk's letterbook is void of any business until May 30, when Sam Gough began sending letters of thanks to various city councils who had donated money to help the families of the dead miners. The letter was the same for each but the sentiments heartfelt. Gough wrote these words:

> The Mayor and Council desire me to express their hearty appreciation of the substantial sympathy that the Council of ... have so generously extended to the widows and orphans of those killed in the lamentable coal mine accident that occurred in the city on May 3, 1887, and they feel that your liberal donation will be gratefully accepted by those who through this melancholy catastrophe have been deprived of their support and protection.[13]

Wellington No. 5 Pit Explosion

The grief the community felt after the No. 1 Esplanade event can only be imagined. Numbness probably settled in, but emotions were abruptly re-awakened on January 24, 1888, when another explosion killed 77 miners. Archibald Dick's report noted that there were 82 fatalities that year. Once again he attached no blame: "I have not discovered that any blame or negligence could be attached to any one—all [the accidents] took place when men were at work."

This latest explosion happened in the newest and best-ventilated mine in the Wellington Colliery, the No. 5 pit, on Diver Lake. There were 46 Chinese and 31 white men working.

Again, people agitated against the Chinese. Management held a mass meeting with miners of the Wellington and Nanaimo mines. Samuel Robins and William McGregor presented a list of measures that could be taken to ensure safety in the mines. Someone suggested excluding the Chinese from the mines. More meetings followed, and it was finally decided that the Vancouver Coal Company and the Wellington Colliery would exclude all Chinese. Robert Chandler of the East Wellington mine reluctantly agreed to go along with the decision when his own miners refused to work until he fired his Chinese employees. Nanaimo mines were now gaining a reputation as being among the most dangerous in the world.

Dunsmuir Expands to Cumberland

Dunsmuir continued to develop his empire. The 1889 mining report noted the coal discovery near Comox Lake, "two miles from the flourishing Comox settlement." The coal operation, the No. 1 slope and the No. 1 shaft, came under the name Union Colliery Company. The company constructed eleven miles of standard-gauge railway from the mines near Cumberland to the terminus at Union Bay, where it built deep-sea wharves. Dunsmuir inaugurated regular passenger service between Union Bay and Cumberland. The report also noted that No. 1 Pit, Esplanade, now belonged to the New Vancouver Coal Mining and Land Company Limited (NVCML). There were four fatalities this year and 33 serious accidents.

The New Vancouver Coal Mining and Land Company

The Vancouver Coal Company changed its name in the mid-1880s, when the company's fortunes were in decline and money put aside for the equalization of dividends had disappeared. The company had to borrow to expand its operations and reduce costs. By November 1885 it was unable to repay some debentures when they fell due and had to renew them at 6 percent interest. Additional shares were sold at discount prices, well below par. The company got a wake-up call when a court ruled in a similar case that subscribers were liable for the difference between the amount they had agreed to pay and the par value of their shares. The Vancouver Coal Company took steps immediately to protect its shareholders from such a liability. On January 30, 1889, it reorganized itself with a capital of $215,000 and changed its name by adding "New" to its title, becoming the New Vancouver Coal Mining and Land Company. This corporate manoeuvre did not affect operations, but it did relieve shareholders of the possibility of finding themselves in trouble with creditors.

The new company faced the same problems as the old; the coal field was badly faulted and added greatly to the cost and uncertainty of mining. Still, Chairman John R. Galsworthy had faith in the operation. He remarked, "Vancouver [Vancouver Coal Company], with all thy faults, I love thee still."[14] There was less demand for coal, and now the company had to share markets with Robert Dunsmuir. The bulk of sales for both companies went to California. Reports about the quality of the coal have differed. Even though the coal won a silver medal at the Antwerp Exhibition in 1885, one company director said it was "rather dusty so what are called in America 'the helps' complain."

The presence of Chinese workers also presented problems. Director John Wild complained that he was "one of the first to introduce Chinese labour on Vancouver Island and instead of 20 or 30 men, there are now swarms of them, and they look to the company to protect them, because the whites are determined to put them down. But the 'heathen Chinese' was sharp in other things beside[s] the celebrated game of cards, and he was playing tricks with the company. They were being paid at a rate of over $1 per day."[15] In 1889, B.C. passed legislation that had the effect of preventing coal-mining operations from employing Chinese underground.

Protection Island Mine

The Vancouver Coal Company expanded about two miles under the harbour from the No. 1 shaft to the south side of Protection Island, and built a new wharf about 400 feet from the shaft. Contracts for

Protection Island Mine in full production.

sinking the shaft were let in the spring of 1891 and finished the following January. The first ship to load coal from the Protection Island wharf was the *General Fairchild* on March 9, 1893.

The number of fatalities continued to be of concern. There were fifteen fatalities and 71 serious injuries during 1891. Half of the accidents resulted from falling rock and coal. According to Dick, this showed "a reckless and venturesome disregard of propping of the roof and spragging of the coal."

The mining report of 1892 and 1893 bragged that the Protection Island shaft was the deepest in the district: "On all the shifts there are nearly 400 men and about 40 miles, besides steam engines, pumps and three electric locomotives, all in motion and much of these works lighted by electricity." The slope went east under Nanaimo Harbour. From the north level was another slope driven in a northeasterly direction under Northumberland Channel, which separates Gabriola Island from Protection Island. Here the water was two miles wide. Dick speculated that by the time the mine reached under Gabriola Island, it would be 2,000 feet below the surface. The Vancouver Coal Company owned land at the north end of the island.

Northfield and Southfield Mines

The Vancouver Coal Company developed another mine at Northfield, close to Wellington; it also owned the Southfield Mine, on the other side of the estate. The coal at Northfield was of very good quality and was very hard. It commanded the highest price

19

Vancouver Coal Mining and Land Company, later Western Fuel Company No. 1 Mine.

in Victoria and California for household coal, but it was expensive to produce. A new mining town developed close to the mine, with the usual number of stores and saloons. The town was often called Belgian Town because of its large population of European immigrants. An estimated 900 people lived in Northfield in 1893.

New Market Competition

By 1892 B.C.'s coal market had competition from other places. An oversupply of "cheaply produced" coal "from countries recklessly competing with the collieries of the Pacific Coast"[16] resulted in restricted output and lowering of exports. Australian and British coal flooded the San Francisco market just as the staggering output from Washington State mines reached California. This situation continued for a couple of years.

The Dunsmuir Company could now transport coal by rail. The No. 5 pit of Wellington Colliery was the only mine connected directly with the E & N Railway. Company railcars running directly under the mine chutes received the coal and transported it to Victoria, saving handling and reducing breakage.

By 1894 the Vancouver Coal Company had closed all its mines with the exception of the No. 1, Protection, and the No. 5 shafts. All others had been worked out and flooded.

Five Acres Development

Vancouver Coal Company had held the Harewood Estate in trust until the time came to develop the coal there. But fire was a constant problem, so in 1892, in an effort to protect the town, Samuel Robins decided to clear the former site and subdivide the area into five-acre lots for the miners and their families. Chinese were put to work logging the magnificent stand of timber; some of the trees were used for pit props, and the remainder were burned. For the first several weeks a cloud of ugly black smoke hovered over the city. The clearing continued for several years. In 1894, 7,000 trees were logged. When someone inquired why "the trees were not cut up for fuel, Robins said his company was in the coal business, not forestry."[17]

Five-acre lots, and some much larger, were offered for lease. The rent was $2.50 a year for the first two years, then $12.50 for the next three. After that the payment was between five and ten dollars an acre per year. At any time during the first ten years, miners could purchase the land at the stated price and according to certain conditions: The land must be cleared, made fit for cultivation, fenced with post and rail, and no businessperson need apply. Robins' strategy was designed to assist the miners in becoming independent. The price averaged about $200 an acre, or from $125 to $400 an acre. Should a miner be forced through circumstance to give up the lease, the Coal Company reimbursed him for the value of any improvements made to the land. The demand far exceeded the allotments. James Hurst Hawthornthwaite, or Big Jim, as the miners liked to call him, administered the plan on behalf of the Coal Company.[18] Hawthornthwaite was married to Mark Bate's daughter Elizabeth.

The leases were issued from 1887 to 1897. Former mayor Richard Gibson constructed the first home on Howard Avenue, near the Nanaimo Cemetery. He and his family lived there until 1905, when his home was destroyed by fire. He then moved into an apartment above the Gibson Block on Commercial Street.[19]

Chain Gang Improves Road

The company improved the old Harewood Mine road and built new roads into the development. Much of the roadwork was done by a chain gang of men from the Nanaimo jail. Many were deserters from sailing ships that had called in at the port for coal. Names of deserters were left with local police, and the men were kept in jail until the ship returned for another load of coal. To finance their stay in jail, it was necessary to raise money to purchase food and clothing, so the men were hired out to various projects around town. Each morning police paraded them—complete with leg irons—through the streets to the site and returned them in the evening.

By 1892 the road was completed halfway up Mount Benson, where from the 3,323-foot summit one could see "most magnificent views after a few hours of walking, or climbing."[20] Many hiking parties made the trek up the mountain.

Robins Park—A Legacy to Nanaimo

Samuel Robins, the "Godfather to Nanaimo," was the last manager of the Vancouver Coal Company. Robins' sentiments lay with the miners. Because of his co-operation with the Miners' and Mine Labourers' Protective Association, there were no strikes during his nineteen years as superintendent. Not only did he keep labour peace, he also endeared himself to the community by developing Five Acres.

Just after the turn of the nineteenth century, Robins Park was created at the corner of Fifth Street and Park Avenue as a memorial to him. Robins previously lived in the mine superintendent's house at the corner of Milton and Esplanade across from the No. 1 mine

Some Nanaimo residents made the trek up Mount Benson to admire the beautiful view, 1904.

with his wife, Maria, who had joined him from England. Here he developed a large garden with plants and shrubs from around the world. Ships' captains brought him exotic specimens to add to his collection. His garden was once described as "a horticultural marvel" and was admired by everyone.

Robins had Lombardy poplars planted along the Esplanade and along Wakesiah Avenue to mark the boundaries of the company farm. He planted holly trees throughout Harewood and English oak seeds along property lines. He grew sycamore trees from seeds he'd received from England, and put eleven of the trees along the Commercial Street boardwalks. When the boardwalk was replaced, all but one of the trees was cut down. James Hirst saved the only remaining tree by transplanting it to his garden on Commercial Street. Robins also planted monkey puzzle trees and Spanish and Chinese chestnut trees for future generations to enjoy.[21] The man who had endeared himself to the community also provided walking and horseback riding trails along the north bank of Chase River and arranged for paths to be cut on Newcastle Island. Today, only one of the five-acre lots remains intact. All the others have been developed into the community of Harewood.

CHAPTER TWO

Transportation by Sea

Vancouver Island's history is rich in maritime stories of ships large and small that have plied the waters of the Strait of Georgia and the treacherous waters off the Pacific coast. Legends have been told of swift, beautifully carved canoes filled with warring Natives descending on unsuspecting enemies and carrying away trophies, or of sleek sailing ships of the British Royal Navy, with guns mounted, throwing terror into the hearts of riotous tribes.

Commercial sailing ships loaded with furs, spars, and other items of trade carried cargoes from Vancouver Island to countries around the world. Immigrant ships of the Hudson's Bay Company brought miners and settlers from Great Britain around the arduous Cape Horn, taxing the determination of the bravest men and women, who were bone-weary when they finally came ashore to their new home, Nanaimo. Not to be forgotten are the gallant little steamers that carried freight and passengers to remote locations along the coast of British Columbia.

The Beaver, 1835–1888

The *Beaver* is still ranked as one of B.C.'s most historic vessels.[1] She was a regular visitor to Nanaimo and served as a sort of mobile trading post for the Hudson's Bay Company, transporting furs, merchandise, passengers, and mail between the company's northern post at Fort Simpson on Chatham Sound and Fort Victoria. But in 1888 the gallant little ship met an untimely end. She was outbound from Vancouver when a strong current swung her onto a rock off Stanley Park's Prospect Point. She remained lodged there for the next four years, slowly disintegrating, until she finally dislodged and sank from the backwash of another ship.[2]

The *Beaver* was originally built for the HBC in 1835 and was described as "the wonder of her age." At first Natives thought the strange craft was evil, but still they watched her with awe and admiration. One paid tribute to her by saying that "since the Beaver could do anything but speak, the white men must have been assisted in their work of building her by the Great Spirit!"[3] Dr. John Sebastian Helmcken described her as giving the appearance of a "small man-of-war with brass cannon, muskets, and cutlasses in racks around the mainmast and hand grenades in safe places."

The *Beaver* burned 700 pounds of coal per hour.[4] She was also able to burn wood, which she did at the rate of 40 cords in 24 hours. She was not a pretty vessel. Marine historian Ruth Greene described her as being "most uncomfortable, too small, too heavy, she used too much fuel and wore out nearly a dozen boilers in her life."[5] A Nanaimo company, Bolton and Cook, once hauled the old ship up on the ways to do some extensive repairs to the vessel. [6]

The SS Otter, 1852–1890

Another gallant little ship was the *Otter*, which also did yeoman service among the HBC's forts along the Pacific Coast. In her final days, the *Otter* was relegated to freighting and barging coal. She was burned for her copper in Victoria Harbour in 1890.[7]

The *Otter* was the first propeller vessel on the coast. She mystified the Natives, who could not understand her propellers, which were unlike the paddle wheels of their friend the *Beaver*.

Between the two ships, the HBC was well served. Together, they had kept law and order in the new colony.

The SS Maude, 1872–1915

The steamer *Maude* could be called the first ferry on the Strait of Georgia. In 1873 she sailed between Victoria and Burrard Inlet, and in the middle of August she switched her route to New Westminster and Vancouver Island. In 1874 she was placed on the Nanaimo–Comox–Victoria run.[8] She also served the west coast, making monthly trips to Port Alberni. Her first skipper was Captain Peter Holmes. The ship was built at the Albion Iron Works in Victoria. She served Vancouver Island well by laying cables and carrying steel and lumber for docks, piers, bridges, and railroads. During the gold rush she carried gold, mail, fish, fur, and all manner of goods.

The SS Maude *docked at Nanaimo in 1895.*

Later, the *Cariboo Fly* under Captain Rudlin was placed on the same run, alternating with the *Maude*.

The *Maude* ended her days as a salvage vessel. She was sold in 1903 to B.C. Salvage Company and rebuilt by B.C. Marine Railway Company at Esquimalt.[9]

Nanaimo—A Port of Call

Following Nanaimo's incorporation in 1874, administrative staff were appointed to oversee the Nanaimo Harbour. Captain John Sabiston was appointed the first harbour master, a position he held until his retirement in 1896.[10] He had been a deck hand aboard the HBC's historic *Beaver*. Thomas E. Peck was appointed Nanaimo's first customs collector.[11]

Nanaimo was a frequent stop for many ships delivering passengers, mail, or freight. It was not unusual to see several ships waiting in the harbour to load coal, or "black diamonds," for delivery to markets in San Francisco and other U.S. ports. The harbour had been under the jurisdiction of the Canadian government since Confederation. By 1886 new wharves had been built, impediments to shipping had been blasted away, and Cameron Island had been connected to the main island.

Prior to this time, it had been the HBC, then later the Vancouver Coal Company and Dunsmuir and individuals such as John Hirst and David William Gordon, who built the wharves and

View of Commercial Inlet, circa 1910.

made the improvements. Coal wharves were built off Cameron Island and Departure Bay to accommodate ships loading coal from the Nanaimo and Wellington collieries.

Ownership of the Nanaimo Harbour was a muddy issue until 1924, when B.C. signed the Six Harbours Agreement with Canada, allocating only a portion to the federal government. The federal area extended from "the British American Oil (now Petro-Canada) down through Newcastle Passage, including the main body of Nanaimo Harbour, to a line from Gallows Point across to the present CPR wharf."[12] The federal portion also extended up the ravine known today as Commercial Inlet. Departure Bay and the outside of the islands, the mudflats, and Northumberland Channel remained within the jurisdiction of the province.

Commercial Inlet had always been a problem because it reeked at low tide. In 1892 city council discussed filling it in, but the work needed the approval of the Department of Marine and Fisheries, a branch of the federal government. Three years later, money was raised to fill the portion between Commercial Street and Victoria Crescent, allowing for the replacement of the Commercial Street Bridge with a permanent roadway.

Another three years passed, and the ravine still generated offensive odours. Provincial Health Officer Dr. R.S. McKechnie reported to the city on July 26, 1897, regarding complaints he had received about "the stench arising from the Ravine." He recommended that the city health bylaws be enforced "and that the privy and stable nuisances be remedied."[13] The New Vancouver Coal Company again offered to help fill a portion if council supplied drainage pipes. This did not happen. It was not until the New Vancouver Coal Company had been sold to the Western Fuel Company that council negotiated a deal. Western Fuel Company would do the work and be reimbursed for the cost of moving and dumping refuse material.

Entrance Island Lighthouse

A lighthouse was built at Entrance Island in 1874. For many years, ships carrying coal out of Departure Bay and Nanaimo Harbour had been at the mercy of fog or gale-force winds. Local MP David William Gordon lobbied for navigational lights similar to those employed at Victoria and Esquimalt. Tenders were called and the contract was awarded to Nanaimo contractor Arthur Finney. The beacon was lit on the evening of June 8, 1875. The *Nanaimo Free Press* reported the event, observing that no notice had been given to mariners. Editor George Norris hoped, for everyone's sake, that there would be no casualties over the "cheese-paring policy of the Dominion Government."[14]

John Kenney was the first keeper in 1876, followed by Robert Gray, who remained on the job until 1907 at a salary of $148 per quarter. He had to provide his own transportation to and from the light.[15] Tending to his farm on Gabriola Island and looking after the light was difficult for the Irishman, but he managed with the help of an assistant. In 1894 the Vancouver-based company of Baynes and Horie built an engine room to house the new steam foghorn that bellowed for eight seconds at 45-second intervals. Gray kept careful logs of the ships entering and leaving Nanaimo Harbour. He must have been frustrated at some of the bureaucratic mumbo-jumbo coming from Ottawa. He noted: "Received a note and form from William Smith Esq., Deputy Minister of Marine and Fisheries Department accusing me of not returning ... forms previously sent to me which I never received so I could not return [that] which I did not get."[16]

In 1888 another impediment to shipping was removed when Pioneer Rock, situated off the coal wharves on Cameron Island, was blasted out of existence.[17] Later, in 1900, a fixed red anchor light was moored off Gallows Point on the south end of Protection Island to assist pilots bringing in large steamers. Pilots complained that the light reached only a mile; therefore, a more powerful beacon was installed on a platform atop copper-sheathed piles. In 1906 the Western Fuel Company, which operated the Protection Island mine and wharf, requested a mechanical fog bell. This was promised provided the miners would wind the bell in thick weather for ten dollars per month pay.

The Gap–Gabriola Island Link

During the early years, transportation in the Gulf Islands was usually by canoe. Thomas Degnen used his dugout canoe to carry people and freight between Nanaimo and Gabriola Island. In stormy weather the crossing was very dangerous, especially when rounding Jack Point, and it often took several hours to travel through rough water. Carrying cattle or farming equipment to the island was no easy task. Scows made of logs were lashed together to provide a flatbed for the animals.[18] Island farmers eventually petitioned government to open a passage through "The Gap" about half a mile from the point. In 1883—again through the efforts of David William Gordon—a canal was made through Biggs Portage, the present location of Duke Point ferry terminal. This water passage not only shortened the distance to Gabriola Island, but also made it a much safer journey, as boats could glide through the canal into the quieter waters of Nanaimo Harbour. The canal was enlarged in 1888, but as larger boats arrived, the passageway proved too shallow. Gordon also erected a wharf where the Canadian Pacific Railway Company's dock is today. For many years it was known as Gordon's Wharf.[19]

Canadian Pacific Navigation Company

As the town grew, the number of ships using Nanaimo Harbour and Departure Bay increased. In 1883 the HBC fleet joined the Pioneer Line to form the Canadian Pacific Navigation Company Limited (CPN). The steamer *Robert Dunsmuir*, owned by Captain William Rogers (brother of Jerry Rogers, the logger for whom Jericho Beach is named), ran a regular triangle service between New Westminster, Vancouver, and Nanaimo. On the return trip from Nanaimo, it carried coal, earning the nickname "Dirty Bob."

The SS Cutch, 1884–1908

The Union Steamship Company entered the Nanaimo service with the steamer *Cutch*, a vessel brought here from India in 1890. The

Cutch was described as a "taut, smart, handsome vessel having a resemblance to the *Danube*,"[20] a CPN vessel. Built as a cruising yacht with graceful lines, she had an enclosed passenger lounge and sported two funnels. She was licensed to carry 150 passengers and had space for over 150 tons of general cargo in two capacious holds. Her first master was Captain Peter Johnson.

On Monday, July 7, 1890, the *Cutch* made a special trip to Nanaimo, where the Union Steamship Company hosted a party for over 50 city notables and friends to inaugurate the new service. The ship made the crossing in three hours. A newspaper account of the event noted that the majority of the passengers had never visited Nanaimo before and were surprised "at the fine site the place occupies, possessing as it does every qualification necessary for an important seaport."[21] The Silver Cornet Band played as the vessel approached and later played selections on the deck of the *Cutch* during the official luncheon. Mayor John Hilbert and council welcomed the ship to Nanaimo. The ship was fast, fresh, clean, elegant, and so reliable that the people of Nanaimo kept time by her whistle as she left the wharf daily at 7:00 a.m. for Vancouver.[22]

The *Cutch*'s new service began in February 1891. The advertisement for the Vancouver-to-Nanaimo run noted that the ship "left the Company wharf at noon and the CPR Wharf at 2.30 p.m. daily except Saturdays, returning from Nanaimo at 7:00 a.m. except Sundays."[23] The skippers of the *Cutch* and the *Robert Dunsmuir* were bitter rivals, and the *Dunsmuir* soon lost business to the faster and more powerful vessel.

The City of Nanaimo, *1891–1926*

In 1891, in order to compete, Captain Rogers and the Dunsmuirs invested in building a new wooden steamer, the *City of Nanaimo*, at Leamy & Kyle's sawmill on False Creek, Vancouver. The *City of Nanaimo* would eventually force the *Cutch* out of service, but it also precipitated Captain Rogers' bankruptcy. The Dunsmuirs foreclosed on the mortgage and took over the ship. Again, there was bitter rivalry between vessels, this time between the crew of the *Cutch* and the *City of Nanaimo*, the more spacious vessel.

There was a lot of opposition to and criticism of Robert Dunsmuir and his Esquimalt & Nanaimo Railway Company. Various business groups on Vancouver Island and in Vancouver did not want Dunsmuir holding a monopoly over the shipping business on the east coast of Vancouver Island, as he had with the railway. This was evident in a press report of *The Province* on September 12, 1896:

Our Nanaimo correspondent recently drew attention to a proposition then before the ratepayers of the City to bonus the Union Steamship Company in the amount of $30,000 in consideration of their guaranteeing a daily service between Vancouver and Nanaimo, for five years at the rates for freight and passengers at present charged, the avowed object being to prevent the possibility of the entire steamboat and railway service on the east coast of Vancouver Island falling into the hands of the Esquimalt and Nanaimo Railway Company. (That Company having announced their intention of placing the SS *Joan* and the *City of Nanaimo* on the Vancouver-Nanaimo route.)[24]

The rivalry between various factions literally crashed in 1892.

Collision of the Cutch and the Joan

On November 12, 1892, three vessels were scheduled to leave Nanaimo at the same hour. *Joan*, another Dunsmuir vessel, was headed for Victoria; the *City of Nanaimo* and the *Cutch* were headed for Vancouver. The *City of Nanaimo* left first, and the *Joan* purposely delayed leaving, holding up the *Cutch* so that the *City of Nanaimo* would get well out into the Strait of Georgia. When *Joan* finally left, the *Cutch* took off as quickly as possible, trying to make up for the delay. In the race to get away first, the two vessels collided as they headed for the south channel of the Nanaimo Harbour.

The Joan *and* City of Nanaimo *at wharves in Nanaimo.*

The *Cutch* did not stop, even with black smoke pouring from her funnels. She headed after the competition without offering assistance to the stricken *Joan*, apparently in bad shape with clouds of steam coming from her engines. Each had left Gordon's Wharf at the same time, although it was later ruled that the *Joan* had cast off first. As the *Cutch* had not stopped after the collision, she was judged at fault in a court case that came before Chief Justice Sir Matthew Begbie.[25] The collision cost the Union Steamship Company, as the repairs to the ship were heavy. The company also lost trade, and the run between Vancouver and Nanaimo was dropped after 1896.

The *City of Nanaimo* was sold in 1912 to the Terminal Steam Navigation Company, which renamed her *Bowena*. For a time she serviced Bowen Island, Britannia, and Squamish. Later, the Union Steamship Company of Vancouver purchased her and renamed her *Cheam*. Four years later, in 1926, she was scrapped. The *Cutch* was wrecked during the Klondike gold rush era.

The People's Steam Navigation Company

The People's Steam Navigation Company was formed in May of 1884 in direct competition to the CPN. Businessmen from Nanaimo, Chemainus, and Victoria invested $100,000 in the company. Joseph Webb was one of the shareholders, and this investment proved to be one of his less successful ventures. The SS *Amelia* was the company's first major acquisition; she was a side-wheel steamer built in San Francisco and previously used on the Sacramento River. Just bringing the vessel into British Columbia cost the owners 10 percent of the value of the hull and another 25 percent on the ship's machinery.[26] She was placed on the Victoria-to-Nanaimo run in opposition to the CPN's *R.P. Rithet*. As the competition increased, fares plummeted to 25 cents per person return. Eventually the two companies agreed that the CPN would withdraw its vessel from the route in return for 25 percent of the gross receipts of the *Amelia*. The timing could not have been worse for the venture; as soon the E & N Railway reached Nanaimo, it made the sea route uneconomical. In July 1889 the *Amelia* was bought at auction by the CPN.

Nanaimo's Shipbuilding Industry

For a time Nanaimo was known for its shipbuilding industry. The town had an excellent shipyard located at the mouth of Millstone

River, where the first vessel, the *Alpha*, a 58-ton schooner, was built in 1859. A group of local businessmen, including Adam Grant Horne, Edward Walker, and Dr. Alfred Robson Benson, had formed a company to build the *Alpha* to carry coal to Victoria and return with merchandise.[27] The ship also carried mail and messages from Governor James Douglas in Victoria to the officer-in-charge in Nanaimo. Edward Walker and Enas Sabiston were captains of the vessel. At times, when the weather was foul, the captains had difficulty finding the harbour, so Walker installed a beacon on Gallows Point and another on Satellite Channel. Walker Rock in Trincomali Channel is named in his honour.[28]

The HBC had hired Edward Walker as a miner, but a leg injury prevented him from mining when he arrived in Nanaimo. At first, he worked as a carpenter and, along with Robert Dunsmuir, received the first free miner's licence to work independently. At age 40, he married eighteen-year-old Selena Sage, daughter of Jesse and Mary Ann Sage, *Princess Royal* pioneers.[29] Walker held a variety of jobs. He did try mining on Newcastle Island and Protection Island, but was unsuccessful. He also supervised the building of the coal wharves on Cameron Island and Departure Bay. Walker retired from the sea and lived to a respectable old age. Enas Sabiston accidentally drowned; he was buried in Nanaimo Cemetery.

The *Alpha* had a short career. She was later sold to a company in Victoria. She met an unfortunate end: On her way to Hawaii in November 1868, she ran into heavy seas and sank off Flores Island, on the west coast of Vancouver Island. The captain and crew survived the wreck, then faced a miserable nine days on the rocky shore before being rescued by Native people. They were given food and shelter and, when rested, were taken to the east coast of the island and shown the route south to Nanaimo. Alpha Passage, west of the entrance to Ucluelet Inlet, is named for the vessel.

The barque *Nanaimo*, built in the same shipyard, was one of the largest seagoing vessels built in British Columbia at that time. She was built by Chauncey Carpenter, owner of the Millstream Sawmill, and launched in September 1882. Constructed with Douglas fir, she was 155 feet in length with a 34-foot beam and was capable of carrying 800 tons of coal or lumber. Mark Bate recalled the day the *Nanaimo* was launched. The Nanaimo Brass Band played as the vessel "glided gracefully with colours flying into the harbour off Dobeson Foundry."[30] As the anchor dropped, the band played "A Life on the Ocean Wave" and continued with several other musical selections on deck. This was a memorable day in Nanaimo, and the brass band added greatly to the event. The *Nanaimo* sailed the Pacific Ocean for 40 years; she eventually sank in the mouth of the Yangtze River in China.

Another vessel launched about the same time was the steamer *Estelle*, built for Andrew Haslam, the owner of the Nanaimo Sawmill. The ship's powerful engines were by Doty of Toronto. She was used as a tug and later sold to Haslam's brother-in-law, Mr. Macdougal, who loaded her with supplies for logging camps. The *Estelle* met an unfortunate end; heavily loaded with supplies, she foundered in riptides, losing all hands, including the owner. Some pieces of the vessel were eventually retrieved, including the beautifully carved and gilded beaver from the pilothouse.

The *Alpha* was the first and the *Estelle* the last vessel to be built in the shipyard.[31] Two other shipyards operated in Nanaimo: In 1918 the Japanese Ode brothers built the Nanaimo Shipyard on Newcastle Island, and during the Second World War the Newcastle Shipbuilding Company constructed a number of minesweepers in Nanaimo.

One Old Seafarer

Captain Arthur Yates spent a lifetime at sea. Most of his childhood was spent aboard his father's sailing ship, the *Albania*, until he was old enough to go to school in Oakland, California. His parents were from Prince Edward Island. He was born on July 24, 1883, at Auckland, New Zealand, the youngest of three children born aboard the ship at various ports around the world. Captain Yates—or "Cappy," as his friends nicknamed him—remembered being with his father as they rounded Cape Horn: "I was taken on deck to see this place. Dad threw a shawl around me. It was a bit foggy and the ship was rolling. Dad said, 'There my boy. That's Cape Horn.'"[32]

In 1900 his father was appointed marine pilot at Nanaimo, and two years later Captain Yates arrived here also. For a time he worked for the Dunsmuir shipping company on the coal ships running between Nanaimo and Alaska or California. He later worked as second officer for the Dollar Steamship Company, hauling wheat and lumber to the Orient.

In 1905 he purchased the steam yacht *Kootenay*, planning to use it for his own pleasure. The *Kootenay* had been a passenger steamer and also the property of the Honourable Edgar Dewdney, who used her in his mining and forest interests along the coast.[33] Captain James W. Troup had built the yacht when he resided in

Captain Arthur Yates' home was at the corner of Fitzwilliam and Wallace streets.

Nelson. The yacht operated on Kootenay Lake, but it was brought to Victoria when Captain Troup moved to the capital city to take over the management of the new coastal steamship service for the Canadian Pacific Railway.

In 1908 Captain Yates started work with the federal fisheries department as a master of the patrol vessel *Alcedo* in Nanaimo. It was on this vessel that he worked with Raymond Collishaw, who received his master's certificate. Collishaw became a flying ace during the First World War.

Captain Yates married Beatrix Margaret Planta on April 14, 1914, in Nanaimo. They had three children, Marion, Nelson, and Annabell. Planta Road is named after Planta's father, building contractor Jeffrey Evan Planta, and Planta Park is named for her uncle, Albert E. Planta.

The Yates residence, called "Hills boro," was the location of many social engagements such as Easter egg hunts and lawn parties. It is now an empty lot sitting high above street level and adjacent to St. Andrews United Church. The lot is known locally as Cappy Yates Park, but it is privately owned and not a dedicated park. From the site, you can look out across town and across the Strait of Georgia toward the mountains of the mainland; this was once a beautiful garden and an excellent vantage point for one of Nanaimo's old seafaring captains.

Captain Arthur Yates celebrated his 100th birthday in 1983. On that occasion he said he owed his longevity to always taking care of himself, adding that "the sea had a lot to do with it" and that "a little coffee of Scotch once in a while doesn't hurt."

Captain Arthur Yates is shown here at 100 years old.

CHAPTER THREE

The Snuneymuxw

The mainly European residents regarded the Snuneymuxw as nuisances, so city council—listening to its constituents—had them removed from town: they were relegated to reservations along the Nanaimo River. This segregation did not happen overnight, but developed through a series of incidents and new laws enacted after Confederation and incorporation.

The Snuneymuxw were employed as labourers in a variety of industries. They helped build the E & N Railway, and they worked in the local sawmills in Nanaimo and Chemainus. The Chemainus mill also employed Snuneymuxw as longshoremen, and they proved their skill at loading ships. Some households and hotels also offered employment as domestics. People who ran boarding houses or had large families hired domestics to help with laundry. This was not an easy chore in the early days, as water had to be carried from springs in buckets. Snuneymuxw were "paid five cents a bucket to carry the water."[1]

The Snuneymuxw and the New Authority

British Columbia's Native people were eager participants in the HBC's fur-trade business. Governor Sir James Douglas noted how friendly they were. He saw them as "kind and friendly, but ready and willing to share their labours and assist in all their toils."[2] This was certainly the case in Nanaimo, where the Snuneymuxw pointed out the coal outcroppings, supplied the fort with food, and worked in the early mines. They willingly shared their fishing and hunting experience, but as more settlers arrived, they began to be shunted aside.

With Confederation had come rules and regulations governing the lives of the Snuneymuxw and other B.C. Native people. Canada, however reluctantly, inherited the responsibility from the imperial government in England through the British North America Act. These rules and regulations allowed the federal government to interfere in all aspects of Native life and assumed that Native people would eventually leave their reserves and live and work among the general population.[3]

The Indian Act of 1876

In 1873 the Indian Lands Branch was created, and in 1876 the federal parliament passed the first Indian Act, which combined all laws affecting Natives everywhere in Canada. The directives in the Indian Act assumed Native inferiority. All "legal" Natives became wards of the federal government and were to be treated as minors without the full privileges of citizenship. Males were considered status Indian; women who married outside and the children of such unions lost their status and membership in the band forever. Only adult males could vote.

The new legislation placed reserve land in the trust of the Crown; it could not be mortgaged, seized, or taxed. The land could only be sold with the approval of a majority of the adult band members and the Department of Indian Affairs. Likewise, forest or mineral resources on reserve land could not be harvested or removed without the same procedure.

There was no provision to accommodate the diverse nature of the different aboriginal governments that existed before Confederation.[4] Other measures were taken to "civilize" the indigenous population. The Indian Act outlawed the manufacture, sale, or consumption of liquor on reserves. In order to become a full-fledged Canadian citizen, a Native had to prove he was literate in English or French, of good moral character, and free of debt. These conditions would have been difficult for most settlers.

In 1880 the Department of Indian Affairs was created as a separate ministry with its own minister. When B.C. joined Confederation in 1871, several treaties were signed; however, most were on Rupert's Land, the agricultural land belt that became the three prairie provinces.

Dr. Israel Wood Powell, a Victoria physician, was appointed Indian superintendent; he administered the Indian Act in B.C.[5] He divided the province into twenty Indian agencies and appointed an agent to each. Each agent had authority to settle disputes and distribute welfare.

Changing Native Ways

The Canadian government tried to change the Aboriginal peoples' way of life by outlawing their potlatch celebrations and by educating their children in English schools. Both policies alienated and destroyed Native culture. A Methodist missionary in Nanaimo is quoted as saying: "The Church and school cannot flourish where the 'potlatching' holds sway ... Thus all the objects or advantages to be secured by good government are frustrated by this very demoralizing custom."[6]

Gilbert Malcolm Sproat, the Indian reserve commissioner of B.C. from 1878 to 1880, also advocated banning the potlatch. He wrote to Prime Minister John A. Macdonald in 1879, voicing concerns about the "evils" of the ceremony. Macdonald took up the cause in the House of Commons in the spring of 1883, when he feared Natives in B.C. might retaliate. He issued an order-in-council on July 7, 1883, directing Natives to abandon the custom. His fear had been for the settlers, but many of them enjoyed watching the ceremony and did not support the war against the potlatch.

Sproat resigned from the commission in 1880 and was replaced by Peter O'Reilly, who served until his retirement in 1898.

Indian Agent William Henry Lomas

The east-coast agency of Vancouver Island, located in Duncan, included Cowichan and Nanaimo. Missionaries throughout the province reinforced this government authority. Historian Jean Barman described the missionaries as "the foot soldiers in the government's effort to manage indigenous peoples."[2]

William Henry Lomas was the first appointee to the east-coast agency in 1881. He was also one of the first teachers in the Cowichan district at the Somenos Mission Chapel School and the first religious instructor at the Anglican Mission Chapel School, Quamichan. He and his wife Jane learned the Halkomelem language and translated the Anglican Book of Common Prayer.[3]

Native Schooling

Early missionaries such as Methodist Thomas Crosby and Anglican Reverend John Booth Good provided elementary schooling and attained limited success in keeping the young Aboriginal people away from the traditional ways. Instruction was mostly in English, although both missionaries tried to learn the Halkomelem language so that they could communicate with their young pupils.

The missionaries' curriculum gave little academic study; girls spent their day learning to sew and be homemakers, while boys were taught farming and manual skills. History has revealed how many children were punished for speaking their language.

By 1900 there were 28 day schools in the province and fourteen residential schools. Churches of different denominations and the Department of Indian Affairs supported the schools. In Nanaimo, elementary students attended the Native day school; later they were sent to the residential school at Kuper Island, near Chemainus. This was not a happy situation, but one that was supported by authorities and the little money that was made available for Native education.

Implementing the Reserve System

The decision soon arose as to how much land would be given to B.C. Natives for their own use and how much would be safeguarded. Elsewhere in Canada, each tribe received a single large tract of land, either 160 acres or one square mile per family, on which they were expected to settle and establish farms. However, in this province each local band was allotted several small reserves that could be used intermittently between migratory activities. The federal government decided that 80 acres per family of five were all that were needed. The B.C. government countered that the coast tribes would never use that much land and set a maximum of only twenty acres per family. The province also insisted on maintaining an interest in reserve lands; if land happened to be cut off a reserve, or if a band gave up its land, the ownership would revert to the province.[7]

The Snuneymuxw Reserves

The Snuneymuxw were given a stretch of land along the waterfront in south Nanaimo, along Eaton Street at Sabiston to just past the present federal government Assembly Wharf. Reserve Number 1 consisted of 46 acres and was the Snuneymuxw townsite. It contained 48 cottages, with about ten acres fenced and cultivated.[8] The population at this time was 223.

Reserve Number 2 at the mouth of the Nanaimo River, two miles from town, consisted of 382 acres, some of which was considered good agricultural land. The Snuneymuxw used this site during the fishing season and for planting potatoes.

Reserve Number 3 was 117 acres on the west side of the river, but it was heavily forested. A Nanaimo Sawmill logging camp located nearby had encroached on the reserve with a rolling way to take logs to the river. A sleeping cabin for the loggers had also been built, with permission, on the reserve. It was estimated that there were about 750,000 board feet of good sawlogs in this portion of the reserve, but the Snuneymuxw attached no value to the timber.

Reserve Number 4 of 200 acres was on the east bank of the Nanaimo River, with fifteen acres of open grassland and the remainder wooded. There were two other small reserves on Gabriola Island: Number 5 was a fishing station, and Number 6 was Burial Island.

In 1876 Mayor Mark Bate requested that a portion of land be set aside for visiting tribes to camp on, because the local Snuneymuxw refused to accommodate "strange Indians in their village. At present, they encamp here, there and everywhere on private property and cannot be well looked after." The Indian Commission did not think much of this idea, as it "would not be a Dominion Government policy, more an undertaking of a purely municipal character."[9]

The problem of how much land was enough would not be settled for three decades. It was not until 1912, during the McKenna–McBride Royal Commission on Indian Affairs, that the allotment of land was finalized.

Snuneymuxw Number 1 Reserve, Nanaimo.

CHAPTER FOUR

The Chinese Community

The first Chinese arrived on Vancouver Island in 1858. Many made their way to the Fraser River goldfields and later drifted back to Vancouver Island, finding work as servants for the HBC hierarchy. There were so few in the beginning that most residents ignored them or viewed them with disdainful superiority. As their numbers increased, due to massive immigration to work on the Canadian Pacific Railway, residents became alarmed. Amor de Cosmos unsuccessfully petitioned the House of Commons to forbid Chinese men from working on the railway.

When B.C. entered Confederation there were 2,000 Chinese living in the province; a decade later the number had increased to 4,000. Before the last spike was driven, there were 8,000 Chinese working on the railroad. When Nanaimo was incorporated in 1874, there were 200 Chinese living there.

There were several classes of Chinese: the railway workers and those who worked in the mines; educated businessmen who were prepared to play an active role in their communities; and a large contingent of agricultural workers who established farms, providing essential food for growing communities.

Despite the animosity from the largely European community, the Chinese in the Nanaimo area were determined to make a living and send money to their families back home. They settled first on land owned by the Vancouver Coal Company in the Victoria and Winfield crescents, Crace, Cavan, and Nicol streets area. Others settled near the mines at Wellington and later at Extension and Ladysmith. A number of Chinese businesses were already established during the 1880s in both Nanaimo and Wellington. They included grocers, butchers, general merchants, tailors, and those who did laundry.

Chinese Enter the Mining Industry

When the Chinese first entered the mining industry in Nanaimo, miners resented the intrusion and saw them as a threat to their jobs. The *Colonist* newspaper reported in 1867:

> Considerable excitement, we hear, exists at Nanaimo in consequence of the introduction of Chinese borers. The colliers threaten with violence the first Chinaman who forgets his Celestial origin so far as to descend to the "bottom pit" of a coal mine.[1]

The Chinese were viewed with suspicion because they looked and dressed differently and their language and culture were foreign. This feeling of unease with the Chinese was universal in B.C. at this time, but the mine operators liked them—they worked for less pay and they worked hard. Pressure was placed on federal and provincial governments to do something about the problem. An editorial in a provincial magazine spewed racial rhetoric, questioning why white jobs were being filled by "beings who can exist on a few grains of rice, live in a pig-sty, work for fifty cents a day, and with whom in many branches of industry it is impossible for white men to compete."[2]

The general attitude toward the Chinese is illustrated in the manuscript of Michael (Mike) Manson, who worked for the Vancouver Coal Company and helped build the railway to Chase River Mine. He was in charge of a night gang of Chinese workers building a road. One of the men insisted on sitting down on his wheelbarrow to smoke. Manson said he found no fault with smoking, but insisted the person return to work as soon as the cigarette was lit. As Manson describes, this time the man insisted on sitting down to finish his smoke:

> After repeated orders he began to curse me in Chinese fashion, so I cut a stick about four feet long and two inches in diameter and I gave him a couple of cracks with it and unfortunately broke two of his ribs. Then the row began in full swing. The other fellows came after me with shovels. I grabbed a shovel and jumped on the top of a stump and kept them off in that way until they calmed down when I

sent four of them to take the fellow home and I got down among them and they surely worked that afternoon.[3]

The next day a lawyer representing the Chinese worker came to Magistrate Mark Bate's office, asking him to sign a warrant for Manson's arrest. Bate refused, but promised he would look into the complaint.

The day after that, Manson explained what had happened. Bate, the manager, exonerated him with a smile and told him not to hit so hard the next time, "but get the road built as quickly as you can."

The Coal Company paid the injured man his wages while he was sick, and as soon as he was well he returned to Manson's gang. There was no more trouble, and the gang worked extra hard until the road was finished.

Royal Commission on Chinese Immigration

Miners and residents of Nanaimo and Wellington petitioned government to exclude the Chinese from working underground in any of the mines. "Your petitioners keenly feel that the presence of Chinese in the mines is a source of grave danger to the lives of those who are employed underground in mining coal."[4] The petitioners drew attention to the lack of accidents in the mines in the past few years, which they attributed to the fact that no Chinese were employed in the Nanaimo and Wellington collieries during that period.

There was so much public pressure on government that a Royal Commission on Chinese immigration was ordered. Several of the mine operators from Nanaimo testified before the commission in 1885. They were asked to answer several questions. John Bryden, general manager of the Wellington Collieries, spoke favourably about his Chinese workers:

The presence of the Chinese has contributed very much to the development of the province. If the Chinese were withdrawn, the effect would be serious, as many of the industries now being carried on would be unable to continue in operation for want of a suitable class of labour.[5]

Samuel M. Robins, superintendent of the Vancouver Coal Company, was not so accommodating. He noted:

It is not necessary to retain Chinese in the province, but their removal should not be sudden. A free immigration of white people of the laboring classes would enable us to do without the Chinese element altogether.[6]

Robert Dunsmuir believed the immigration of the Chinese helped the general development of the country:

If it were not for Chinese labor the business I am engaged in, specially coal mining, would be seriously retarded and curtailed, and it would be impossible to sell this product and compete favorably in the market of San Francisco.[7]

He considered the agitation against the Chinese largely political. No argument yet had convinced him that they were a drawback to the province.

The 1885 Royal Commission on Chinese Immigration reported that in Nanaimo there were 64 miners and cooks, 18 servants and cooks, 6 store employees, 6 merchants, 13 farm labourers, 8 washermen, and 4 barbers. A much larger number, 727, worked in the mines in Wellington. It is interesting to note that there were only four married Chinese women in both communities at that time. Three doctors served the Chinese community in Nanaimo and five in Wellington; each community had one teacher.[8]

Chinese Gardens

Not all the Chinese worked in the mines. Two large Chinese vegetable gardens supplied the community with fresh produce. One was at Departure Bay, above what is now the public beach, and another was behind the present Quarterway Hotel. Wing Lee operated the larger farm, known as the Chinese Ranch, in the Quarterway area, and Wong Gun Sai, also known as Number 4, farmed the Departure Bay operation.[9] Numbers rather than names were often used to identify Chinese workers in the mines. When a disaster occurred, the newspaper recorded how many Chinese were killed, but seldom used their names.

Complaints about Chinese Lifestyle

Nanaimo was not unlike other communities in B.C. in that the whites judged the Chinese based on their own perceptions and those of newspaper reports of the day. The local newspaper in 1884 described the Chinese living quarters unfavourably:

They live, generally in wretched hovels, dark, ill ventilated, filthy and unwholesome and crowded together in such numbers, as to utterly preclude all ideas of comfort, morality or even decency.[10]

This same year, the city introduced a bylaw outlawing Chinese washhouses and laundries that were considered firetraps and public nuisances, but subsequently withdrew it. Council wanted the premises cleaned up and also wanted the Chinese merchants to observe Sunday closing. In 1901 a white steam laundry received city approval, which, according to the owner, would "put white labour on a more equal footing with coolie labour." Before long a bylaw was passed regulating laundries.

The predominantly white community also complained about the noise made by a Chinese theatrical troupe.

Provincial Sanitary Inspector Clive Phillipps-Wolley reflected the attitude of the white population toward the Chinese lifestyle. He wrote of "the hideous condition of Chinatown," saying that the "Chinese should not be allowed to live amongst white people" and that its sanitary problems "can be cured in only one way—by fire. The sooner it is done the better for Nanaimo."[11]

The Second Chinatown

The anti-Chinese sentiment induced the Vancouver Coal Company to move the Chinese living quarters away from the business district downtown. This was easily accomplished, as the company owned most of the land surrounding the city. Eight acres of land were set aside to the south of the city.[12] In the View Street area, homes and shops were built. All but two Chinese stores were removed to the new location. The Vancouver Coal Company charged each employee a dollar per month for rent in Chinatown. The company later claimed that it actually received only $60 to $70 per month rent for the land, which made it an unprofitable venture.

The reasons for removing the Chinese may have been as much economic as racial. As the white business district began to expand southward along the waterfront, the land on Victoria Crescent became too valuable for a rental property. This was also the time for the building of the E & N Railway, and the city expected a large influx of Chinese labourers, thus the isolated site next to the railway line was ideal for relocation. By 1885 almost all Chinese businesses and residents had moved to the south of downtown Nanaimo.

The Chinese community thrived at this new location, particularly during the building of the railway from 1884 to 1886.

Then, two years later, city council voted unanimously to extend the city limits south to include Chinatown. In reflection, it is difficult to understand why the City would take such an action at this time, although city records reveal the reason may have been quite simple: The City resurveyed its land holdings.[13] Chinatown officially became part of Nanaimo on January 13, 1887.[14]

Chinese Social Life

The Chinese had an active social life, often based on social connections from the homeland. There were benevolent associations that looked after the health and welfare of its members in the cities of Victoria and Vancouver. These associations had members in Nanaimo, as there were not enough Chinese in the Nanaimo area alone. The associations were based on surname, dialect, district, and political affiliation. Rooming houses in Nanaimo's Chinatown housed men according to their membership in these associations.[15] If a man was hurt in the mines, the association made sure he was cared for. If he was seriously injured, they raised money for his passage back to China.

The association also managed the Plague House, known also as "the spare room in the spare house." This house was separated from the main areas of Chinatown but still a part of it. When a Chinese person contracted a contagious disease, or when he felt he was about to die, he moved into this house, which contained a kitchen and sleeping facilities.

Associations were also responsible for financing and carrying out funerals and for shipping the deceased's bones back to families in China (after a period of seven years, bones were placed in boxes and returned to their ancestral home). In 1890 the Vancouver Coal Company gave the Chinese land on Stewart Avenue for a burial ground. Unfortunately, springs saturated the area and coffins had to be held down with stones.[16]

Gambling was a popular pastime. There were eight gambling houses operating at the turn of the century. During an evening Chinese gamblers moved from house to house, playing for a period of time at each. They shared the profits and the risks among the various houses. One raid in 1904 resulted in the arrest of eighteen Chinese. There had been no guards on the doors and no means of escape. It was the first raid in eight years and was the result of a crackdown on gambling.[17]

At the turn of the century, there were 1,439 Chinese in the Nanaimo district. In addition to the city population, there were a

47

number of small Chinese camps along the E & N Railway. Workers in these camps came into Nanaimo Chinatown from the mines in Extension, South Wellington, Wellington, and Jingle Pot to shop or do business. They arrived by train on Saturday night, stayed over to Sunday and left on the afternoon train. On Saturday nights Chinatown would be alive with people, talking, shopping, and gambling. Businesses offered imported Oriental art and carvings, rattan furniture, shoes, and work clothes.

Nanaimo Entrepreneur Mah Bing Kee

Chinatown consisted of three main streets: Bingkee Street, named after Mah Bing Kee, a wealthy Chinese landowner, and York and Far streets, named after his two daughters.[18]

Much of the Chinese history in early Nanaimo parallels the life of Bing Kee, who was born in Canton, China, May 16, 1847, and at age fourteen participated in the California gold rush. Later, like so many of his countrymen, he worked at building the Canadian Pacific Railway. In 1887 he married Wong Foon, the daughter of a wealthy merchant in San Francisco. The couple and their three daughters and one son lived in the first Chinatown. In 1890 Bing Kee farmed and logged and built a new house for his wife on View Street, where he owned a large portion of land.[19]

An entrepreneur, Bing Kee was involved in various businesses and partnerships. He provided capital for Chinese to establish businesses as bakers, cooks, tailors, and herbalists, splitting net profits with them on a 50-50 basis. He had interests in two laundries, a tailor shop, a restaurant hotel, a gambling house, and owned residential property. He also invested in a small logging and sawmill operation. The logs from the thousand acres he owned at Timberlands were processed and cut into slabs at his Cassidy sawmill and sent by railway to his lumberyard at the corner of Hecate, Milton, and Kennedy streets, where he wholesaled them to various lumber dealers in town.

After the Vancouver Coal Company was sold to Western Fuel Company in 1903, the new owner began selling off some of the company's property, including Chinatown. On March 9, 1908, Mah Bing Kee and Ching Chung Yung purchased the original Chinatown plus 30 acres of farmland behind it.[20] City records note that Mah Bing Kee and Ching Chung Yung represented themselves as the Hop Sing Company.

The two businessmen hoped that fellow countrymen would purchase their own land and build homes in the way that other

Mah Bing Kee family in traditional Chinese dress.

Bing Kee's Struggle—Mineral Rights to the Ganner Estate

In 1903 Bing Kee purchased the 158-acre Ganner Estate, about eight miles south of the city. The Ganners were *Princess Royal* pioneers. The estate contained valuable timber and coal seams. Along with the title to the land came the rights to the coal. These rights preceded the E & N land grant, the Settlement Act of 1874, which gave "all mineral rights to the coal companies."

Bing Kee wanted to mine the coal, but the executors of the estate appealed to the government to revoke the coal rights. It was alleged the estate executors were prompted and financed by the Vancouver Coal Company. The executors took Bing Kee to court in Victoria. The court ruled that the coal rights passed on to Bing Kee with the land, not to the Ganner Estate. The executors appealed to the Supreme Court in Ottawa, and again the court ruled in Bing Kee's favour. There was no higher court in Canada, so the executors appealed to the court in London, England.

Bing Kee's lawyer was a prominent Nanaimo businessman, Albert Edward Planta, who believed his client did not have much hope of success, as many of the British directors and investors of the coal industry in Nanaimo came from Britain. The two men made an agreement: If Planta won the case, he would be paid; if he lost, he would not be paid. If he lost, the court costs would be awarded against him. Planta did not defend the case any further. He said, "I made my point. Winning two out of three is not bad." Bing Kee lost the coal rights. The coal deposit later became the Granby Coal Mine.

Mah Bing Kee family. Back row, L-R: Douglas, Harry, Mrs. S.D. Mah, Mee Mah, Stanley, David. Front row, L-R: B.C. Wing Mah, Cecil, Toy Won Mah, Mrs. Lung Kee, Toy Mee Mah, Shie Dick Mah.

immigrants did. When the company raised the rents many became angry and bitter, particularly toward Ching Chung Yung, who had made too much money, they believed. Mah Bing Kee garnered a more favourable response, perhaps because he was a wealthy man with considerable influence not only in Nanaimo and in Alberni, but also on the mainland.

A Third Chinatown

Meanwhile, residents of the second Chinatown received notice to vacate by May 30, 1908, and on that day people began tearing down and moving their buildings to the new location. But the move did not go smoothly. Mah Bing Kee had expected trouble and had an injunction to prevent anyone moving the buildings. Then he took them to court.

The Chinese claimed the injunction was never served, but their actions led to the arrest of seventeen Chinese.[21] Their trial was held on June 1, 1908, before a packed courtroom. A copy of the "Chinese Oath" administered in the chief magistrate's court is now in the Nanaimo Community Archives. It employs some powerful imagery:

> To establish a yellow oath I ... the Attester, do swear, at this ... the year ... the month ... the day, that I will give the evidence in court today to speak the truth, pertaining to

the case. If I had any biased mind to invent lies, or to utter falsehood, the high Heaven, the true God, will punish me, sink me in the river and drown me in the deep sea, forfeit my future generations and cast my soul into hell to suffer for ever and ever.[22]

The question of who owned the buildings was referred to the provincial court, which ruled that the buildings belonged to the Chinese who had built them. Mah Bing Kee appealed to the Supreme Court of Canada, but the case was dismissed and the buildings were eventually moved to the new Chinatown.

The exodus from the second Chinatown was led by a group of prominent businessmen who registered their company as the Lung Yick Land Company. The new company included the Yick Chong, Lung Kee, Hop Lee, Wing Fung, Wing Tai, San Chong, and Wong Sun Wo companies. By selling 2,171 shares at five dollars each, the company had raised $10,855 to purchase 11.25 acres from Western Fuel Company located across the E & N Railway line, along both sides of Pine and Hecate streets. Merchants could lease the lots, but they had to erect their own buildings. The land company built rental homes for those who could not afford to build. For this they charged a monthly rent of 90 cents each. Unemployed workers had free accommodation. House rentals remained at a fixed cost of five dollars per month until 1955, when they were increased to seven dollars per month. Business premises rented for fifteen dollars per month. The company maintained the right to run all gambling clubs, an important source of income.[23]

The move was completed by the summer of 1908. The now-familiar array of wooden buildings with overhanging balconies and wooden sidewalks that is depicted in old photographs constituted the beginning of the third Chinatown. Large wooden gates were erected at the entrances to the community.

The City of Nanaimo assessment records of Chinatown reveal a variety of commercial and residential buildings along Pine Street. All were frame-built, with sizes ranging from a small residence of 668 square feet to the 6,360-square-foot Canton Chop Suey House restaurant at 594 Pine Street, owned by Dr. Wong Wah Soon. The land company office was located at 570 Pine Street.[24]

Pine Street ran along the city's boundary, and its northern side was within the City of Nanaimo; its southern side belonged to the provincial district of Harewood. Unfortunately, neither the City nor the Province felt responsible for water or street maintenance services; therefore, the Chinese community eventually paid taxes to both governments. [25]

The 400-seat Lum Yick Theatre was built on Pine, on the Harewood side of the street, to accommodate travelling shows. The Canton Opera appeared here during its west-coast tour. The performances raised funds to pay Chinese teachers.

A two-room school was built on Hecate Street in 1908. It operated as a full-time school until 1910 with one English and one Chinese teacher. After 1910 it was open on a part-time basis, with only Chinese children attending school every day after city school.

Rounding out the growing community were four restaurants, a church, a butcher, and general stores. Herbalist Dr. Wong, father of Chuck Wong, operated the Dai Sang Tong "Keep You Alive Drug Store" at 10 Pine Street. The tailor and dressmaker, Lee Jong, was father of Ed Lee. [26]

After the First World War, the province was in an economic recession; returning soldiers were unemployed and white workers blamed the Chinese for taking away their jobs. This resentment heightened as the number of Chinese immigrants increased, from 650 in 1918 to 4,066 in 1919. [27] The $500 head tax imposed years before did not appear to be curtailing immigration. In June 1919, immigrants of any nationality belonging to a labouring class were prohibited from landing in Canada at any of B.C.'s ports of entry.

Nanaimo Chinatown Parade.

The final assault came on July 1, 1923, when the head tax was revoked and replaced by the Chinese Immigration Act, which virtually halted all emigration from China. Chinese came to know the day as "humiliation day."

Chinese Mission School, 1900.

CHAPTER FIVE

Farming, Fishing, and Forestry

Nanaimo had always been known for its coal production, but it did have another economy, albeit a smaller one, in agriculture. The mild climate free from severe winters made the area ideal for mixed farming. Fruit, dairy, poultry, sheep, and cattle farming were all profitable. With a growing population, improved transportation links, and good marketing, Nanaimo's future looked bright. Potatoes, first cultivated by the Coast Salish on Vancouver Island during the HBC era, became a staple for many pioneer settlers. Many small farmers also made a profit from poultry, eggs, and milk sales in the community.

Clearing the Land

Clearing even a small acreage of heavily forested land to make it ready for the plough was not easy, especially for men with limited capital. They used fire to bring down some of Vancouver Island's giant trees—a formidable task. It often took days to burn the interior before the fire would eat away the tree. The undergrowth had to be cleared and burned, and there was always the fear of fire spreading. Then the area had to be fenced, if cattle were involved, and gradually the farm became productive.

Miners brought to Nanaimo from Great Britain were promised acreage after they had completed their contracts with the Hudson's Bay Company. These lands became some of the first farms in Nanaimo. The *British Columbia Gazette* of 1859 advertised the sale of 30,000 acres of agricultural and mineral lands in Nanaimo. This same year a group of "cattle holders" petitioned HBC representative Alexander Grant Dallas for a portion of meadowland. They agreed to take either 50 or 100 acres. Some of the petitioners were miners who had arrived on the *Princess Royal*: John Meakin, John Biggs, Joseph Webb, Joseph Bevilockway, John Thompson, John Richardson, Richard Richardson, Edwin Gough, Thomas Hawks, Elijah Ganner, George Baker, and Matthew Miller.[1] Baker, Biggs, Miller, and Bevilockway made another application for more land.

There were regulations on who could pre-empt land in the colony. An unmarried eighteen-year-old British subject could pre-empt 150 acres. A married man with a wife already in the colony could have 200 acres, and for each child under 18 he was entitled to an additional 10 acres.

The area surrounding Nanaimo was divided into the Mountain, Cedar, and Cranberry districts; these designations referred to the "character of the prevailing wild produce grown in each."[2] By 1863 there were six farms in the Mountain and Cranberry districts, producing only small potato crops, and employees of the Vancouver Coal Company owned an estimated 250 head of cattle.

The district around Nanaimo was known as the "North Pacific hay and pasture region,"[3] but it never managed to produce enough food locally to support its population. A British newspaper in 1861 summed up the agricultural situation:

> In Vancouver's Island very little is grown. No attention is paid to agriculture, except by a few of those who were, and still are, in the service of the HBC. A conclusive proof of this is afforded by the fact that the whole annual agricultural produce of the colony would not supply the demand in Victoria for more than one month of the year. Almost all the flour and cattle consumed in Victoria, and shipped thence to British Columbia, come from Oregon and Washington Territory.[4]

Perhaps the main reason for the lack of agriculture was that mining captured most of the labour market. As well, shipping costs would have been high for importing heavy farm equipment. However, farms owned by the Vancouver Coal Company and the Dunsmuir enterprise provided food and pasture for the animals working in the mines.

Mark Bate noted, "Cattle and sheep raising in the district have not kept pace with the requirements of the increasing population.

There is evidently room for more 'Ranchers' and maybe more modern methods of farming."[5]

Some agricultural statistics for 1865 are available in Magistrate William Hales Franklyn's papers in the British Columbia Archives. There was a total of 1,069 acres suitable for cultivation in the Nanaimo area, all free of timber. Seventeen owners worked more than 200 acres—half in pasture, half in hay. The chief crops were oats, barley, and the old staple, potatoes. The area had a large number of livestock, including 231 pigs, 88 bulls and cows, 112 steers and calves, 55 sheep, 28 oxen, and 9 horses.

Cedar District Pioneer Farms

Farms thrived in the Cedar district south of Nanaimo. Before transportation links were improved, these early farms kept Nanaimo stores stocked with dairy products, fresh vegetables, and fruit.

Magistrate William Hales Franklyn owned Cob Tree Farm at Cedar and had 70 acres under cultivation in 1864, with 70 cattle plus a few pigs and sheep. His farm was considered a model farm for the time. After Franklyn moved to Nanaimo, Englishman Thomas D. Jones purchased the farm. The next occupant was Edward Henry Michael, a veteran of the Crimean War. The Michael family had lived in the Falkland Islands, Peru, and Panama before settling in Cedar in 1878. Within a few years Michael established his own farm, known as Lake View Farm. He later became the justice of the peace for Cedar.[6]

In 1862 an Englishman and a Scot entered a partnership to establish the Riverside Farm near York Lake. Charles York was from Barnsley, Yorkshire, and his partner, James Gordon, came from Lanarkshire, Scotland. Theirs was a dairy farm with a herd

Horses grazing at the York Farm, Cedar, in 1890.

of 50 cows, although the 400 acres provided ample opportunity for various field crops.[7] Produce from the farm was ferried across the Nanaimo River and sold in Nanaimo. The pair dissolved their partnership in 1880 when Gordon established his own farm at the end of Gordon Road (where Harmac is presently located). Gordon's son Kenneth, who was born in Cedar in 1871, recalled a particular important social gathering held in the York barn on July 1, 1878. Gordon and York had sponsored the successful Conservative candidate Arthur Bunster; this, coupled with Dominion Day celebrations, was a good excuse for a barn dance. Nanaimo piper Robert Jameson and Harry Bolton, who played the mouth organ, supplied music for the event. Friends and neighbours danced the night away.[8]

Sam Fiddick, who is known for building the Occidental Hotel near the E & N Railway station in Nanaimo, "the only brick fire-proof hotel in the city, and situated in the healthiest portion of the city,"[9] also had a farm in the Cedar area. Fiddick was a sailor when he first visited Nanaimo. He married Elizabeth Grandam. The young couple settled on a farm near the Nanaimo River in 1873 and raised their family there. They had two blocks of land of 100 acres each alongside the HBC grant. After Fiddick's death, his farm was sold to Herb Armishaw and became known as Baby's Own Dairy Farm.

William M. Thomas's farm on Yellow Point Road was on the east arm of Quennell Lake in Cedar. When the Nanaimo Creamery opened in 1905, Thomas was one of three farmers shipping cream to the dairy. He also raised horses and took great pride in being a "driver" who could make the ten-mile trip to Nanaimo in one hour.

Edward Quennell lived on the shore of the lake that bears his name. He came to Nanaimo in 1864 and worked at various jobs in the mines and on steamboats, before becoming a rancher and butcher. On his 425-acre farm he had 200 sheep and 50 cattle. Quennell employed twelve men and had two retail shops in Nanaimo. In his butcher shop, Quennell & Sons, he processed ham, bacon, and lard at the rear of the store. His butcher-shop operation was a partnership with Frank Veale, his neighbour at Quennell Lake.

Edward and Julie Wilcox married in 1870, and they had three children. After Julie's tragic death from typhoid fever, Edward married again, in 1875, to Maria Biggs, whose parents were *Princess Royal* pioneers John and Jane Biggs. Edward and Maria raised ten children.[10] As a businessman, Edward kept a keen eye on city affairs. By 1900 he had served two terms as mayor of Nanaimo and four as alderman and was chairman of the school board and president of the Union Brewing Company.

One of two butcher shops operated by Edward Quennell.

Louis Stark, an African-American, pre-empted 160 acres in the Cranberry district in 1873 and established a farm there. He had left Saltspring Island after some violence aimed at his black farm workers. William Robinson, a Sunday-school teacher and labourer on the Stark farm, was found murdered in his small cabin on the Stark property. Giles Curtis, the worker who replaced Robinson, was also found murdered, his throat cut. A Cowichan Native paid the ultimate price for the crime in July 1869 when he was hanged at Chemainus. The evidence was considered dubious, as it had come from a young Native girl. Upset over these incidents, the Stark family decided to move to Ganges. Later, Louis moved to the Cranberry district, south of Nanaimo. Two years later his wife, Sylvia, and their children joined him. Their daughter Emily was the first teacher at North Cedar School.[11]

Gabriola Island Pioneer Farms

Gabriola Island had several farms producing meat and vegetables for the Nanaimo market in 1874. The *Nanaimo Free Press* reported on May 15, 1875, that there were 22 settlers on the island, "four of whom were about to enter into the hop business," and there was still more land available for farming. "Most of these settlers have made comfortable homes for themselves and families."

A number of fruit trees on the island produced apples, plums, pears, and peaches.[12] The difficulty for island farmers wishing to sell their produce was getting it to market. This was partially solved when Biggs Portage opened.

Two early Gabriola Island farmers were Thomas Degnen and Robert Gray, who met when they worked in the Nanaimo coal mines. Both men had come from Ireland, so they had much in common.

Degnen pre-empted 160 acres in 1862. The land was forested, with heavy undergrowth and brush—backbreaking work to clear, even with a couple of oxen. The soil was rich, however, and Degnen successfully raised crops and market produce. He then added sheep and a few cattle to the enterprise. He married Jane Janimetga, the daughter of the chief of the Cowichan tribe. The couple had nine children, all born on Gabriola Island. The farm eventually expanded to more than 600 acres. Degnen lamb was a welcome addition to the dining tables in Nanaimo. Pigs, chickens, and turkeys thrived, and Degnen cleared more land for an orchard.[13]

Robert Gray also had hundreds of acres under cultivation. He too kept sheep, and, like Degnen's, his lamb was very much prized in Nanaimo. Beef, poultry, and eggs were also taken to market. Gray had another occupation as the lighthouse keeper on Entrance Island, a position that often kept him away from his wife, family,

Tragedy on the Stark Farm

The Stark farm in Nanaimo's Cranberry district was adjacent to that of Ephraim Hodgson, a friend of James Dunsmuir. Hodgson was "known to deal with recalcitrant homesteaders whose land lay in Dunsmuir's way or whose pre-emption entitled them to a part of the coal Dunsmuir regarded as his sole preserve."[4] In 1896 Louis was 85, and still a successful farmer. He had no interest in mining or in mineral rights. Hodgson offered to buy his farm, but Louis refused to sell. Not long after, the body of Louis Stark was found at the bottom of a cliff. Evidence presented at the coroner's inquest was contradictory, and when the police took no action, his son John hired a private detective to investigate the circumstances of his father's death. Police arrested Hodgson in August 1896, but there was little evidence implicating him, so he was released. The irony of the case was that Hodgson later became a provincial police officer. The Louis Stark case was never solved.

and farm. After Gray's death, his son James remained on the farm, married, and raised his family there.

Nanaimo Pioneer Farms

There were three early farms off the Comox Road—those of Peter Sabiston, William Westwood, and a man named Brown—plus the Chinese farms of Wing Lee at Quarterway and Wong Gun Sai at Departure Bay and the two company farms. Nanaimo businessman John Hirst also operated farms at Englishman River and Gabriola Island.[14] Mine manager Charles Nicol had his own 160-acre farm where he employed several farm workers to look after the livestock and crops.[15]

Wakesiah Farm, owned by the Vancouver Coal Company, produced hay and oats to feed the mine animals. A large red barn had the capacity to store at least 200 tons of hay. Teams of horses pulling hay wagons could drive through one end of the barn and out the other, unloading the hay inside. The company farm manager was a man named Cunningham, and under his direction the farm was able to produce enough vegetables and fruit, including strawberries, to be sold on the local market. Eventually 560 acres came under cultivation, nine of them in oats, producing 134 bushels per acre.

The Dunsmuir Farm, owned by the Robert Dunsmuir family, occupied the Millstone Valley on both sides of Jingle Pot Road and extended south as far as East Wellington Road.[16]

Promoting Agriculture

The Vancouver Island Development League, the forerunner of the Board of Trade and present-day Chamber of Commerce, was a booster of agriculture:

> Vancouver Island has an area of 15,000 square miles … something over one million acres of arable land under improvement and … a very large area available for pastoral purposes. Millions of acres now occupied by standing timber will be further available for farm lands when the timber is cut off.[17]
>
> Vancouver Island lands are very productive and the climate and other conditions being so congenial a great many settlers are coming from the Prairie Provinces to take up land in the district of Nanaimo. A 50-acre Vancouver Island farm is the equal of a 200-acre farm in the middle-west, price and productiveness considered.[18]

The government agricultural inspector compared the land around Nanaimo with the famous Okanagan fruit lands and said, "Equally good if not better fruit can be grown around Nanaimo."

The first evidence that agriculture had become an industry to be celebrated was the Nanaimo Dairy Agricultural and Horticultural Society fair, held on October 6, 1894, in a log building near the present-day Bowen Park complex.[19]

By the turn of the century, agriculture played a significant part in the economy of the province. Although not as important as elsewhere in Canada, where it was a major employer, the industry had developed, particularly on southern Vancouver Island and the Gulf Islands and in Cowichan, Comox, Courtenay, and the Alberni Valley. The government actively promoted farming as a way of life. Former HBC men and miners who had fulfilled their contracts often turned to the land to make a living, and new settlers arriving in the province could easily obtain sufficient land to start a small farm. Many of the farms remained small and were passed down from generation to generation, while others grew enough produce to sell at market. Still, in Nanaimo and elsewhere in the province, produce continued to be imported from the United States.

A post office was a good barometer of a community's agricultural growth. If there was one, it usually meant there were sufficient settlers to warrant the service. The first post offices were housed in small general stores. As Jean Barman says in her history of B.C.: "The number of post offices in the Vancouver Island and the Lower Mainland regions tripled from 34 during the 1870s to over 100 in the next decade and then to twice that number in the 1890s. By the mid-1890s a dozen of the most populous Gulf Islands had postal service. In almost every case, these communities were based on agriculture."[20] By 1884 Nanaimo finally had a beautiful new Dominion Post Office building on Front Street. This did not, however, come about through the growth in agriculture, but out of necessity for a growing city. This building perhaps demonstrated that the city had come of age.

Fishing—Harvesting the Sea

The fishing trade was already established when the HBC first arrived on Vancouver Island. Natives had fished in coastal waters for thousands of years. The HBC recognized the importance of the salmon fishery, and the company traded with Natives as early as 1821.

At first, salmon mainly augmented food supplies at the fur-trading posts. When it was cured, salmon became another addition to the HBC's articles of trade. Local markets also absorbed the early catches of cod, sole, and halibut. Cured salmon was first traded to the Orient, because Britain was too far away to make shipment economical. Another market opened when the gold rush brought new settlers to Vancouver Island.

The HBC obviously attached importance to the salmon fishery, as it signed on John Flett, from the Orkney Islands, to a five-year contract to make barrels for the salmon fishery on Vancouver Island.[21] The first shipment to England of 300 cases of B.C. salmon was made in 1870.

Native Fishery

The Snuneymuxw considered a weir the most simple and efficient method of catching salmon. A fishing weir was being used on the Nanaimo River when the miners arrived and was still in use in 1887. The Department of Fisheries report for 1886–87 has an entry dated October 6, 1887: "Nanaimo River weirs and nets at work." The report also credits the Snuneymuxw with observing "the weekly close time set regarding the opening and closing of weirs on small streams."[22]

Nanaimo miners learned a great deal from the Snuneymuxw about harvesting the sea, and a healthy system of trading developed. Several entries in the Joseph William McKay portion of the Nanaimo daybook during the first two years of the HBC's tenure in Nanaimo relate to trading with the Snuneymuxw for fish, particularly salmon. On November 8, 1852, McKay traded 300 salmon with the local tribe. On occasion, the Native fishery cut into the production and loading of coal. On July 11, 1854, McKay noted: "Most of the Indians away gathering shell fish being much in want of provisions and the remarkable low tides of this full moon affords them an opportunity of getting a supply although it much retards the loading of the *Cadboro*."[23] McKay's successor as officer-in-charge, Captain Charles Edward Stuart, also complained that the Snuneymuxw's move to their fall fishing site greatly hindered coal loading. His diary reveals their fishing activity:

March 16: Shoals of herring arrived. Indians all fishing.

March 17, 1856, Isbister, Finlay and Rich engaged salting herrings, which we trade off the Indians at a rate of five barrels for a blanket.[24]

For centuries the Snuneymuxw harvested the herring that crowded the waters of Departure Bay and Nanaimo Harbour during the first few months of each year. The first fish captured were the best quality, but as the season advanced the product deteriorated. Quantities of herring spawn were collected and dried and used for a food called "skoc." Natives had a unique way of gathering the glutinous eggs on cedar boughs placed in shallow spawning grounds. Salmon, cod, and herring were preserved using the salt from the Nanaimo salt spring.

Dogfish oil was also a very important commodity in Nanaimo, because the oil was used in miners' lamps as well as for greasing skid roads for loggers. The dogfish is a small shark about five feet in length found in abundance along the coast. Oil from the fish livers was one of the earliest products of the fishing industry in B.C. Nanaimo required large quantities of the oil for lubricating and lighting, as did steamers and sailing vessels.[25] The oil was also used in lighthouses, as it produced a brilliant light and was cheaper than any other oil that could be imported.

A dogfish refinery located on the east side of Newcastle Island produced enough fish oil for the mines. Miners paid 35 cents for a gallon of the oil, which would last a month. In 1908 the Dominion Fisheries Commission of B.C. recommended that dogfish carcasses be marketed as fresh fish. This helped alleviate fishermen's complaints that dogfish cut through fish lines and ate fish from the hooks, leaving only the heads. Dogfish were marketed, mostly in the U.S., as "whitefish" or "greyfish" or sometimes as "salmon shark." This market declined after the First World War.

In the 1860s the Snuneymuxw began shifting from traditional subsistence fishing to commercial fishing in response to the demand for salmon and the emergence of the fish-canning industry. The increased demand also brought white fishermen into the industry, which meant competition for the available fish.

One British author noted the lack of interest in Vancouver Island fisheries: "No attempt has yet been made to develop them, and, with trifling exceptions they still remain in the hands of the native fish-eating Indians who subsist almost entirely on salmon, cuttle-fish, shell-fish, etc. caught in the vicinity of the Island."[26] He further noted that the "development of the fisheries of Vancouver Island [was] both necessary and judicious."

New Rules—Fishing after Confederation

After Confederation, the Canadian government took charge of B.C. fishing, and set new regulations on how and where Native people could fish. The regulations particularly affected subsistence fishing. In 1878 charges were made that Natives destroyed millions of young salmon and also wastefully destroyed salmon in the spawning grounds. Fisheries inspector Alex C. Anderson repudiated this claim, stating that any deterioration in fishing stock must be ascribed to other causes. Fourteen tribes under distinct treaty had their fishing rights secured. He recommended they be exempt from the general fishery law.

New rules introduced in 1889 prohibited Natives from using drift nets and spears in subsistence fishing. More changes in 1891 allowed Natives to fish during closed season for food purposes only, "but not for the purpose of sale, barter, or traffic. No trader, peddler, hawker, or any other person whomsoever shall engage in buying, trading or being in possession of fish of any description, caught or killed by Indians, half-breeds, or any other person, or any Indian reserve, or elsewhere during the close seasons fixed by law."

Fish Canneries

The Native population represented the largest labour pool in the canneries along the Fraser River during the developing years of the industry. Men crewed the cannery fishing boats while their wives cleaned the fish and filled cans with salmon. In 1884 there were 1,280 Natives employed in the canneries.

When the Chinese workers entered the industry, they soon displaced the Natives. White workers usually acted as managers, supervisors, or mechanics. After the gold rush, white settlers—Norwegians, Scots, Newfoundlanders, and Nova Scotians—joined in the harvest of the sea; however, it was the arrival of the Japanese in the industry that made officials take notice.

Fishing Guardians

By 1886 "fishing guardians" were appointed to oversee the rivers of Vancouver Island and report on how the regulations were being observed. Fisheries superintendent Thomas Mowat toured Vancouver Island aboard the schooner *Pathfinder*. He saw a future for the fishing industry if only there were enough fishermen. Presumably he meant white fishermen! His report of the expedition concluded that if fishermen immigrated to Vancouver Island and received a subsidy from the government for a couple of years, "the fisheries would be developed much quicker than by any other mode."[5]

Fisheries District Number 3

As the fishing industry developed, the province was divided into three districts. In District Number 3, which included both the east and west coasts of Vancouver Island, the east-coast centres of the herring fishery were in Nanaimo and Victoria; the west-coast centres for cod and salmon were at Ucluelet and Tofino. The regular fishing season lasted about seven months, from the middle of April to the middle of November.[27]

The Early Forest Industry

During the early years of Vancouver Island, HBC sawmills produced lumber for the company's mines and housing. The first HBC sawmill was erected in 1847 at the head of Esquimalt Harbour. Captain Grant, the first settler, built a small water-powered mill at the northeast end of Sooke Basin. John Muir, one of the first miners hired in Scotland to work at Fort Rupert and then later at Nanaimo, purchased the sawmill after he had completed his mining contract with the HBC. Former HBC Nanaimo officer-in-charge Joseph William McKay and provincial surveyor Joseph D. Pemberton were partners in the Island Steam Sawmill Company at Albert Head, Victoria. This sawmill was destroyed by fire in August 1859;[28] it had not been a profitable venture for the young men.

Most of the water-powered sawmills operating on Southern Vancouver Island in the 1850s failed because they could not compete with the Puget Sound sawmills. It was not until the demand for building material increased during the gold-rush days of 1858 that the British Columbia forest industry gained a foothold. William Sayward, a lumberman from Maine, cut logs at Mill Bay for buildings in Victoria. He later operated a sawmill at Rock Bay, closer to Victoria.[29]

In 1862 Adam George Elliott operated another small water-powered sawmill at Horse Shoe Bay, later named Chemainus, in partnership with J.A. Bradshaw and Harry Guillod.[30] The Anderson Sawmill at the head of Alberni Canal operated from 1861 to 1864, producing lumber for export. During its short life, it shipped lumber to ports around the world. Incredibly, the mill ran out of easily accessible timber. Technology had not advanced sufficiently to harvest logs from the mountainsides.

The Nanaimo Sawmill

The HBC sawmill at Millstone River in Nanaimo, near the salt-spring shed, was completed in 1854. The Snuneymuxw supplied most of the logs at the price of eight logs for a blanket, delivered at high water when needed. Each log had to be no less than fifteen inches in diameter at the small end and fifteen feet long. If logs were smaller than that, sixteen of them were needed to purchase a blanket. When there was plenty of water, the mill ran night and day to keep up with the demand for lumber. However, there was often a shortage of water. And sometimes it was not lack of water that stopped the operation, but a good bottle of HBC rum brought to the site.[31] By 1864, the sawmill could barely meet local demand, so lumber had to be shipped from a mill on the Fraser River.[32]

Chauncey Carpenter

Chauncey Carpenter purchased the Nanaimo Sawmill in 1875 and continued to satisfy local trade. The mill produced 5,000 board feet of lumber a day. The logging camp was located in the Nanaimo River area. Carpenter established another sawmill and logging camp about seven miles up Millstone River for the convenience of the Wellington mines. He employed about 60 men in both mills.[33]

Under Carpenter's management, wages were $30 per month plus board. But when the mill was idle, board was deducted—a dollar per day. Carpenter managed the payroll so that at the end of the month workers never received more than $10. Eric Duncan, a Scottish immigrant who worked at the sawmill for a short time in 1878, provided information on the working conditions:

> The whistle woke us at 5 a.m., breakfast at 5.30 a.m. and start work at 6. Whistle blew for dinner at 12, work resumed at 12.30 and continued till 6, when we had supper and were free for the rest of the day. Lodging was two ancient block-houses of hewed square logs, built by the Hudson's Bay Company on the bank of Millstream. They had two stone fireplaces in each, and small windows with iron-bound shutters, and rows of wooden bunks for which we brought our own bedding. They were infested with rats, which scampered over us all night long, but we got used to them.[34]

Despite the long hours and uncomfortable surroundings, Duncan said the food was good "and of considerable variety."

Andrew Haslam

Andrew Haslam arrived in Nanaimo in 1874 to work for the Nanaimo Sawmill. Originally from Northern Ireland, Haslam emigrated in

1861 with his parents, who settled in New Brunswick. He left there in 1870 for Winnipeg, where he found work with McArthur & Co. in the lumber industry. A year later he moved to Texas for two years, where he again worked in forestry. After two years at the Nanaimo Sawmill he moved to New Westminster and invested in Hendry, McNair, Haslam & Kelly. The company was successful, operating a box factory in New Westminster and a small sawmill and sash-and-door factory in Nanaimo. The company discovered it had to incorporate in order to hold any real estate, so it reorganized and became known as the Royal City Planing Mills (Limited).

The company purchased the Nanaimo Sawmill in 1885 and operated it until 1886, when Haslam and a partner, Mr. Lees, bought it out after selling their interest in the parent company. Eventually Haslam bought out Lees and became the sole owner of the Nanaimo Saw & Planing Mill.

In 1884 Haslam married Eva Macdougal of New Brunswick. The couple had three children, Charles, William, and Ian.[35] During his time in New Westminster, Haslam was elected to city council three times.[36]

The business prospered, but Haslam's luck changed drastically in May 1904 when fire destroyed the sawmill, representing a loss of $70,000. The mill reopened two months later and Haslam had just begun to recover from the first fire when a second one struck. Unable to recover financially, he lost all his Nanaimo properties, including his home (which was later named Haslam Hall). In November 1905 the Ladysmith Lumber Company purchased the sawmill for $72,450.[37] Haslam moved to Vancouver where he was employed in the government log-scaling department. He became B.C.'s first log-scale inspector in 1906.

Dangerous Playground

As young boys, Samuel Gough and George Bevilockway often played on the logs on the river. Sometimes they rode the logs as they were pulled upstream by oxen or by Snuneymuxw workers. This was a dangerous playground for youngsters. Tragedy hit the small community in August 1855 when Elijah Ganner's son William Henry, aged eleven, drowned after falling beneath logs in the river. Attempts were made to rescue the boy, but it was too late.[6] Another young boy drowned in a similar accident in April 1883. John Renwick Horne, almost six years of age, the eldest son of William and Jane Horne, slipped on some planks and drowned.[7]

Haslam Hall at the corner of Wallace Street and Comox Road. Inset: Andrew Haslam.

Haslam House—A Grand Victorian Mansion

In 1893 Andrew Haslam built one of the finest homes in Nanaimo at the corner of Wallace Street and Comox Road. For decades the grand Victorian mansion on the hill facing the water was an imposing landmark. It was designed by James Kelly, a local architect, and built by Mr. Summerhayes at a cost of $6,000, and like the earlier Franklyn House, it became the setting for many social events in the community. When the building was completed, Andrew Teit and other sawmill employees attended a housewarming party. Teit was very impressed by the mansion's beauty—the etched glass doors, gleaming wooden balustrades of the stairway, a candelabra that kept all the rooms bright, and the domed ceiling of the large front hall where relief cherubs, entwined with scrolls of ribbon and flowers, swam in a pale blue sky.[8]

Logging by Ox, Horse, and Rail

Logging was initially done with oxen during the summer—in winter, the men worked in the mines. One of the last men to log using oxen was Benjamin Brown, nicknamed the "Last Bullpuncher" for having logged with oxen from 1890 to 1909. He owned his own team. Many times he told stories to his family of the bulls that would not move until he swore at them.[38] Oxen were notoriously stupid and slow animals, and their drivers readily reverted to swearing to get them to move.

It became obvious that another method of logging was needed to make the process faster; this brought horses into the industry. Horses like the Clydesdale were more intelligent, could work on steeper grades and were also very strong and fast.

Many local families were involved in horse logging. Ben Morgan worked in the Yellow Point, Cedar, and Boat Harbour area along with his teamster, Harry Crane. William Marwick operated in the Chase River area, and William Turner was also known to use horses in his logging operation.

The arrival of the E & N Railway opened up vast timber resources and made logging accessible by rail. The demand for ties, trestles, and lumber for bridge building gave the forest industry its first foothold in Nanaimo and Chemainus.

A number of entries in the railway company logbook indicate that logging by rail began in Chemainus as early as July 1887. One, dated August 1, 1887, notes: "Engine Number 2 logging for Croft & Angus (1 train) gone to Chemainus to unload logs."[39]

Henry Croft and William Angus had operated a sawmill in Chemainus since 1884. The sawmill did business with Robert Dunsmuir when the railway needed lumber for bridges and railway ties. This business connection gave Croft an opportunity to meet other members of the Dunsmuir family. On July 1, 1885, the young Australian civil engineer and mining specialist married Robert Dunsmuir's daughter Mary Jean.

When Croft's sawmill enterprise began losing money, Dunsmuir purchased it from his son-in-law for $100,000. He then sold the sawmill to Wisconsin lumberman John Alexander Humbird, with whom he had entered into an agreement to purchase 100,000 acres of forest from the E & N Land Grant. Humbird picked the best timber from Chemainus and from the Nanaimo River valleys to an area north of the Courtenay River. Under the terms of the agreement, Humbird had to build or purchase a sawmill on Vancouver Island. He considered locating the mill in Victoria, but decided instead on Chemainus.

George Gartlley with his team of oxen. Logging by oxen was a difficult task, as the animals were notoriously stupid and slow.

The Victoria Lumber & Manufacturing Company Ltd. (VL&M) was incorporated on April 6, 1889. Edmund James Palmer became manager and under his direction a new sawmill was built. Theirs was the first land taken out of the E & N Land Grant, and timber cruisers picked some of the finest timber on Vancouver Island. Noted forester Martin Allerdale Grainger said of the selected forest: "I have seldom seen such a beautiful Douglas-fir forest as the Victoria Lumber & Manufacturing Company possessed. However, this is what one would expect, knowing that it was the first selection any timbercruisers had the opportunity to make out of about one and one half million acres of Douglas-fir forest between Shawnigan Lake and Campbell River."[40]

New Ladysmith Lumber Company

The Ladysmith Lumber Company that purchased the old Haslam sawmill on Millstone River was itself taken over by the New Ladysmith Lumber Company Limited in March 1911. The new company also purchased the Red Fir Lumber Company, located on the waterfront just south of the Brechin mine. It also had another sawmill and shingle mill in Ladysmith.

John W. Coburn was president and managing director of the combined mills; he also held controlling interest in five lumberyards in Saskatchewan and was director of the Shawnigan Lake Lumber Company.[41] Coburn had previously been managing director of the Ladysmith Lumber Company.

The Red Fir Lumber Mill, Nanaimo, was purchased by the New Ladysmith Lumber Company in March 1911.

The company holdings consisted of the Nanaimo sawmill—with a capacity of 70,000 board feet per ten-hour shift, a planing mill, and a sash-and-door factory—as well as two acres on the E & N Railway, tracking facilities, and nine acres of waterfront granted by the federal government for the construction of wharves and mills.

Near East Wellington, in the Mountain district, the company operated its Number 2 sawmill, covering more than seven acres. It had a capacity of 40,000 board feet per ten-hour shift as well as planing and kiln capabilities. The Ladysmith plant had a lumberyard and shingle mill on five acres; part of the acreage was leased.

The three mills employed a total of 320 men; about half were white. The mills manufactured long, heavy timbers suitable for constructing large buildings and railway bridges, plus flooring, ceiling dimension, lath, and moulding supplies. These were shipped largely to Ontario, Quebec, and the prairie provinces, as well as to parts of the United States.

Strait's Sawmill at Red Gap

In 1912 Joe and Max McKeicher operated a small sawmill at Red Gap, Nanoose Bay. Within a short time they sold it to the Newcastle Lumber Company and the Merchant Trust Company. After those companies went bankrupt, the sawmill was bought by Strait's Lumber Company in 1916. It reopened in 1917 under manager Frank Pendleton Sr.[42]

Today, Nanoose Bay seems an unlikely place to load lumber, but for several decades ships from around the world waited there

New Ladysmith Lumber Co's Staff. 1925.

New Ladysmith Lumber Company staff; president James W. Coburn is in the centre.

to do just that. They could not load directly from the mill wharves because of shallow water, so they anchored out in the bay and had the lumber brought to them on scows. This double handling of the lumber added to the overhead and brought about the eventual economic downfall of the mill.

Workers at the mill built homes along the E & N Railway tracks and across the road in a gulch in the hillside. They named their little community Red Gap after the popular novel of the day. The sawmill village had a company store, post office, school, and several boarding houses. Wooden sidewalks connected the buildings. The mill employed not only white workers, but also hired Japanese, Chinese, and East Indian workers who were housed in separate buildings. Fresh water came from the creek that flowed through the gulch. A concrete dam was constructed to collect water, which was carried in wooden pipes.

Markets for the lumber were Great Britain, Australia, the U.S., and Japan, the latter being one of the biggest customers. The mill was known for producing large timbers that were remanufactured in Japan.

Finding New Markets for B.C. Lumber

Forestry took on new importance after the First World War. Before then most sawmills in the province had not been interested in exporting lumber; they were quite content to serve the local market that had flourished during the first decade of the century. During the war years, however, the industry almost came to a standstill as workers left the logging camps and sawmills for military service.

In 1916 Edmund J. Palmer hired H.R. (Harvey Reginald) MacMillan as his assistant manager at the Victoria Lumber & Manufacturing Company (VL&M) in Chemainus. MacMillan had been the province's first chief forester in 1912, and under his direction forest-management practices were introduced.

During the First World War MacMillan became special trade commissioner to Great Britain and found an ally in the new B.C. trade agent in London, Sir Richard McBride. Together they convinced Britain to purchase lumber from Canada rather than from the U.S. Due to MacMillan's efforts, lumber from B.C. found a new and ready market.

Strait's Lumber Company, (Red Gap) Nanoose.

CHAPTER SIX

City Boom and Law and Order

N anaimo grew from a few hundred people in the 1860s to over 6,000 by 1900. During this time the city experienced an unprecedented boom. Yearly coal production rose from 18,000 tons in 1863 to a million tons a year with a record of 1,298,445 tons in 1923.[1] In 1874 there were an estimated 400 workers in the mines, but by 1900 this number came close to 3,000.

In the 1890s the city took measures to deal with the problems of an increasing population. In 1891 Albert Thrall and city clerk Samuel Gough devised a house numbering plan. Homeowners paid 25 cents to have a number placed on their houses. After the numbering project Thrall offered to supply street signs, but because of the cost the signs did not get installed until 1894, and then the street committee did the work.

In 1894 the British Columbia Annual Report noted a tannery, a cigar factory, an explosives factory, and a carriage-and-wagon works. There were also two breweries, two foundries, machine shops, and gas and electric-light works. Saloons, restaurants, and boarding houses accommodated the hundreds of young single men employed in the mines.

Law and Order in Nanaimo

Canada's most western province was still a wild frontier, and justice was dealt swiftly. Under the HBC's dominance, Nanaimo normally took care of its own offenders. Prisoners were locked up in the two cells of the

74

Bastion, or were punished according to the crime. Three men served as jailers: Edwin Gough, William Stewart, and William Weston. They made some attempts to make the prisoners useful. There was the ongoing road construction—the chain gang—or, in the early days, Magistrate William Hales Franklyn's garden, a duty that angered the miners.

The chain gang became a familiar sight in the streets of Nanaimo during the latter part of the nineteenth century. The prisoners wore leg irons and blue dungaree overalls, stamped on the back with the letters "NP." The chain gang also built the approaches to the new bridge over the Millstone River. There were reports of overcrowding in the lockup as sometimes four or five men passed the night in the "Black Hole" of Nanaimo. One visitor to the Bastion jail wrote: "I pity the poor fellow who has to pass a night in such a loathsome den, with dirty Siwashes. His olfactory nerves must be strong to stand the effect of the odor."[2]

Later the criminals were shipped to Victoria to await justice, that is, until the skippers of early vessels refused to carry such a dangerous cargo. In 1863 the *Alpha* was fired upon while transporting a Native convict to Victoria. This incident united the skippers in their refusal to carry criminals and led to the establishment of a permanent jail in Nanaimo.

By 1874 the Bastion colonial jail had become outmoded, so a new jail was constructed on Front Street, using logs and heavy timber. It contained fourteen cells and accommodation for 42 prisoners.[3] Until it was built, Adam Grant Horne's store became the community's first courthouse with accommodation for troublesome prisoners. Horne had been posted to Fort Simpson in 1864, leaving the building vacant. The whitewashed high board fence that surrounded the new facility disappointed some citizens who delighted in attending public hangings. However, on one occasion the screams of a man being hanged were plainly heard from the street outside the fence.[4]

Reluctant Police Constable—Edwin Gough

The first full-time police constable was appointed in 1863. Edwin Gough was a strong man with a reputation for bravery and fairness who abhorred weapons. He preferred settling quarrels with his fists.[5] Magistrate Franklyn thought Gough was a rough type who was irresponsible when drunk, so Franklyn fired Gough in 1865 for insolence and neglect of duties.[6] An alternate story is that Gough resigned, as he did not like being a constable; he had been a carpenter in England and probably wanted to put his skill to work. He built a number of houses in Nanaimo; then in 1870, when some miners went on strike, he and his friend Joseph Bevilockway tried their luck at a mine near Seattle. Only a month into their stay there Gough broke his leg, and his friend cared for him until they could get to Victoria, where his leg was amputated below the knee. Mark Bate noted that this friendly social man then became sullen and his wonderful singing voice was seldom heard again.

Gough opened the Nanaimo Hotel with partner William Wall in 1874, but a year later the partnership dissolved. He continued to operate the hotel with his wife Elizabeth until his death that year. Elizabeth carried on until misfortune struck in 1878, when the hotel was destroyed by fire. Her son Reuben Gough was killed in the 1879 explosion at the Wellington Colliery.[7] Another Nanaimo Hotel was built on Commercial Street, but it too was destroyed by fire in 1894. Elizabeth soldiered on and built yet another hotel, which she operated until her death in 1899.[8]

Sergeant Blake followed Gough as constable, but Magistrate Franklyn fired him too. It seemed that law and order had almost disappeared in 1866; Nanaimo was wide open to robberies and assault, and bootlegging flourished. The two Nanaimo justices of the peace wrote to the colonial secretary for assistance. William Stewart was appointed special constable; he eventually became police chief, a position he held until his death in 1904.

New Provincial Jail Built

By 1892 the provincial jail could no longer accommodate the number of prisoners assigned to it. The previous year the city had had its own lockup because of lack of space. A new brick jail was subsequently constructed on Skinner Street in 1894, containing 46 cells with accommodation for 100 prisoners. City police also used the lower part of the Bastion as a lockup from 1891 to 1897, until it could lease the old provincial courthouse and jail on Front Street for $50 a year. That building was later renovated for police offices, a lockup, a city pound, and horse stables. Since the Bastion was no longer needed, city council proposed converting it into a morgue.

By 1896 the city had a fine new courthouse, designed by Victoria architect Francis M. Rattenbury. Two years earlier the provincial legislature had voted to put $25,000 towards its construction.[9]

The Nanaimo Courthouse is today one of the city's finest historical buildings. With the Bastion, the Dominion Post Office, and the Globe Hotel, all in the vicinity of the courthouse, Front Street had shed its frontier image.

The Police Commission Takes Control

The city may have had new law courts, but keeping law and order was not an easy task in early Nanaimo. Between 1872 and 1904 the "Municipality Act, 1872," gave the city the mandate to hire police officers. The Act was amended several times, and in 1893 the management of the police force was taken out of the hands of city council and placed under the control of a police commission board. The chief of police position was created about the same time. Police were still under the direction of the superintendent of provincial police, but the administration of the force, including its payment and clothing, remained a city responsibility.

City council looked to the City of Victoria for guidance in establishing the rules of conduct for its police force; those rules were altered slightly to suit Nanaimo's requirements. The Board of Commissioners of Police for the City of Nanaimo held its first meeting on Monday, January 1, 1894.[10] Joseph Planta, police magistrate, took his oath of office as required under the Municipal Act of 1892. Mayor Andrew Haslam confirmed city clerk Samuel Gough as commission secretary, and the first order of business was the appointment of Chief of Police Alex McKinnon. Two weeks later Henry Brown was appointed police constable.

From 1894 to 1905 the police and police commission experienced many problems, especially from a public who looked to them to enforce liquor laws, Sunday closing, and public morals by-laws. When laws were not strictly enforced, residents claimed that the police were participating in gambling, prostitution, and other vices. Even police magistrate Planta was not immune to accusation and innuendo.

By the end of 1894 both Police Chief McKinnon and Constable Brown had been removed, and William Stewart was appointed temporarily as constable. The two men had committed an indiscretion that in the opinion of the police commissioners reflected on their authority. In the eyes of the commission they would not be able to carry out their duties until the courts disposed of the charges against them. The minutes of the board did not reveal the nature of the indiscretion.

The commission appointed a new police chief, James Crossan, along with Constables Jacob Neen and George A. Thompson. Crossan had come to Nanaimo from Scotland in 1876. He had worked in the mines and had been the customs officer before

William Stewart (on far left) was police constable, jailer, and lamplighter. This is the Battery on Front Street.

William Stewart—Police Constable and Lamplighter

From 1875 to 1881 William Stewart doubled as provincial police constable and jailer, and for these services he was given a small monthly wage. In 1882 city council appointed its own police constable, whose duties included not only policing but also sanitary inspection and night patrol. The night patrol, or night watchman position, was established in 1877 when hotel owners and merchants appointed a night watchman. Although council dictated patrol duties, the salary was raised through resident subscriptions. From 1879 until the mid-1880s, the night watchman also served as lamplighter. He was often sworn in as a special police constable, and eventually his position was united with the police force to come under the police commission; however, his salary was still paid partially by local businesses and the Vancouver Coal Company. Stewart got some help when a second police constable position was created.

accepting the appointment of chief of police in December 1894.[11] At this time the police commission, established for less than a year, had already lost the "rules for police" and had to send for a replacement copy from the City of Victoria.

A year later Chief Crossan and Constable Thompson were drawing fire from the Reverend D.A. McRae, the minister of St. Andrews Presbyterian Church, for their "unbecoming conduct and illegal actions."[12] McRae documented three actions he deemed "should not be tolerated in men occupying public positions." The two police officers had been seen in the Crescent Hotel on Victoria Street, playing games of chance until the early hours. On another occasion the police chief tried to enter 61 Fraser Street by the front door and, failing to do so, entered by the back door. Fraser Street had the reputation of being the red-light district where prostitution, gambling, and drinking took place. The police chief spent an hour in the house, and during this time "intoxicating liquor and cigars were bought and paid for contrary to the law." The third accusation was that he endangered the health and lives

Nanaimo Courthouse, built in 1896, was designed by architect Francis M. Rattenbury.

of citizens by failing to carry out the instructions of the medical health officer .

The investigation of the charges continued with no action taken to remove the two police officers. On February 8, 1897, the police commission received a letter from city council with a copy of a resolution requesting the board immediately remove the chief and constable. At a meeting between city council and the police commission, the latter made it clear that the action of appointing, dismissing, and management of the police rested solely with the commission and not with the city council. The commission could not comply with the request, as there were no grounds for dismissal. Mayor Joseph Davidson voted against the motion, but it was carried. City council had tried to overrule the fledgling police commission and had lost.

Council then attempted to have Police Magistrate Simpson removed from office. The 1898 council went so far as to petition the premier and the Attorney General to abolish the police magistrate position to help solve "the crisis which we have reached, in the financial condition of our city."[13] Council did not succeed, but it did manage to have the magistrate's salary cut in half.

Problems in City Council

There was more excitement at the end of November 1898 when a number of ledgers in the Collector's office were mutilated. A week later, Adam Thompson was arrested and convicted for having shortages in the accounts he kept as city treasurer. At the time of his arrest he was 24 years old. After serving his sentence, he went into the real estate and insurance business and became a notary public for British Columbia. He eventually served as commissioner for Manitoba.[14]

These events occurred as reports of the gold discovery in the Klondike spread. Following the arrest of Thompson, Mayor Davidson requested a leave of absence and left for the Klondike. At the final council meeting that term, George Campbell, the acting mayor, remarked: "The Council of 1897 had had a rather peculiar experience. The goldfields of the far north had attracted the mayor and two aldermen, while another alderman had gone to the neighboring city expecting to find a better field." Looking at all the difficulties, trials, and temptations of the year, he thought that council had made a good showing, and he hoped the incoming council would be able to straighten things out and get the city cleared of its debt.[15]

Mayor Mark Bate Returns

In the following election in 1898, all aldermen were elected by acclamation. The municipal election garnered little interest from the public. Who could blame it after the incidents of the previous year? Mark Bate was re-elected and Samuel Gough unanimously re-appointed city clerk/treasurer. These two men brought some stability into city affairs.

Mayor Mark Bate.

In 1899 city council finally regained control of police management when the statute changed the composition of the police commission to consist of the mayor and two people appointed by the lieutenant–governor in council, one of whom was to be an alderman. Police Magistrate Simpson's appointment was cancelled on March 31, 1899, and in 1900 Edmund Montague Yarwood became the new police magistrate.

The police commission settled down to deal with more mundane items such as houses of prostitution, new jail premises, gambling, and underage drinking and smoking. During the month of October 1899 there were fourteen offences reported: driving a wagon over the sidewalk, using insulting language, obstructing the sidewalk, vagrancy, causing disturbances, and allowing cattle to run at large.

Nanaimo Police Force Resigns

Nanaimo was not a city with major crime at its doorstep. The chief of police's report for the month of January 1905 showed there were eight cases of crime on the books, including charges of carrying a concealed weapon, one assault, three people charged with vagrancy, another for selling liquor to a minor, and two people for drunken conduct.

When the entire police force resigned on January 5, 1905, Mayor William Manson was happy to leave the problem to his successor. Manson had been mayor since 1901 and was not seeking another term in office. The new mayor was Albert Edward Planta, the manager of V.C. Securities Ltd. and the son of former magistrate Joseph W. Planta who had died the previous November. Mayor Planta could count on the experienced city clerk, Samuel Gough, who was first appointed in 1880 and was a valuable resource person on city affairs.

The police resigned because of an "alleged neglect of duty" complaint. This new charge may have resulted from a gambling incident, but Chief Crossan refused to discuss the subject publicly.[16]

There was no written complaint, only a verbal one, but it was enough to have the police commission advise the police force to resign. The men did just that, and the board accepted their resignations. Mayor Planta assumed that the resignations had been voluntary and that the next course of action would be to call for new applications for the positions. A spokesman for the police force called for an investigation and asked city council to reinstate the men. When he learned the policemen had been advised to resign, Mayor Planta expressed his surprise: "Am I to understand that the resignations were forced without any cause being shown?" Council subsequently granted an inquiry.

The wrangling over such a petty complaint that led to the resignation of the entire police force was certainly fodder for a *Free Press* editorial.

The position was a very delicate one, in spite of the contention that no charge was levied at the former Commissioners it virtually put them on trial. It is questionable if the present Board should have touched it at all. The resignations had been accepted and there was not a thing to show that any charge of neglect of duty lay against the police. It seemed to us that the proper remedy was to appeal, not to the Board, but to the Attorney General, asking for a Royal Commission, if the police considered they were badly used.[17]

Mayor Planta invited new applications for the position of chief of police, with a salary of $90 a month, including a free home, exclusive of fuel, water, or light; and one constable who would be paid $80 a month. The police commission, still trying to assert independence over city council, decided the people of Nanaimo should appoint the new force by voting in a plebiscite. The vote was scheduled for February 28 at the old courthouse.

Five applications for chief were received, including one from the former chief, James Crossan, and the constable, George Thompson. Twelve applications were received for constable, including one from Jacob Neen. It was clear the former police force members wanted their jobs back. Another five applications were received for either position—chief or constable.[18] On the day of the plebiscite, the police commissioners suddenly abandoned the idea of a public vote and instead decided it would make the appointments. Chief Crossan got his old job back, as did Constable Jacob Neen. Crossan remained police chief until 1912, when he retired from the force and ran for alderman. Constable Neen succeeded him and served until 1920.[19]

The Notorious Flying Dutchman

There was some revulsion to public executions in Nanaimo, depending on who was being hanged. A man designated as the official hangman travelled across the country, officiating at such sentences. The law required there be present a chaplain, doctor, warden, and witnesses. B.C.'s first hanging took place at Gallows Point, Protection Island, in 1852, when two young Natives were hanged for the murder of the Christmas Hill shepherd Peter Brown.

A hangman's noose now in the collection of the Nanaimo District Museum is a grim reminder of an execution that took place in 1913. Etched in the history of early Nanaimo is the story of Henry Wagner, a flamboyant German. The hangman, Mr. Ellis, had been in the community for a few days and had erected the scaffold on which Wagner would be hanged. Ellis was "a medium sized man, spectacled, [who had] the bearing of the professional class, being cautious, quick and methodical in plying his gruesome task."

August 28, 1913, was a beautiful summer morning in Nanaimo. On a large, bare patch of ground in the corner of the provincial jail yard on Skinner Street, the grim apparatus of death stood waiting. The scaffold was connected to the ground by a long gangplank, and from a centre beam hung a coil of rope and the gruesome black cap.

Only jail officials and those in an official position were allowed to enter the jail yard. Still, crowds gathered outside the yard to hold witness to the end of the notorious "whiskey smuggler, pirate and general bad man" who had terrorized communities along the West Coast.

Henry Wagner, also known to B.C. police as "Ferguson," and to U.S. authorities as "the Flying Dutchman," was said to be "one of the most notorious criminals who have infested the waters of Puget Sound and the Gulf of Georgia in many years."[20] It was said he had once ridden with Butch Cassidy. He was wanted in the U.S. for robbery and murder, but to residents of Lasqueti Island he was a new and harmless resident. Wagner and his wife had bought a float house there in 1912. They also owned a boat, the *Spray*. Their friend, Bill Julian, had moved into a little cabin on the island. Islanders considered them "quite ordinary folk, attending the regular meetings of the Farmer's Institute whenever they were able." They were shocked when police came and arrested Julian; Wagner was already in custody.

For several months during 1913, Wagner and Julian robbed isolated communities along the east coast of Vancouver Island. They arrived with lightning speed and efficiency, then made their getaway in their fast motorboat. Chief Constable David Stephenson with the B.C. provincial police, in charge of the northern half of Vancouver Island, was determined to put a stop to the robberies. The robbers had targeted Fraser & Bishop's store in Union Bay before, and Stephenson was convinced they would return, as the store

Arrest of Henry Wagner (centre) after Union Bay shooting, 1913.

was only a short distance from the docks and an easy prize. Two constables were placed there: Harry Westaway and Gordon Ross.

Night after night they waited in the shadows, until the morning of March 3, 1913. Westaway and Ross had sheltered from the rain under a tree and as Union Bay residents slept, the men spotted a light from a flashlight. They moved toward the store and entered cautiously. Only Westaway was armed, Ross carried a nightstick.

As soon as Ross aimed his flashlight and saw the two men behind the counter, the first burglar fired his Colt revolver. The bullet passed through Ross's shoulder and buried itself in Westaway's side. He fell unconscious to the floor. The second burglar ran for the door. Ross lunged at him, with nightstick flying, and made a frantic attempt to get the gun. After a life-and-death struggle, Ross finally succeeded in capturing his opponent and handcuffing him. Just as help reached the scene, Ross fell unconscious beside his fallen partner, Westaway. Wagner was formally charged with the murder of Westaway, was tried, and sentenced to die.

He was placed under guard in the Nanaimo jail, awaiting the arrival of the hangman. Six days before his sentence was to be carried out, Wagner attempted to kill himself in jail by lunging headfirst against the stone wall of the death cell. He was double-shackled and assigned another guard, but even this did not faze him, as he continued to boast that he would never hang.

On the day of his execution Salvation Army officers offered him prayers and spiritual guidance. Wagner asked that they sing "Nearer My God to Thee" and he joined in the singing. Hangman Ellis adjusted the noose and slipped the hood into place. He then stepped back and pulled the trap. Only moments before, Wagner had stood defiant in undershirt and coveralls, unshaven, with his long hair matted. Not a tremor was seen on the rope; death had been instantaneous.

CHAPTER SEVEN

Nanaimo's Political Leaders

*T*oward the end of the nineteenth century, the men who represented the constituents of Vancouver Island federally and provincially had a difficult task. Their ridings were large and communication was not as simple as it is today. Under the terms of Confederation in 1871, five federal constituencies were established in B.C.: the Cariboo, Yale, New Westminster, Victoria, and Vancouver Island. Victoria District had two members, but "all the remainder of Vancouver Island and all such islands adjacent thereto as were formerly dependencies of the old Colony of Vancouver Island shall constitute one District, to be designated 'Vancouver Island District' and return one member."[1] Six members would be returned to the House of Commons and three to the Senate to represent Canada's newest province.

Nanaimo had the largest population of the Vancouver Island constituency after Victoria. For some reason the "Island" part of the name was dropped and in all the official returns of the chief electoral officer the constituency is listed simply as "Vancouver," a little confusing today, but at that time the City of Vancouver did not exist as a centre of population.

The First Senators and Members of Parliament

One of the three B.C. senators was Dr. Robert William Weir Carrall, a mainland supporter of Confederation. Carrall had practised medicine in Nanaimo before moving to Barkerville in 1867. The other two were Clement Francis Cornwall, who later served as B.C.'s lieutenant-governor from 1881 to 1887, and William John Macdonald, who had been in the colony since 1851.

The first Members of Parliament (MPs) were Robert Wallace, Vancouver Island; Hugh Nelson, New Westminster; J. Spencer Thompson, Cariboo; Henry Nathan and Amor de Cosmos, Victoria; and Charles F. Houghton, Yale. These men sat for only one session, but in the next election of July 29, 1872, those of the Cariboo, New Westminster, and Victoria were re-elected. Newcomers were Edgar Dewdney, returned in Yale, and Sir Francis Hincks, who represented Vancouver Island. In 1873 dual representation federally and provincially was abolished. This ruling brought about the resignation of de Cosmos and Arthur Bunster. The latter was elected to represent Vancouver Island in the 1874 election.

Confederation blotted out the past and joined the two former colonies at the hip into a new entity; everyone was expected to put aside personal and geographic differences and speak for the province as a whole. The old battle cry of Island versus Mainland survived somewhat. Yet, there was also a feeling of renewal and recovery after the depression of the previous few years.

From Confederation to 1900, the province saw twelve premiers take office; nine resigned, three died while in office, and one was dismissed. George Anthony Walkem became premier twice and resigned both times. Each man left his mark on the province. Without a party system of government these were turbulent years in B.C. politics. Perhaps this period established the wackiness of West Coast politics in the eyes of the rest of Canada.

Members of the Legislative Assembly

John Robson, 1871–1875

The first provincial election after Confederation saw two Victoria candidates vie to become members of the Legislative Assembly (MLAs) for the Nanaimo riding. John Robson, editor of the *Daily British Colonist*, ran against Joseph Westrop Carey. It seemed Nanaimo would continue to be represented by outside interests, as it had before Confederation. Records show 90 people voted in this election: 57 for Robson and 33 for Carey. Robson was the same man who had earlier dismissed Vancouver Island as an "insignificant little island." He has the distinction of being the first MLA to represent Nanaimo.

Robson was born in 1824 at Perth, Ontario, of Scottish parents. He married Susan Longworth of Goderich, Ontario, in April 1854 and in 1859 they came to B.C. They settled first in New Westminster, and in 1861 Robson established the *British Columbian* newspaper. Through this journal he fought the battle for constitutional government, which was not always an easy task. He entered politics in 1864, serving on the New Westminster council, and in 1867 he was elected to the Legislative Council of B.C. and served until Confederation. By this time the couple had moved to Victoria, where John became editor of the *Daily British Colonist*, a position he held for six years. After Confederation he served as Nanaimo's MLA from 1871–1875, when he accepted a federal appointment as paymaster and commissary of the Canadian Pacific Railway surveys until that position was abolished in 1879. He returned to New Westminster in 1879 and resumed publishing the *British Columbian*. But politics was in his blood and he was again elected, this time to represent New Westminster as MLA. During this period, he was appointed provincial secretary, minister of mines, finance and agriculture, and was re-elected in 1886 and 1890. He became premier of B.C. in 1889.[2]

John Bryden, 1875–1876

The next election, held in 1875, had three candidates, all from Nanaimo: John Bryden, Joseph Ferguson, and David William Gordon. In this election the Natives and Chinese were disenfranchised and could not vote, and before long Japanese were added to the list. Voting seemed to be a privilege only of the white male population; women did not get the vote until 1917. Schoolteachers were also prohibited from voting or campaigning. Bryden won over his nearest rival Gordon, a local contractor. A year later Bryden resigned, saying he had to look after his business interests. A by-election in January of 1877 returned Gordon to the legislature. His two opponents in that by-election were James Harold, a miner, and Peter Sabiston, the manager of the Miners' Hotel. Gordon lost the next election in May 1878, beaten at the polls by James Atkinson Abrams.[3]

James Atkinson Abrams, 1878–1882

Abrams was born in Napanee, Ontario, where he apprenticed as a tanner. He worked for two years in New York and three years in San Francisco before coming to Victoria in 1867, where he was foreman in Rock Bay Tannery and afterwards in Belmont Tannery. He moved to Nanaimo and established the Nanaimo Tanning Company in 1878; he married Georgina Wenborn the same year. He retired from public office in the 1882 provincial election to give more attention to his business. In 1886 he joined a partnership, Abrams & McLean, in Vancouver, but still kept his Nanaimo business. In June the fire that destroyed part of Nanaimo also consumed his tanning business. He sold his partnership in Vancouver and what remained of his business in Nanaimo. Abrams became a justice of the peace and served on Nanaimo city council in 1889.[4]

David William Gordon, 1877–1878; MP 1882–1893

David William Gordon came to Victoria in June 1858. He was born in Kent, Ontario, on February 27, 1832. His parents were United Empire Loyalists. He had previously apprenticed with a contractor, learning the building and carpentry trade. When he arrived in Victoria the city was just starting to grow, so he did well in the building trade. In 1862 he decided to move to Nanaimo, and two years later he married Emma Robb, who was the daughter of a Comox family and whose mother had been matron aboard the bride ship *Tynemouth*. Of the eight children born to the Gordons, two baby daughters died.[5]

Gordon was a close friend of Robert Dunsmuir, and they often talked business or politics. He built a house for Dunsmuir at Departure Bay, not as grand as the one later built in Victoria, but a grand house, nonetheless. Ardoon was one of the finest homes built in 1876. The two-storey house had a deep verandah and delicate gingerbread clinging to its steeply pitched eaves. It seems likely Dunsmuir first talked Gordon into public life.

The *Colonist* of January 1877 reported: "The Nanaimo election—return of Mr. Gordon, the reform candidate. The election to fill the seat in the local House made vacant by the retirement of Mr. J. Bryden took place at Nanaimo on Friday. The result: D.W. Gordon, 103, James Harold, 86, Peter Sabiston, 71."[6]

Gordon first tried for the federal seat in 1878 but lost the election. He was first returned to the House of Commons on August 4, 1882, winning out over a powerful politician, Arthur Bunster. Earlier that year his wife Emma died. In politics Gordon was a Liberal Conservative, and was a prominent member of both the Freemasons and the Oddfellows. He remarried in 1886 to Statora Kitty, of Lansing, Ontario. They had three children. In the general election of 1887 he ran against a formidable opponent, magistrate Joseph Planta, the former schoolteacher.

The *Nanaimo Free Press* reported that all the saloons were closed for the election and "the 'old stiffs' who had neglected to replenish the 'pocket pistol' the night before got thirsty during the day and they voted the election a 'very dry' one."[7] *Nanaimo Free Press* founder George Norris kept the *Free Press* office open because of the demand for news of the election. The returns showing Gordon ahead were met with cheers, but when it became clear he had carried south and north Wellington by a majority of only 22, the excitement became more intense. Cheers followed when it was announced he had carried Saanich by a majority of one. "In the evening a torchlight procession headed by the Nanaimo Brass Band and Chemainus Drum and Fife Band was formed at the Dew Drop Hotel and, accompanied by a large concourse of citizens, marched through the principal streets to the residence of Mr. Gordon on Prideaux Street."[8]

Gordon had won another term in office.

William Raybould, 1882–1886, and Robert Dunsmuir, 1882–1889

The provincial election of 1882 was a rather strange one for the leading candidate, Robert Dunsmuir, who was off on a trip to Scotland. He never campaigned, nor did he have to suffer tedious door knocking or public meetings to garner support. However, he could count on the recognition factor, as his name was a household word in Nanaimo. Before he left he happened to mention his possible candidacy. There were four other candidates for what was now a two-seat riding. They were William Raybould, who with his wife operated a clothing shop in town; a local butcher, Edward Quennell; William Hinksman, a Wellington coal miner; and John George Barnston.

The most important election issue was the construction of the E & N Railway, and Dunsmuir seemed to have that firmly in hand. Without government party affiliation, Barnston and Hinksman supported the government of the day under Premier Robert Beaven, while Quennell, Dunsmuir, and Raybould supported the opposition. Dunsmuir and Raybould garnered the largest number of the 770 votes cast.

Labour Issues

The Dunsmuirs were getting very rich and, as some viewed it, it was on the backs of the miners. The community seemed to be divided along class lines, and politicians did not appear to be interested in social reform. These feelings became abundantly clear in the 1886 election when the Workingmen's Protective Association felt strongly enough to run candidates in two elections, in Victoria and Nanaimo. Noah

Coal Mines Regulation Act

During David William Gordon's term as MLA he was responsible for pushing through the bill known as the Coal Mines Regulation Act, 1877. A coroner's jury report of 1876 into "Black Damp" deaths in the mines urged the province to introduce the legislation. This bill regulated who could or could not work in the mines and prohibited the hiring of Chinese in dangerous positions. Mine owners did not like the restrictions, but their petition was ignored and the new bill passed. After a term in the provincial legislature, Gordon turned his eye toward Ottawa, no doubt again influenced by Dunsmuir.

Shakespeare, a former miner from Nanaimo, and brother to Phoebe Raybould, formed the labour group in Victoria in 1879. The objective of the association was to protect the working class against the influx of Chinese.[9] Shakespeare also presided over the Anti-Chinese Society. The two candidates in Nanaimo representing labour were James Lewis, a former miner and now Gabriola farmer, and miner Samuel Henry Myers. They found themselves in stiff competition from Dunsmuir and Raybould, who easily took the election.

The labour movement was not yet well organized in Nanaimo, but the candidates did succeed in putting Chinese exclusion on the agenda of the election. The miners did not give up, and despite being dejected over Dunsmuir's success, they decided to organize the Miners' and Mine Labourers' Protective Association and fight for the eight-hour day, the recognition of their union, a limit on Chinese immigration, the arbitration of industrial disputes, and other benefits.

Dunsmuir's Dominance Continues

When the public learned of the E & N Land Grant awarded to Robert Dunsmuir, many were outraged that such a large portion of Vancouver Island had been given over to private interests. Prime Minister John A. Macdonald shrugged off all criticism. "We want more Dunsmuirs, more men of action, less men of straw and cheek, and more men of brains and energy to complete our provincial destiny."[10]

After their father's entry into provincial politics in 1882, Dunsmuir's sons, Alex and James, became more involved in the management of the company. Robert Dunsmuir moved to Victoria.

Dunsmuir had not forgotten a promise made to his wife Joan to build her a castle. In 1882 he bought a piece of land overlooking Victoria. He added to this more acreage until, by 1885, he owned 28 acres—a spectacular residential building site ten minutes from the city's business sector. The fact it was high above Victoria did not escape him. He had grand designs to build a landmark, a castle that would dominate the skyline "as he had come to dominate the business and political life of the province."[11]

The dream mansion with a tower was named Craigdarroch after the Scottish home of Annie Laurie, the woman made famous by Scottish poet Robert Burns. No one knows how much it cost to build, but it probably was the most expensive residence in B.C. at the time. Perhaps Dunsmuir visualized himself firmly ensconced in the palace as Sir Robert Dunsmuir, for there was a movement afoot to give him such a knighthood.

Dunsmuir was flush from his success in building the Esquimalt & Nanaimo Railway. The conservative-thinking *Colonist*, which had supported both Sir John A. Macdonald and Dunsmuir, came out publicly with a pronouncement: "If her Majesty were to bestow upon him the dignity of a knighthood, few would be found to begrudge this progressive man the honor."[12]

The timing for a knighthood would have been perfect for the following year, 1887, when the country planned to celebrate Queen Victoria's Golden Jubilee. There was speculation she would mark her 50th year by bestowing honours on some of her loyal subjects. Unfortunately the executive council delayed passing the formal motion until the actual anniversary of the date Queen Victoria ascended to the throne, June 28. Council suggested it would be fitting to bestow a knighthood on the leading citizen of B.C. "Besides taking an active part in public affairs, he is always to the fore in private enterprise." The communiqué noted Dunsmuir had not sought the honour, but he had been advised and had agreed to accept it. Alex Davie, the president of the executive council wrote: "I presume that financial standing as well as social status is taken into consideration in these matters and in this respect Mr. Dunsmuir is well qualified for he is one of Canada's millionaires."[13] The council's recommendation arrived in Ottawa too late to make the honour list. When the Queen's Honour List was announced on New Year's Day, only the name of Joseph Trutch was included.

Death of William Raybould

William Raybould died December 3, without ever taking his seat. The businessman and politician died as a result of an unfortunate accident. On that fateful morning, his neighbour heard a strange noise and went out to the rear of his shop to investigate. He found the crumpled body of Raybould. The doctor was called; Raybould was found to have suffered a fractured skull and was rushed to hospital. He died later that day; he was 50. An inquiry speculated that Raybould had been taking stock and accidentally opened the rear door and fell to the ground.

On the day of his funeral, all the stores in town closed for the day. His wife Phoebe sold her millinery business to Richardson & Horner, but she stayed on for a time as seamstress until another person was hired, then moved to Vancouver. A by-election held on January 3, 1887, returned George Thomson, a government supporter.

Death of Robert Dunsmuir

Nanaimo and Wellington once again grieved, this time not for lost miners, but for the man who had been so much a part of their working world. Robert Dunsmuir died in Victoria on April 12, 1889, with Joan by his side, never having seen the completion of his castle, or having the knighthood bestowed by the Queen. However, he had seen the E & N Railway finally arrive in Victoria the year before; this was probably the most satisfying achievement for the indentured miner from Scotland.

Robert Dunsmuir's funeral was held April 16, 1889, in Victoria. The mines at Wellington and Nanaimo closed. Hundreds of men and women took advantage of free passes on the E & N Railway to attend the funeral. In Wellington, Nanaimo, and Victoria all the schools and shops closed and the flags flew at half-mast. Dunsmuir lay at rest in Fairview as mourners paid their last respects. At two o'clock every bell in Victoria rang as the hearse attached to "a rope of sufficient length," and pulled by 200 employees of the Albion Iron Works, the E & N Railway, the CPN Company's tugboats and steamer *Isabel*, and the Wellington miners, began the funeral procession. It has been estimated that there were 12,000 people lined along the route to St. Andrew's Church and on to the Ross Bay Cemetery. At his final resting place the Wellington band played "Nearer My God to Thee."[14]

Press accounts of the day paid homage to the veteran miner who had won a place in the hearts of almost all in B.C. There were those who had not such flattering praise, but few could deny his accomplishments. The canny Scot died a millionaire, the richest man in the province, with an estate worth $15 million. Dunsmuir had died while still a member of the Legislative Assembly; Andrew Haslam was acclaimed to fill his seat with another year to go before the next election.

The Dunsmuir estate was left to his wife Joan, and sons Alex and James continued to be directors with shares in the company. However, Joan held the purse strings. James became president of the Wellington Colliery and Alex became president of the E & N Railway Company. Alex continued to reside in San Francisco while James moved to Victoria to replace his father at their Store Street office. Joan turned her home, Fairview, over to James and his family, and after signing over power of attorney to her sons she sailed for Europe, leaving them to complete the castle and manage the mines. When she returned she moved into the completed castle with her daughters and shocked everyone by announcing she had decided to sell the Wellington Colliery.[15] In November 1891, James was 40 years old and Alexander was 38. They had spent their working lives involved in the mines, helping the family estate prosper only to see all the profits go directly to their mother, who had no inclination for expanding or diversifying.

Provincial Politics in the 1890s

In 1890 Nanaimo was still represented federally by David William Gordon and provincially by Andrew Haslam. The federal election that year saw Gordon returned as MP.

Provincially, labour forces were at work changing the face of the riding. The most dominant force was the Miners' and Mine Labourers' Protective Association (MMLPA), which worked closely with its Vancouver affiliations. There were two seats in the riding: Nanaimo District and Nanaimo City. The sixth B.C. general election campaign began in Wellington with a mass meeting and parade attended by 800 miners.[16] The MMLPA protested against the E & N Land Grant and advocated for safety measures within industries, the protection of wages, the need for arbitration, and a shorter workday.

Three people vied for the two seats in the Nanaimo District. Candidates were farmer-labour supporter Colin Campbell McKenzie, independent Dr. William Wymond Walkem, and miner-farmer Thomas William Forster, who suggested miners had "lost the power over the land." The only candidate running for Nanaimo City was Irish-born miner, Thomas Keith, who was acclaimed. Keith told the crowd they needed a working man to represent them against the capitalists. The labour candidates Forster and McKenzie were victorious in Nanaimo District. Although there were no organized political parties in B.C. at this time, the Nanaimo labour members functioned as independents in the legislature. Keith fought them, alone against the government, but failed to pass taxation reform and restrictions on Oriental immigration. However, the mere presence of labour representatives in the legislature forced the government to make new concessions to the miners.

David William Gordon's Death

When MP David William Gordon died in office in 1893, Andrew Haslam once again stepped in to fill the vacancy, as he had done provincially after the death of Robert Dunsmuir a few years earlier. The simple announcement of Gordon's death was carried in the *Colonist* in February 1893:

> Mr. Gordon's death is universally regretted. His long residence in Nanaimo, the active interest he took in all that concerned Nanaimo's welfare, and his many amiable qualities had endeared him to a large circle of friends and acquaintances who will long mourn his loss. He was a man of strong convictions and great earnestness of purpose. He never did things by halves and he always knew his own mind.[17]

Gordon had earned the respect of his constituency. Nanaimo City Council took the unprecedented action by calling an official day of mourning.

Ralph Smith, Party Organizer and Politician

In the next provincial election, held in July 1894, there were three seats in the Nanaimo riding: Nanaimo City, Nanaimo North, and South Nanaimo. This time the government candidates defeated all three labour candidates. John Bryden, Dr. Walkem, and James McGregor defeated Ralph Smith, Tully Boyce, and Thomas Keith. It was Boyce who had advocated for the celebration of Labour Day. McGregor was the son of Nanaimo's pioneer mining family.

Ralph Smith was born into a mining family at Newcastle-on-Tyne, Northumberland, England, on August 8, 1858. At age eleven, he joined his father and four brothers in the mines at Newcastle.[18] His first wife died when their daughter was born. He then married Mary Ellen Spear, a young elementary school teacher and the daughter of a miner from the village of Framlington, near Newcastle-on-Tyne. Ralph and Ellen had three sons before Ralph's health began to deteriorate. The young family decided to come to Canada, hoping the climate here would be beneficial, and Nanaimo seemed like a natural location for a coal miner to settle.[19] Smith said they did not plan to stay, only to recover his health, make some money, and then return home in five years. Many years later he commented, "For two years I was a dying man, came to Nanaimo and found that treasure, health."[20] His daughter was eleven when they came to Nanaimo. Another son was born here.

In 1895 he was appointed general secretary and agent for the Nanaimo Coal Miners' Association of B.C. He ran again in the 1898 provincial election and this time was successful in securing the South Nanaimo seat as a Labour-Oppositionist.[21] He joined John Bryden in North Nanaimo and Dr. Robert Edward McKechnie in Nanaimo City.

Smith's political success in Nanaimo came as a party organizer, and he looked to the working men of the mines for his power base. In 1900 he again sought re-election for Nanaimo City. At a political meeting held in the Opera House, Dr. McKechnie nominated Smith, referring to him as "the old war-horse of many political fights." Smith spoke about his adversary James Dunsmuir and made the charge that "the throats of the people of the province had been grasped by a corporation that was prepared to throttle them without mercy."[22]

James Dunsmuir had told him that his company had experienced a change of heart and in future would treat its miners differently. He intended to establish reading rooms and look after the interests of his men generally, and especially to see that complaints against the underground management were personally investigated. If these promises were carried out, Dunsmuir would find no warmer supporter than Smith. But Smith did not think that would happen; the "rights of the people would have to be as jealously watched in the future as in the past."

Smith won the seat in Nanaimo City along with James Dunsmuir in South Nanaimo and William Wallace Burns McInnes in Nanaimo North.

Mary Ellen Smith supported her husband's political ambitions wholeheartedly. She also interested herself in the local hospital, being elected first vice-president of the Women's Auxiliary to Nanaimo Hospital at the organizational meeting. She was re-elected as president in three succeeding elections.

After only a few months as MLA in 1900, Smith ran federally and was successful in winning the Vancouver Island seat. He was now MP Ralph Smith, with Mary Ellen by his side. James Hurst (Big Jim) Hawthornthwaite was acclaimed in Smith's seat provincially. Within a few months James Dunsmuir would be premier.

CHAPTER EIGHT

Nanaimo's Sporting and Adventurous Young Men

Sports Days were the happiest of times for the residents of Nanaimo. Families brought picnics. They watched and they cheered and they celebrated athletic ability, and then they stayed to dance the night away. Each ethnic group brought its own special sporting interest to the town. The Green, now the location of Port Place, formerly Harbour Park Mall, was the centre of many sporting events held to celebrate special occasions like Queen Victoria's birthday and, later, Dominion Day. Even the Fourth of July was a special day for the community so tied economically to its neighbours to the south.

For many young single miners with a competitive spirit, these events would have been a release from the boredom that surely resulted from spending days in darkness, mining for coal. They enthusiastically joined in the foot races, boat races, horse races, or shooting events. Competition was strongest between the teams from the various mines, but they also matched their prowess with other communities' teams.

With a sheltered harbour close at hand, boating and water sports were also popular. Below the Bastion (in the area of the present Nanaimo Port Authority), HBC workers had carved out steps in the steep bank that led to an anchored scow, which had been fenced in to protect anyone from falling overboard while watching the water sports. Both whites and Snuneymuxw competed in these sports.

The earliest celebration recorded is of Queen Victoria's birthday in 1859. This was an exciting day for six-year-old John Meakin. There were foot races held on a ploughed-up trail from the Bastion along Bastion Street to City Hall where the course ended, as there was no bridge over the ravine. There was a variety of races, sprint and novelty, such as the wheelbarrow race, both full-vision and blind.[1]

Horse racing on Haliburton Street was also a regular occurrence. The judging stand on the balcony of the Dew Drop Inn overlooked the finish line. All horses had to be in a field adjacent to the hotel for inspection one hour before the start time. George Baker's horse Sleepy Dan was considered the best and was often banned from entering local races. Sleepy Dan was a delivery horse used by Baker's butcher shop to deliver meat to Nanaimo households.[2] Many a hard-earned wage was lost betting on the horses.

Clubs, Sports Grounds, and Parkland

There are archival references to a cricket club being in existence in Nanaimo in 1864, 1889, and 1899. The game was introduced by a number of Englishmen working in the mines and became an important part of the city's early sporting life.

Records of the cricket matches are sketchy: on June 22, 1889, the single men beat the married men; in 1899 the Nanaimo team beat a Vancouver team by five runs. During one particular cricket match against a Vancouver team, the judgement of the Vancouver referee so enraged the Nanaimo team that they chased him all the way down to the boat, and the game was never finished.

Robins Park, located in the south end of Nanaimo, had a cricket field cultivated by Robert Hilton. The field was described as having "magnificent turf." It was created when businessmen John Hilbert and G. Crutchley met with mine superintendent Samuel Robins on June 5, 1889, and negotiated permission for the club to use a cleared area of over seven acres for cricket matches. The land lay in the Daisy Field area, between the E & N Railway tracks and Chinatown at Needham Street. A month later, in July 1889, W.S. Chandler, who acted as president, formed an East Wellington Cricket Club.[3]

Horse racing found a new audience when an oval-shaped track was laid out on Daisy Field. Future plans for the park included a half-mile track, four tennis courts, a lawn-bowling green, and a grandstand with the capacity of seating 5,000. These plans were eventually shelved in favour of development at Bowen Park.[4]

About the same time as the Cricket Club negotiated for its land, the Nanaimo Athletic Football Club was formed with William McGregor as the first president. William was active in track events, especially high jump and long jump. The old wooden courthouse

Nanaimo Cricket Club. The game was introduced by young Englishmen working in the mines.

Nanaimo Sailing Club. Nanaimo's sheltered harbour provided ideal conditions for water sports.

became the home of the club. The building housed almost every form of sport from billiards to championship boxing, wrestling, cycling, basketball, rugby, football, and lacrosse. Until the beginning of the First World War, it was a hive of activity and the sporting home for many young athletic miners.

Several other sporting clubs were established in Nanaimo during the latter part of the nineteenth century: the Curling Club in 1874, the Nanaimo Lawn Tennis Club in 1889, the Lacrosse Club in 1891, the Gun Club in 1892, the Yacht Club in 1897, and the Lawn Bowling Club.

Establishing Bowen Park

When the HBC purchased land from the Crown, 724 acres were dedicated for public purposes. Part of that land was the 89.4 acres that lay between the bank of the Millstone River and Comox Road. When the Vancouver Coal Company purchased the HBC land holdings in 1862, the company decided to reserve that tract of land

The Wrestling Swanson Brothers

Wrestling was popular in the early days, and the Swanson family—Bob, Sinclair, and Sandy—were tops in their field. Bob was a heavyweight, Sinclair was a welterweight, and Sandy a lightweight. They wrestled everyone who came to town. Sinclair, nicknamed Sinc, cared little about the weight category, and he put up some memorable fights against a young strong Japanese wrestler named Matsuda.[9] The pair wrestled three times, with Sinc winning the rubber match in Vancouver. Unfortunately he injured his back in this match and this curtailed his wrestling activities for some time.

Sinc had a memorable match with Charlie Kileen. The latter was over six feet tall and weighed about 240 pounds. Sinc weighed only 145 pounds. Charlie had challenged Sinc, who "looked like an ant alongside an elephant." Sinc flopped Charlie right on his face, and then he tugged, pulled, and twisted, until time was nearly up, with the crowd booing Kileen, who just lay on the mat like a log. Sinc was still trying when suddenly a booming voice yelled, "Get bloody crowbar Sinc, get crowbar that's the only way you'll turn him over." Amidst a great roar of laughter, Sinc turned him over.[10]

According to one sports commentator, these wrestling matches were hard on the competitors: "When you finished one of those old time matches—usually two out of three falls—you were lucky if you could wrestle again in a month."

Sandy wrestled Johnnie Billiter, the world lightweight champion, in the Athletic Club. Sandy lost the first fall in a very short round, and the second after 27 minutes. A number of people lost a lot of money betting on the loser, "but it was one of the sporting highlights of that time."[11]

until a decision could be made for its use. No one objected to anyone using the land as a picnic ground. A dance platform was constructed and archery contests were held on the ground. The Nanaimo Foresters Lodge held its first annual picnic there in 1876.

Samuel Robins, mine superintendent, was instrumental in having many parks dedicated for public use. He fully intended to turn over the deed to the land by Millstone River as soon as the company decided there was no coal in the area, but the deed was never processed. Even after Western Fuel Company purchased the New Vancouver Coal Company in February 11, 1903, the park continued to be used by the public, and the new company voiced no objections—that is, until May 8, 1915, when Western Fuel Company challenged the ownership of the land. The city was advised that the public was trespassing on company property. City council withdrew its support, and the park reverted back to nature within a few years.

By 1918 Western Fuel Company had been taken over by Canadian Western Fuel Company, and the new owners were George W. and James Bowen. Company carpenter Joe Kneen, who had been with the company for over ten years, was invited to meet with George Bowen, a personal friend. Bowen asked Kneen if he knew of the land in dispute and if he would be willing to take a tour to view it. Bowen was impressed with the land and promised to take everything into consideration. He would discuss matters with his brother James, who was the purchasing agent for the company.

A letter from Bowen to the city dated June 10, 1918, made the official offer to convey to the city the "125 acres of land between Comox Road and Millstone Stream ... without compensation, reserving the coal rights to the same ... land to be used for a public park."[5]

On April 28, 1919, Canadian Western Fuel Company Limited conveyed the deed for the land to the city for a public park.[6] At this time Bowen also gave title to various squares in town: Dallas Square, Milford Crescent, Lubbock Square, and Comox Park. Bowen noted in his letter to the mayor: "It was evidently the intention of Mr. Robins, representing former owner, to convey these tracts to the city."

Mayor McKenzie graciously accepted the land for a city park. Then he asked for volunteers to help clean the paths and gardens. The response was overwhelming, as young and old showed up with garden tools, and in no time the park was ready for visitors. The parkland was given the name Bowen Park in recognition of the generous gift.

Bicycle Craze

The invention of the bicycle soon overshadowed all other Nanaimo leisure activities. For the first time there was an affordable vehicle that could provide freedom and mobility. And it was not socially restricted; anyone could ride—the housewife, miner, businessman, or farmer. For women it meant a change to more sensible clothing, such as divided skirts or bloomers.

Nanaimo's Bicycle Club had several members who were considered professional riders. Teacher Jack McGregor cycled to school at Cedar every day and was a professional cyclist: "The Swansons were good bicycle riders too, perhaps not as good as the Demings and the Grays, but I have heard it told that when they went to the Yukon in 1897 or 1898—they took their bicycles and rode them over the ice wherever possible."[7]

On August 24, 1896, the city regulated the use of bicycles by passing a bylaw that restricted when or where they could be used. "No person shall ride or drive a bicycle at a pace exceeding 8-miles an hour on the streets or lanes, and at intersections at a pace exceeding 6-miles an hour."[8] Pedestrians were not to be inconvenienced and there was to be no riding on sidewalks. "All riders of bicycles shall have a lighted lantern attached to such bicycle, when within the city limits, from sunset to sunrise." For any infraction the fine was $25.

In January 1893 a young Nanaimo physician, Dr. Robinson, bragged that he was going to be the first to ride a bicycle across

Nanaimo Bicycle Club. The introduction of bicycles gave freedom and mobility as never before.

Vancouver Island. George Bird, then 26, overheard the comment and decided to "change the doctor's ambition." Bird had worked as an engineer for the Nanaimo Boat House, operated by Foreman & Campbell, on one of their steamers before deciding to move to Alberni to work at the new paper mill being constructed there.[9] Dr. Robinson made regular trips into the Alberni Valley before a doctor opened a practice there; perhaps it was during one of those trips that Bird heard of the young doctor's plan and decided to beat him to the record.

Bird purchased his bicycle in England. The bill of sale records he paid 16 pounds, 15 shillings sterling, for the Ivel Safety bicycle. It was one of the first to be driven by a chain to the rear wheel and had solid rubber tires about 7/8ths of an inch in diameter.

Bird had a sense of adventure as he set off for Nanaimo. He had never travelled the road, having arrived in Alberni by ship, so he knew nothing of its condition. The road was better than he had expected, although very narrow: "Generally the strip between the wheel-rut and the edge of the road was better for a cycle."[10] Parts of the road still had snow, so he could see footprints, hundreds of them, and realized wolves had made them. The forest edged the roadside. After a stop at Joe Carter's Halfway House, near today's Parksville, Bird continued on to Nanaimo. Except for several settlers who had located along the road on small clearings, the road was desolate until he reached the Somerset Hotel and the town of Wellington: "The road between the two towns [Wellington and Nanaimo] was alive with horse-drawn vehicular traffic."

Bird dropped in on George Norris at the *Nanaimo Free Press* office. The newspaper of January 18, 1893, duly recorded the event that had taken 13.75 hours. The story's headline read: "The First Bicycle across Vancouver Island." Bird would have been glad he had not waited until February to make his trek across the island, because 52.5 inches of snow fell in Nanaimo between January 28 and February 8 that year.

George Bird, first man to ride a bicycle across Vancouver Island.

Nanaimo Hornets, 1893. Formerly known as the Rovers, the Hornets thrilled many with their winning ways.

Soccer and Rugby

There were a number of notable soccer and rugby teams who did battle against other island teams. The prowess of the Nanaimo Hornets rugby team was well known. The team began in 1888 as the Rovers, with Edwin W. Pimbury and Dr. Davis as vice-presidents, Albert Edward Planta as secretary, and James Hurst Hawthornthwaite as captain. The first game, played against Victoria on October 6, 1888, resulted in a draw. The Nanaimo team included E. Potts, Hovaloque, James Hawthornthwaite, L. Jones, Honeyman, Frank Garrard, Chalmers, Burdett Garrard, Arthur E. Planta, R. Watson, C. Martin, T. Cole, J. Norton Pettigrew, and W. Halliday. The return game against Victoria was played on Bevan's Swamp, part of Wakesiah Farm.[11]

In 1889 the Rovers ended the year by losing to the Vancouver team by four points. By 1890 the Rovers were known as the Hornets, and so began their winning ways. Bill Roper and Edgar Snowden were outstanding players.[12] The Hornets won the provincial championships in 1891–1892; 1892–1893; 1893–1894; 1894–1895; and 1897–1898.

The Garrard Brothers—Adventurers

Two brothers, Frank and Burdett Garrard, from Hertfordshire, England, joined the Rovers team in 1888. Frank had spent

William Good—A Snuneymuxw Champion

Nanaimo also had its share of individual sports champions: Charles Trawford was a Canadian wrestling champion; and William Good was the world's fastest sprinter in the 400-metre race at the San Francisco World Fair, but he never received his medal because he was Native. William was the son of Louis Good, the hereditary chief of the Snuneymuxw, the same man whom Reverend Good looked upon as his adopted son. William's daughter Hazel said of her father: "My dad had a dream when he was a boy. He was running across a field of grass and when he looked down he saw snakes. Many snakes! And so he ran so his feet just touched the snakes and were up before they could get him."[12]

William Good and his daughter Hazel.

his life at sea; he had made sixteen voyages to Australia and travelled seven times around Cape Horn before deciding to settle down in Nanaimo. He purchased 100 acres for $100 and worked clearing land. Frank joined a local drama group that gave benefit performances for victims of coal mining disasters. He called the group a "company of Nanaimo amateurs." They performed in Nanaimo and Victoria. Both brothers enjoyed sports and eagerly joined their countrymen in the game of rugby. Frank wrote in his journal about the game against Victoria. "Victoria thought they would win easily but they did not know that Nanaimo had some of the top players from the Old Country."[13] Frank's seafaring experience earned him jobs on the *Rainbow*'s Gulf of Georgia service, the *Cutch*, and later, the paddlewheeler *Isabel* before he decided to prospect for gold at China Creek. The brothers moved to Alberni, then later to Tofino.

There were other sporting teams such as the Nanaimo Thistles soccer team, who became the intermediate champions of B.C. for 1899–1900, and the Nanaimo Rangers, who were B.C. champions in 1893.

Nanaimo and the Klondike Gold Bug

When the outside world received news of gold on the Klondike River in the Yukon, the rush was on; gold fever swept the country. Men who had been businessmen, bankers, bakers, farmers, teamsters, and factory workers came from all over—the Pacific Coast, Eastern Canada, Winnipeg, Edmonton—and about 50 men came from Nanaimo, even the mayor.

Many old vessels were patched up and sailed to Alaska, carrying as many people and as much cargo as they could hold. The ships carrying the gold seekers were as interesting as their passengers. The Canadian Pacific Navigation Company (CPN) seized the opportunity and expanded its fleet. The *Queen City*, the *Princess Louise*, the *Danube*, the *Tees*, and the *Willapa* all left for the Klondike, bulging at the seams with prospectors and their gear.[14] The *Islander* and the *Danube* alternated weekly sailings from Victoria to Alaska. It seemed for a while that everything that floated was heading north.

Victoria merchants, already experienced in coping with gold-rush prospectors, perhaps reaped the greater benefits because they did not have to leave town to make money. They stocked up on picks and shovels and assorted mining paraphernalia. Vancouver was a newer city but had equally astute businessmen. Every horse, mule, or dog was purchased as a pack animal. The HBC quickly jumped into the fray. Those going to the Klondike could purchase a complete miner's outfit at any of the company's western stores. The outfit included everything from flour to wool underwear to gold pans. There was money in the gold rush, but it did not all come from digging gold.

Nanaimo miners were not immune to the lure of gold. Many left the mines, pooled their resources to outfit their trek, and boarded the *Islander* for their trip to the Klondike. Fifty men boarded the *Islander* in Nanaimo on July 27, 1897. The wharf was reportedly "black with men."[15] There was excitement in the air as the ship sailed with the Silver Cornet Band playing in the background. An estimated hundred friends and family members said goodbye and burst into song, joined by those aboard the ship. The Nanaimo steamer *Joan* blew her whistle in salute. It was truly a worthy send-off for potential millionaires. Newspapers reported in September an estimated 20,000 miners were on their way to the Klondike before winter closed in.

Many of the Nanaimo men were descendants of the first pioneer miners. Jack McGregor left with his cousin Arthur

The Silver Cornet Band played as the Islander *sailed for the Klondike in 1897.*

McGregor, James Pender, and David Elliott, who married Jack's sister Bertha. Also joining the contingent were sons of *Princess Royal* pioneers: Samuel, son of John and Elizabeth Thompson, and Albert Henry, son of John and Mary Ann Meakin. Others included John D. Stewart; George Muir; George Gibbs; Gus Steffin; Thomas Hunter; Sam Mottishaw; William Gray from Gabriola Island; Richard Gibson, former mayor; Thomas Keith,

The *Cutch*—Aground in Alaska

Even the *Cutch*, which had been out of service for some time, was remodelled with more cabin space, new engines, and new boilers. The Union Steamship Company put her back in service on the Alaska run. In July 1898 she set a speed record of about 88 hours for the journey from Vancouver to Skagway—estimated to be 1,100 miles—by using the outside passage and thus avoiding Wrangell Narrows. The ship kept up her fast schedule until August 24, 1900, when she ran aground on Horseshoe Reef, south of Juneau. Fortunately, there was no loss of life; all the passengers were safely transported to shore over two miles away. Reports of the shipwreck noted the ship had "$100,000 in Klondike and Atlin treasure."[13] An American company had the *Cutch* towed to Juneau for repair and made ready for further Alaskan service. She operated out of Seattle as the *Jessie Banning*, then was sold to the Colombian government and converted into the gunboat *Bogota*.[14]

former MLA for Nanaimo; the three Scouse brothers; and John Wilkinson, Thomas Flack, and Sam Fiddick, who had built the Occidental Hotel. Fiddick was 65 years old.

After experiencing a difficult time with the police commission, Mayor Joseph Davidson abruptly resigned, leaving acting Mayor George Campbell in charge of city affairs. Davidson and two aldermen also joined the contingent leaving for the Klondike.

Nanaimo Merchant Stakes a Claim

Not all with the gold fever were miners. William Sloan of "Sloan and Scott," a dry-goods merchant in Nanaimo, left with three friends. After prospecting in the vicinity of the Stewart River for a good part of the season without success, his group came to Eldorado Creek, where he staked Claim Number 15 and his friends staked adjoining claims. It was Claim Number 15 that first reached bedrock; it proved the fabulous richness of the creek and led to the gold rush. However, Sloan had already sold his interest for $50,000 and turned his back on the Klondike to invest his money in other interests. The *Nanaimo Free Press* reported July 18, 1896, that William Sloan and John Wilkinson had returned from the Klondike, Sloan with $85,000.

William Sloan's house, Eldo Villa.

Back in Nanaimo, Sloan purchased all eight lots of Block V and constructed Eldo Villa. He and wife Flora McGregor Glaholm, the daughter of pioneer Margaret McGregor Glaholm, whom he had married in October 1891, moved into the beautiful mansion on the Newcastle townsite. The decorative gateposts on Stewart Avenue are all that is left of the mansion today. The Sloans' son, Gordon, became a chief justice of the B.C. Supreme Court. William entered federal politics by becoming a candidate for Nanaimo, then known as the Vancouver District, but was defeated in the general election of 1900. The dry-goods business was still in operation in 1900.

Soapy Smith's Gang

There are many adventure stories told of prospecting for gold, but the frontier experience of John D. Stewart of Nanaimo was not one of adventure but of misadventure. Stewart arrived in Skagway on his way back home to Nanaimo, clutching a poke of gold dust valued at $2,700. Friends warned him about the Skagway gang headed by Captain Jefferson Randolph Smith, known as Soapy Smith. They urged him to lock up his gold in a hotel safe until he got his passage home. Smith's gang included confidence men, gamblers, pimps, and thugs. Somehow these scoundrels talked him out of locking it up.

Stewart was perhaps a little naïve, for within a short time "the Reverend" Bowers and "Old Man" Tripp had assured him they were buyers for a fake assaying company in Colorado. They convinced him that he could get a better price for his dust if he took his poke to Jeff Smith's Parlour. At the parlour Bower's accomplices jumped Stewart and stole his gold. The citizens of Skagway had had enough of Soapy Smith's gang and told him Stewart's gold must be returned and that Smith and his gang must leave. A deadline was given for the return of the gold.

A citizens' committee was formed, and a meeting was planned for that evening to decide how to get rid of Smith and his cohorts. Heading the committee was Frank H. Reid, the city surveyor.

Soapy Smith figured he could bluff his way out of the touchy situation that developed, but drink had clouded his judgement. The hall was packed as he and a dozen of his men strode defiantly in; Smith had his rifle slung over his shoulder and a revolver in his pocket. He swaggered up the aisle and pointed his rifle at Reid's head. Reid grabbed the muzzle and pulled it down while reaching for his own gun, then fired. Reid's shot misfired; Smith then shot Reid in the groin. Reid shot back, hitting Smith three times, once in the heart. The gang was then rounded up. Smith's premises were searched, and Stewart's stolen poke of gold dust, found in

Smith's trunk, was returned to him.[16] Back home in Nanaimo, John Stewart often told the story of how Soapy Smith stole his poke.[17]

Jack McGregor's Klondike Adventure

John (Jack) McGregor's experience was a little different from John Stewart's. His was a story of adventure, hardship, camaraderie, and sadness. With his cousin Arthur McGregor, friends William (Bill) Gray and Richard Gibson, he left on July 23, 1897, sailing north on the SS *Queen* from Victoria and landing at Skagway on July 26. They spent five days in Skagway, the city of tents, before deciding to go over the Chilkoot Pass to Dawson City.[18]

Their trek to Dawson City was fraught with danger, from climbing the snow-covered pass with tons of gear to rowing lakes and rapids and portaging over the rugged country. The frontier town was crowded with prospectors with gold on their minds, willing to believe the impossible was attainable and fiercely determined to make a fortune. Unsavoury characters preyed on the innocent; saloons, gambling, and dancing halls exploited the lonely. This was not a town for the weak of heart.

McGregor and friends staked their claim, but it would not amount to anything of value. Two winters in the Klondike tested their resolve mentally and physically, although the beauty of the evening sky lifted up their spirits. Jack wrote in his journal:

> Often the Aurora Borealis appeared in all its glory and magnificence, bright colours of every hue shooting out in long ribbons that seemed to reach the ground in all directions.

For their second Christmas in the Klondike, about a dozen men from Nanaimo got together to have a Christmas dinner. Gus Steffin and Jack McGregor were delegated to cook, as Jack describes:

> We had everything except the turkey. However, two lovely roasts of beef with lots of rich gravy filled the bill. All kinds of canned vegetables were on hand, and best of all the plum pudding with sauce that contained a whole bottle of the best whisky that could be bought. One did not need drinks during the meal, for the sauce gave all that happy feeling required.

As New Year's Eve approached, the men looked forward to the sun returning and a trip home. A load of outside mail and papers arrived. Jack normally received mail, but this time he got none. Jack dropped in at the cabin next to his, where the Nanaimo men discussed the latest news from home, even though it was three months late. No one spoke; all made themselves busy putting letters away and folding newspapers. Gradually conversation began, but no one offered him a newspaper, so he returned to his own cabin.

One of the Nanaimo men came into his cabin and remarked that there had been a small explosion in No. 1 mine in Nanaimo, and he named some fire-bosses who had been burned slightly. Jack noted it was strange that his father, William McGregor, who was general manager, was not listed. A few days later a stranger working on the next shaft called over to him, saying it was too bad that his father had been killed. Jack asked who had told him that; he said he heard the Nanaimo boys talking about it.

Jack contacted his friend Bill Gray, who gave him his mail, including two letters advising him to return home as early as possible. Jack's father, William McGregor, had been badly burned in the explosion in No. 1 shaft on November 12, 1898, as were six other miners. He died five days later on November 17. The 43-year-old miner had entered the mines at age eleven on the death of his father John, working his way up the chain of command to become manager of No. 1 mine. His wife, Amanda, was left to mourn once again. The explosion of May 3, 1887, was still fresh in her memory; she had lost her father, brother, brother-in-law, and William's cousin. But she was resilient and put aside her own sorrow to focus on their five children: Jack, Mary Alice, Maude Agnes, Kate, and Ernie. Thousands attended William McGregor's funeral; four railway coaches were filled with people from Wellington. The funeral was one of the largest in Nanaimo's history to date. Among the mourners were James Dunsmuir and John Bryden with his son Robert.[19]

Back in the Klondike, all thoughts of gold were quickly forgotten. Jack left Eldorado Creek on February 15 and walked to Dawson City to prepare for the trip over the ice up the Yukon River. He met a Chicago detective and noted, "He being a big active fellow, I was only too pleased to have his

Jack McGregor wrote about his experiences in the Klondike.

company on the long cold hard trip." Together they covered 600 miles, often in below-zero weather. At one point a snow blizzard almost cost them their lives; they floundered around in circles and nearly froze. They covered some distance by dog sleigh; at other times they walked. At Skagway they boarded the steamer the *City of Topeka* for Seattle. Jack arrived home in Nanaimo 27 days after leaving the Klondike.

Jack McGregor studied to become a master mechanic and was employed at the Pacific Coast Coal Company in South Wellington. Later he worked at the Canadian Collieries No. 5 mine as chief engineer.[20] He served as alderman for ten years and chairman of the parks and recreation board for fourteen years, and was the first commodore of the Nanaimo Yacht Club.

McGregor, Stewart, Sloan, and other Nanaimo Klondikers returned home, perhaps not richer but a good deal wiser. They had been part of an historic event that was indelibly stamped on their characters. No doubt stories of their exploits were told to their children and grandchildren. They came back to their everyday jobs, happy in the fact they had dreamed, were capable, and had tried. Their lives were set apart from others, and they would forever be known as Klondikers.

CHAPTER NINE

Reverend George Taylor

At this time the natural resources of British Columbia were freely exploited. No one took an interest in preservation of stock, in pollution, or even in documenting the flora and fauna of the province. Certainly there was no political will to alienate businessmen bent on making a profit marketing fish or amassing large tracts of forest for industry. For only a few cents an acre plus a small royalty on cut timber, anyone could lease forests for as long as 30 years. On Vancouver Island, the E & N Railway Company owned most of the east coast and its mineral wealth through its railway land grant. However, the west coast was another matter. Here, fishing was the major resource, as it was on the Fraser River on the mainland. The difficult decisions of who could fish and where were usually left to the local fisheries officer. There was no scientific knowledge on which to base these decisions or to plan for the future. It was economics, not research, that was the critical factor in persuading the federal government to spend money on fisheries and science.[1]

One man who did much to increase this knowledge was the Reverend George William Taylor, who, through a twist of fate, became a world-famous amateur marine biologist and founder of the Pacific Biological Station in Nanaimo. He was born in 1854 in Derby, England, and was a trained mining engineer with a remarkable knowledge of shells. He was also an accomplished collector of insects. He had a consuming interest in the natural world, an interest that remained with him for his whole life and led to his turning away from a mining career. He worked for a time with the museum in Derby and earned a reputation as a conchologist. When offered a senior position at the British Museum as an entomologist in 1882, he declined, deciding instead to visit his cousin Ted Wilkinson in Victoria. On his visit he marvelled at the untamed natural wilderness that was then Vancouver Island and decided to stay.

Taylor continued collecting shells and insects. His first paper in 1884, entitled "Notes on the Entomology of Vancouver Island," appeared in the Annals of the Entomological Society of Ontario. However, scientific papers did not put food on the table, and he was forced to look elsewhere for work. He visited Nanaimo to check out opportunities and discovered that here a miner had a three times greater chance of dying in the mine than he did anywhere else in the British Empire.[2]

When he came to Victoria, he had brought with him a letter of recommendation from the Bishop of Derby, a family friend. The Reverend Bishop Hills took an immediate liking to the young Englishman and persuaded him to enter a training program at Christ Church Cathedral. For two years, while continuing his scientific research, Taylor augmented his income as a minister of the church. Somehow he managed to juggle the two careers; he was made a deacon in 1884 and licensed as a missionary clergyman, becoming rector in 1886. He was the first man to be ordained in the Anglican Church in B.C. rather than in England. The following year he was appointed honorary B.C. provincial entomologist. Within the next four years Taylor built or improved churches: St. Luke's Church at Cedar Hill and additions to St. Michael's Lake Church and All Angels, Royal Oak. He also raised money for the construction of Holy Trinity Church in Patricia Bay.

Taylor was described as a striking figure—handsome, with a distinguished moustache. "He never rose to his feet without commanding respectful attention. His speeches were always clear, incisive and well thought out. He was a stalwart champion of the rights of women to vote at Church meetings."[3]

In 1885 Taylor married Elizabeth (Bessie) Williams, the daughter of an Anglican minister and headmistress of Victoria's Central Girls School. The young couple had four children: Fred, Ted, Helen, and Willie. Their first son died at birth. Fred was born on August 4, 1887. For the next three years Taylor was seconded to St. Barnabas Church in Ottawa East. Ted was born there in 1889. On the family's train journey to Ottawa, Taylor learned of the fossils in Alberta and was determined to see them for himself. When it was time to return to Victoria, he sent Bessie and the children on ahead while he stayed in Alberta to study the fossils. The Alberta visit resulted in another scientific paper, "A Survey of the Land and

The original building of the Pacific Biological Station and its founder, Reverend George Taylor.

Fresh Water Shells of Alberta," which he presented to the Royal Society of Canada in 1895. The previous year he had been elected a fellow of that Society.

On his return to Victoria, Taylor designed and built St. Barnabas Church at the corner of Cook and Caledonia streets. It opened in January 1891, with the Reverend Hills preaching the sermon. The new church resembled Taylor's former church in Ottawa. Helen was born December 13, 1891, and was the first baby christened in the new church. Taylor was now a charter member of the newly formed Natural History Society of B.C.

In 1893 Taylor was appointed rector of St. Alban the Martyr Church in Nanaimo, the breakaway church from St. Paul's. These were difficult years for the two churches; they struggled financially, partly because of their division. The Taylors' youngest son, William, was born February 24, 1895, and ten days later Bessie died at 38 years of age. Saddened at her passing, Taylor resigned his parish in 1896. Unable to care for four young children alone, he made plans to return to England.

Just as he contemplated the move, Samuel Robins, superintendent of the Vancouver Coal Company, offered him 100 acres on the north end of Gabriola Island if he would stay. Taylor had been a good friend of the miners and often went down into the pits to administer last rites or to comfort injured men. He had also christened many new babies in the community. Taylor accepted the gift and paid one dollar for the area known as Gabriola Sands, now a provincial park, and this became his new home.

Bishop Hills gave Taylor a posting to the parish on Gabriola Island. His youngest child Willie was sent to Victoria to be cared for by Bessie's sister Millie. The eldest son, Fred, took on the role of caregiver to his younger siblings, Ted and Helen. A modest two-bedroom cabin was built without insulation; cracks were filled with rags to keep out the wind, rain, and snow. Daughter Helen recalled, "We had a few rabbits and grew a few vegetables. Our good and reliable sources of meat were fish, ducks, grouse, and clams. We had no milk, as there were no cows near us on the north end. But we were a healthy bunch and we never seemed to be sick."[4] Reverend Taylor conducted services in the north-end schoolhouse at Descanso Bay and once a month walked ten miles to the south-end schoolhouse to hold services there.

For the next four years, while continuing his church duties, Taylor combed the beaches and coves of Gabriola Island, documenting information and collecting specimens. His meticulous records, notes, and writings won the admiration of marine scientists around the world. Son Fred was often by his side, caring for his father's professional needs, constructing showcases for his specimens, and sharing the long walk to church to play the organ during services. During these long walks Fred became close to his father, who was otherwise rarely home.[5] He said his father could spot a small bug on a tree a hundred yards away or more and that books on mathematics were constant bedside companions, read by candlelight.

In 1899 Taylor was given three parishes: St. Philip in Cedar, south of Nanaimo; the combined parish of St. Matthew's in Wellington and St. Luke's at Northfield; and St. Anne's in Parksville. He was given an old horse for his transportation to Parksville once a month. The family lived in the large thirteen-room Wellington rectory with no running water and no electricity. He received an honorarium of $40 a month. Later he purchased ten acres at Departure Bay and with son Ted's help built a four-bedroom house. Taylor communicated with other naturalists and scientists such as James Robert Anderson, the province's deputy minister of

Opening of Pacific Biological Station in 1908. Those identified in group photo: Mr. Spreadborough, Ucluelet; C.J. Keighley, Departure Bay; Thomas Dobeson; A.E. Planta; Prof. A.B. Macallum; unknown; Harry McIndoo, Assistant Fishery Inspector; Mrs. J.M. Miller; unknown; unknown; Mrs. Mary Ellen Smith; C.B. Sword, Chief Fishery Inspector, New Westminster; Edward G. Taylor, Fishery Inspector, Nanaimo; three unknowns; Mrs. H. Skinner.

agriculture and superintendent of B.C. farmers' institutes. Anderson was also one of the founding members of the Natural History Society of B.C. He collected and donated rare plants to the province. Taylor was also a good friend of Canada's first entomologist in Ottawa, Dr. James Fletcher.[6] In 1901 the three naturalists explored the Cameron Lake area and climbed Mt. Arrowsmith. Anderson claimed he was the first person to suggest the preservation of Cathedral Grove, now MacMillan Park. Taylor's circle of like-minded individuals expanded, as did his knowledge.

Taylor saw what was happening on the coastal waters: the whaling industry was expanding. There were no rules or regulations governing whaling on the West Coast. He observed that salmon runs were being destroyed by logging and was concerned that the rivers and their estuaries were also being damaged by the emerging forest industry. In 1901 over a million cases of sockeye salmon were packed; the greatest harvest in the province's fishing history to date.[7] The 1903 Adams River salmon run was wiped out by a log jam, and rotting salmon floated in the Fraser River, so polluting the Vancouver coastline that for an entire year the beaches were closed and swimming was forbidden. Taylor was moved to do something about it.

117

He began a letter-writing campaign, appealing to the government for assistance and recognition of the problem. There was a biological station in Atlantic Canada, established in 1898, but none on the west coast. Fisheries department decisions seemed to focus on the east coast, with little recognition given to problems facing the Pacific coast. When Taylor pleaded for help, others joined in his campaign. He presented a paper to the Royal Society of Canada entitled "A Plea for a Biological Station on the Pacific Coast." The Vancouver Board of Trade endorsed the proposal. Taylor pointed out in his paper: "There is not in any of the papers I have quoted any mention of the Pacific Ocean or of the British Columbian Coast."[8] He argued the value of B.C. fisheries was over $9 million, as reported by the department of fisheries.

Finally a B.C. Fisheries Commission was established in 1905, and Taylor was appointed to the board. The commission recommended a survey of the fishing grounds be carried out as soon as possible, and the results were referred to the Marine Biological Board. The Dominion government recognized something had to be done to regulate the fishing industry and Taylor's proposal seemed like a good starting point. Parliament granted $15,000 to provide for the construction and maintenance of the station.

During the autumn and winter of 1907, Taylor and his son Ted built the Pacific Biological Station at Departure Bay. It was operational in the spring of 1908 with Taylor appointed as curator. His extensive scientific library and zoological collections became the station's principal scientific tools for further research. The station provided living accommodation for eight scientists, some tents, and small boats for collecting specimens and making observations. Scientists did come, many of them in 1909, from Britain, the U.S., and eastern Canada. Taylor was kept busy.

Taylor's busy life building the Biological Station combined with his church responsibilities, travel, and studies no doubt led to his first heart attack in 1908. He recovered, but resigned from his work in the parish to devote all his time to his research. His list of credits continued with the founding of the B.C. Academy of Science. In his inaugural address to the new body on December 3, 1910, he said: "In a new country ... the efforts of the first settlers must necessarily be directed to the pressing problem of how to win a livelihood on land or sea. From agriculture and hunting their attention may turn to trading or mining; but not perhaps for a long time ... to science or literature or art." He thought it was time for thinking people to encourage scientific research and urged all members of the academy to contribute. "Understand the works of the Creator and unravel the secrets of Nature." Another health setback in 1910 left him paralyzed down his left side. He submitted his resignation to the federal government; it was rejected, but he was relieved of responsibility and retained as curator. He died in August 1912.

His old friend from Ottawa, Dr. Fletcher, said of him during his lifetime, "In his parish work he is painstaking, gentle and self-denying, always ready to help. A clear and forcible preacher and an earnest learner, who shows in his work that religion is not an accessory of everyday life but an integral part of it."[9] Reverend Taylor was laid to rest beside his beloved Bessie in Nanaimo Cemetery. The Pacific Biological Station has become one of the world's outstanding fisheries-research establishments. Reverend Taylor left quite a legacy that no doubt inspired his son Fred, who is remembered for his campaign to build the Lions Gate Bridge in Vancouver.[10]

CHAPTER TEN

Premier James Dunsmuir

As the Victorian era drew to a close, Dunsmuir's geologists turned their attention to the Wellington seam. They reasoned there should be another coal seam to the south of Nanaimo. When this seam was finally discovered eight miles southwest of Nanaimo, on the southern slope of Mount Benson, development got under way, and another town—first named Wellington Extension, later shortened to Extension—was constructed.

In 1897 the Newcastle townsite was studied for a possible railway route to ship Extension coal from the mouth of the Millstone River, but the water there was not deep enough.[1] A few months later the *Nanaimo Free Press* reported that Dunsmuir planned a "big project" to make Departure Bay a terminus:

> It is learned that the E & N is to be extended from Wellington to Departure Bay and that speedy steamers will be put on to connect to Vancouver. Extensive new wharves are to be built at Departure Bay. It is proposed to make the passage of water and land from Vancouver in less than five hours. The extension of the line to Departure Bay is only an undertaking of two miles.[2]

The railway plan was stymied, however, by the refusal of the Vancouver Coal Company to give access to its property. James Dunsmuir swore vengeance. He decided to build his wharves at Oyster Bay for the shipment of coal from the Extension and Alexandria mines. A new railway was constructed to Oyster Bay, about fifteen miles south of Nanaimo. This turn of events now enabled coal to be shipped directly from the docks to the mainland.

Three large seaside bunkers were built to hold 8,000 tons of coal at a time. At Oyster Bay harbour another new town developed. When news came of the relief of Ladysmith in South Africa after a 118-day siege by the Boers, Dunsmuir was inspired to call his new town Ladysmith. Another new Wellington Colliery railway was constructed. The town of Extension grew as miners located their homes close to the pithead. Others who made their homes in Ladysmith were transported daily by company train.

Both the Cumberland and Ladysmith coal operations were lucrative and had virgin coal seams, while the Wellington mine had become obsolete and costly to operate. The decision was made to shut the Wellington mine down and move the town to Ladysmith. Homes, businesses, and hotels were barged to the new location. James Dunsmuir made sure his miners had little contact with those living in Nanaimo by ruling that all employed at Extension must live in Ladysmith. The town of Wellington shrank from a population of 5,000 to only 100. Old pit workings were sealed off, and the town's coal mining era was committed to history.

Family Difficulties

On June 19, 1896, James and Alexander convinced their mother Joan to relinquish her control over the San Francisco operation, which Alexander managed. For a token payment of $10 she conveyed R. Dunsmuir & Sons to a new company to be known as R. Dunsmuir's Sons, a small but significant change.[3] James and Alexander now turned their attention to the Union Colliery and the E & N Railway. After six months of arguments, on December 11, 1896, Joan finally relented and gave her sons what they had asked for—a share in both enterprises.

Only the Wellington Colliery remained in her control, and she wanted to sell. The brothers tried to convince her the colliery was rightfully theirs, but they also knew that after 30 years the mine was about played out. They had already decided to abandon it and move the coal operation to the Extension mine south of Nanaimo. Joan asked $500,000 from her sons if they wished to purchase the Wellington Colliery. When she dropped the price to $410,000 James decided to accept her final offer.

Alexander, who had been the first white boy born in Nanaimo, and the young man who successfully petitioned government for the incorporation of the city, died on January 31, 1900. Years of his excessive alcohol consumption had finally taken their toll. Eighteen months later, his wife Josephine also died, leaving James the sole heir to his brother's million-dollar fortune—much to the dismay of mother Joan, his sisters, and Alexander's stepdaughter Edna Wallace Hopper.

For the next five years a number of lawsuits reverberated through the courts. Dunsmuir versus Dunsmuir and Hopper was heard in one court or another in Canada, the U.S., and Great Britain. The Dunsmuir family was divided as family scandals were unearthed and charges and counter-charges were made.

This was a very difficult time for James Dunsmuir. His mother Joan still controlled some of the family's holdings, including the Albion Iron Works and the Canadian Pacific Navigation Company, as well as Craigdarroch, Fairview, and other properties in Nanaimo and Victoria. However, James controlled the mines and the E & N Railway and all the profits generated from them.

Now approaching middle age, James Dunsmuir was a fine figure of a man. He had added a few extra pounds, giving him an appearance of prosperity; the few grey hairs on his head and beard only added to his distinguished look. He looked and acted the successful businessman; however, the outward appearance only disguised the quiet, cautious, and wary man he really was. Many associates regarded him as "cold and haughty, a tough-minded businessman—impatient, imperious and demanding."[4] James lacked the ambition of his father and missed the counsel of his brother Alex. He wanted to be rid of all responsibilities and contemplated selling off his holdings and retiring to the life of a country gentleman.

Political Voice

Elected as the provincial member for Comox in 1898, James Dunsmuir took the road last travelled by his father, ensuring a voice in government. Like other politicians before him, he promised Nanaimo better roads—something close to his constituents' hearts. It is difficult to know clearly Dunsmuir's political affiliation because he was said to contribute to both the federal Liberal and Conservative parties. B.C. was still without a party system of government; members were either for or against the government. The first general election along party lines was held in 1903.

These were turbulent days in the B.C. legislature. Between 1895 and 1900 there were four premiers. John Herbert Turner, who had served for three years, received only fifteen supporters in a house of 38 in the 1898 election. Lieutenant-Governor Thomas McInnes dismissed Turner and called on Charles Augustus Semlin to form a government, but even he lacked support. Semlin was a cattle rancher from Cache Creek and the leader of the Opposition in the House. It was a difficult proposition forming a coalition of like-minded individuals. His tenure was further eroded when the Attorney General Joseph Martin resigned to join the Opposition. Joe Martin was new to the province; he was "egocentric, headstrong and brusque."[5] Semlin battled on, constantly under attack from Martin, and sometimes managing to stay in power by only one vote. A non-confidence vote in 1900 forced the lieutenant-governor to ask Semlin to resign and call an election. He refused, leaving Lieutenant-Governor McInnes no alternative but to dismiss him.

Lieutenant-Governor McInnes then called on Martin to form the next government, but the legislature had no confidence in him. What happened next was without precedent even in this stormy legislature. The *Colonist* of March 2, 1900, reported on the proceedings: "Shortly after, when His Honour arrived to prorogue the House, every member, with one exception, (Martin) rose and left the Chamber. The Speech from the Throne was read to empty benches."[6] James Dunsmuir had led the exodus from the House. He later insisted the exit had not been prearranged. As the shaken lieutenant-governor left the hall, the members filed in again, singing, "God Save the Queen." "An uproarious scene followed—resolutions condemning his conduct were mingled with patriotic songs and general disorder."[7] This single act of defiance made Dunsmuir appear to have leadership qualities.

Martin, or "Fighting Joe" as he was nicknamed, tried to form a government composed of men unknown in public life. Three months later an election was called for June 9, 1900. Of the 38 members, only thirteen supported Martin.

Dunsmuir decided to seek re-election, this time in the South Nanaimo riding that included Extension and Ladysmith. He promised the miners he would rid the mines under his control of Chinese labour. The Labour Regulation Act of 1898 had excluded Japanese and Chinese from working in the mines; however, the courts had dismissed the anti-Chinese legislation as being outside provincial authority. In a packed hall at Extension, miners cheered as Dunsmuir promised, "I shall replace Chinese employed underground with white men as soon as I can get them. And I'll go further still—I'll give you my word that so soon as the other industries of the province do away with them, I'll get rid of them altogether."[8]

Adding credence to his promise, Dunsmuir began advertising for 500 white miners and helpers for his mines. He won the vote in South

Nanaimo. Of the 474 votes cast, Dunsmuir received 249 compared to his rival John Radcliffe with 225.[9] Martin retained his seat, but only a few members supported him. On June 14, the lieutenant-governor accepted his resignation and called on the only man who could secure a more orderly government—James Dunsmuir. Dunsmuir's decision to accept the challenge was no doubt influenced by the rising provincial debt, which in 1898 was $7.4 million and which would increase to $12.5 million by 1901. As a businessman he could see the business climate in the province was severely eroded by continual political uncertainty. He agreed to try to bring stability to the office and was willing to give it his best effort, but his stay would be brief.

Dunsmuir Becomes Premier

The legislative members called for the dismissal of Lieutenant-Governor McInnes, who they thought had acted unconstitutionally in dismissing a minister with a working majority and calling on a man with no following. McInnes refused to resign and was dismissed. Prime Minster Sir Wilfrid Laurier had had enough of B.C. politics, so he appointed a new lieutenant-governor from Quebec; he was Sir Henri Joly de Lotbinière. On June 15, 1900, James Dunsmuir became the fourteenth premier of B.C.

Dunsmuir proceeded to gather around him friends like John Turner, a former premier who became his minister of finance, and he named a young politician, Richard McBride, as his minister of mines. Wellington Colliery surgeon Dr. D.M. Eberts joined the executive team as attorney general. McBride resigned, and the former inspector of mines, Edward Prior, was called on as his replacement.

The following year Dunsmuir and Eberts decided a visit to Ottawa was in order to put B.C.'s concerns before Prime Minister Wilfrid Laurier. The usual western problems were raised such as Chinese immigration, railways, and the need for a better share of federal revenue. This feeling of having to fight Canada for recognition still resounds in the province today. Dunsmuir argued the province paid three times the average contribution to the Dominion and got less than half of it back. "If the people of British Columbia were able to retain all they contribute in taxes ... they could support every public utility of the province ... build their own railways and still have a surplus each year to their credit."[10]

The province was also concerned about the fishing industry. There were no rules and regulations governing west-coast fishing.

This was a fight Reverend Taylor would champion. Dunsmuir refused to negotiate with the U.S. State Department over the fisheries question; he said this was a federal matter. The Ottawa meeting solved nothing.

Dunsmuir and his family attended the coronation of King Edward VII following the death of Queen Victoria the year before. They were soon swept into the social whirl of London life during this special year. Dunsmuir's great wealth and political prominence ensured his family was included in special events. When he returned to Victoria, it was clear he intended to give up his office as premier. In November 1902 he resigned, and his old friend, Edward Prior, was invited to form a new government. Prior's was the last of the old governments without party affiliation.

CHAPTER ELEVEN

Coal Companies
and Stone Quarries

*B*y 1900 Nanaimo was a well-established community with a thriving
coal industry, but the use of fuel oil in California now cut into coal
sales. The Vancouver Coal Company had hoped to preserve its earning
power by getting other mine owners who sold in the same California
market to agree to limit output and raise prices. The company lacked
the capital to get into the coal-oil market and decided to sell to Western
Fuel Limited. The last meeting of the shareholders was held December
30, 1902. Normally when a British company was taken over by another,
the directors made sure they were compensated for loss of office. The
six directors divided the proceeds amongst themselves. Samuel Robins
received a severance of $10,000 and a few other officials were paid lesser
amounts. Rosenfeld and Sons were thanked for successfully selling the
Nanaimo property. The Vancouver Coal Company had mined coal in
Nanaimo for 40 years.[1]

Western Fuel Company was incorporated under the laws of
the State of California. It was registered in B.C. in December 1902
as an extra-provincial company. The agreement for sale was dated
December 15, 1902, and the company took full title on February
11, 1903.[2] The Canadian Western Fuel Company became fully
incorporated under the British Columbia Act on May 9, 1918,
to give it a Canadian entity for taxation purposes. Full title was
conveyed on January 18, 1919.

Coal had been the economic engine that kept the community
together. Vancouver Island mines in 1900 produced 1,383,374 tons
of coal. This output included the combined mines of Vancouver Coal

Company, the Wellington Colliery, Extension mines, the Alexandra Mine in Cranberry, and the Union Colliery in Comox. Mining was the island's major industry, employing 3,701, including 51 Japanese and 568 Chinese. Markets continued to be California, Los Angeles, San Diego, and San Francisco. Despite efforts to make the mines more safe, there were fourteen fatalities and 77 accidents recorded during the year.[3] By 1901 over 6,000 people called Nanaimo home.

The Stone Quarries

Other mining operations at the Newcastle Island Quarry, the Gabriola Island Stone Quarry, and the Biggs Portage Quarry at Jack Point all provided employment for a small work force.

The Gabriola Island Stone Quarry had been in existence for a number of years, possibly as early as 1887, at the north end of the island on the southeast corner of Descanso Bay. There are indications the operation may have been associated with the Vancouver Granite Company. Two Vancouver men, Kelly and Murray, began quarrying the stone in 1889.[4] Mining reports show the two men were still there in 1905. The quarry had three large derricks, a hoisting engine, and a short rail track by which the stone was conveyed to salt water for shipping. The stone was described as "a blue-grey colour, rather coarse, and contains grains of mica and hornblende."[5] The actual cutting of the stone was done in Vancouver. The quarry produced stone for construction of the Victoria Post Office building, the Federal Life Building (Williams

Sandstone blocks being quarried at the Newcastle Island quarry.

Building) in Vancouver, and the Roman Catholic Church on Dunsmuir Street, also in Vancouver.

Biggs Portage Quarry, situated at Jack Point, about two miles from Nanaimo, opened in 1905. After only two months of operation, a quarry about 50 feet high had been exposed and a considerable amount of stone was ready for shipment. The stone was similar in colour to that quarried at Gabriola Island. A derrick ably handled the large blocks of stone, which were loaded directly onto scows.[6]

The Northwestern Construction Company of San Francisco now owned the Newcastle Island Quarry, on the west side of Newcastle Island. The company's representative, John G. Davis, lived at the site. In 1905 about a thousand tons of stone were shipped by schooner to that city. The company received a contract in 1907 to provide stone pillars for the B.C. Permanent Building being constructed on West Pender Street in Vancouver. The *Nanaimo Free Press* reported: "The pillars will be 36 feet high ... [constructed] from solid blocks 16 feet in height. When completed they will be the highest pillars in any building in British Columbia."[7]

The Gabriola Island Brickyard

On November 11, 1911, the Dominion Shale, Brick, and Sewer Pipe Company Limited of Vancouver began producing brick at the bottom of the Big Hill, also known as Brickyard Hill, on the south side of Gabriola Island. The brickyard site had been in use for several decades, but it was not until 1895 that the demand for bricks increased. Plant manager Mr. L.D. Morris was acknowledged as having some experience in "handling men."[8] The company invested $30,000 in the plant, which was expected to produce 40,000 bricks per day and employ up to 40 men. The plant equipment was manufactured and the installation completed by the Nanaimo Foundry. Bricks from the yard were loaded onto wagons and horses, then hauled to Descanso Bay for loading onto scows for shipment to Nanaimo and Vancouver.

Morris stayed only a year; his replacement was R.C. Brumpton of Nanaimo. Under his direction, the plant expanded to produce hollow tile for use in interior decoration. By 1917 over three million red bricks had been barged to Vancouver, and business was thriving. Bricks were shipped by scow from the site, making the operation more efficient. Tugs took the scows from the wharf at high tide.

This same year, Cameron Investment Company bought out the brickyard and renamed the company the Gabriola Shale Products Company. Brothers James O. and D.O. Cameron also owned

Cameron Lumber Company. For a short time Morris was again hired as manager until Mr. D. Campbell of Nanaimo replaced him. It seemed the only concern with the operation was the use of water, for the rights to it belonged to W.N. Shaw, original owner of the property, and when the new owner took over, he raised the rate from $6 to $20 per month. Campbell and Shaw could come to no resolution, so the matter ended up before Justice McDonald in the Nanaimo Courthouse. The plaintiff was awarded $200; the case was dismissed June 11, 1920.

No. 1 shaft and WFC's offices, Nanaimo.

The steam engine San Francisco *at the No. 1 Mine.*

CHAPTER TWELVE

The Hub City

*A*s other communities on Vancouver Island grew, Nanaimo became an important junction and distribution point for goods and services. The E & N Railway had a regular passenger service linking the "Hub City" to Victoria. Ferries connected to Vancouver, New Westminster, and points along the Island's east coast. Steamers such as the *Joan* called on a regular basis from Vancouver, the *City of Nanaimo* from Comox, and the *Dunsmuir* from New Westminster.[1] The Sidney and Nanaimo Transportation Company steamer *Iroquois* offered transportation three times a week between Nanaimo and Sidney, north of Victoria. The return fare by ship was $2.50.[2]

The E & N Railway Company's big white tug *Czar* towed rail barges between Ladysmith and Vancouver, a service that allowed the company to ship carload freight to and from the mainland without having to load and unload the cargo onto steamers. The financial savings were significant and helped many Vancouver Island businesses stay competitive with those on the mainland.

An extract from a Vancouver Island Development League brochure, 1910, describes the City of Nanaimo as:

> ... the "hub" of Vancouver Island: the place where all roads meet and where steamer connections are made with all parts. A more charming place to idle a few days would be hard to find. It is one of the oldest places in British Columbia being founded away back in the fifties. The city is most beautifully situated, the townsite sloping gently towards the Gulf; in the rear Mt. Benson, to the fore two

Tug's Legal Battle

James Dunsmuir had a "long and unending legal squabble" before he took ownership of the *Czar*. The tug was built by Captain Joseph Spratt of the Albion Iron Works in Victoria and sold to the Klondike and Columbia Goldfields Company. Dunsmuir first chartered it from the company and claimed he had the first option to purchase. The dispute between the two parties ended up in court, which decided in Dunsmuir's favour. The tug was virtually a new vessel when he took ownership and practically gave him a monopoly of the towing in the area. His fleet now consisted of the *Lorne*, which he had built in 1889, the *Czar*, and the new tug *Pilot*.

large harbours, perfectly land-locked by the islands of Newcastle and Protection which shelter them from the Gulf. Beyond the twin harbours the mountains on the mainland rise up majestically in the blue mist.

Nanaimo presents a good example of the old and the new prosperous city in British Columbia at the turn of the century. As a residential town it stands prominent among the cities of the Pacific Coast. A visitor would be hard pressed to see evidence in the city of the most important mining industry on the Coast. Mining families take pride in their homes and gardens.[3]

Nanaimo's Business District

The city's natural development was along the waterfront; coal wharves crowded the busy harbour as vessels of various sizes waited to load coal or to pick up passengers outbound for Vancouver or Victoria. The business district was centred along Victoria Crescent, Commercial, Church, and Front Streets. Little changed along the streets with the passage of time, only the tenants of the buildings. Brick buildings replaced some of the old wooden structures.

On Front Street, the Globe Hotel and the Nanaimo Courthouse anchored the street on the west, and on the east side stood the imposing Dominion Post Office building with its new addition. All three buildings provided a sense of well-being in the community. The Nanaimo Athletic Club now occupied the old wooden courthouse and jail. These fine buildings also encouraged other development, particularly during the second decade of the twentieth century.

The former HBC's Bastion sat smugly amidst the growing community as a reminder of the city's humble past. The fortress building, on the east side of Front Street, was the only reminder of the first tenant. In 1904 the Native Sons of B.C., Post Number 3, purchased the historic building from Western Fuel Company. Members renovated the interior of the building and maintained it on behalf of the community. Every year descendants of the *Princess Royal* mining pioneers gathered here on November 27 to remember their ancestors who made that horrific voyage to Nanaimo in 1854 from the "Black Country" in England.

Banks Established

In 1864 the Bank of British Columbia arrived, the first to be established in Nanaimo. From 1887 to 1889 the bank occupied the old Stone House built by William Isbister in 1852. A new bank building opened in 1889 at 55 Front Street.[4] Soon it offered a "bank savings department."[5] A rather exclusive club, the Nanaimo City Club, was next to occupy the old Stone House. The steward-custodian was a Japanese gentleman who knew all the foibles of certain members, and he earned a reputation for his diplomacy.[6] The Elks lodge then occupied the building until October 8, 1917.

In 1901 the Canadian Bank of Commerce took over the bank, and manager Mr. Cruckshank announced that a new bank building would be built on the triangular corner of Church, Chapel, and Commercial Streets. An old wooden frame building on the site, once used as a warehouse, was removed. The Nanaimo architect for the new red-brick two-storey building was Mr. Kelly. The building was completed in December 1901. Police assisted in the transfer of the bank deposits, files, and documents from the old building. During the first week of January, the bank was back to business as usual.[7]

In 1914 another building replaced the 1901 one. The bank's own architect, Victor D. Horsburgh of Toronto, designed the building, which was completed under the direction of building superintendent John Madden. This became the building known today as the Great National Land Building.

The Royal Bank of Canada, Nanaimo branch, was opened originally as a branch of the Merchants' Bank of Halifax on February 9, 1898, on the ground floor of the old Doon Hotel in the Gibson Building on Commercial Street. On January 2, 1901, the bank changed its name to The Royal Bank of Canada.[8]

In 1917 the bank purchased the Vendome Block on the northwest corner of Bastion and Commercial Streets; the stores on the ground floor were vacated, and the building was remodelled for bank use. In May 1919 the bank announced it would construct a new branch building on the same site. The bank's manager from 1917 to 1920 was Mr. F.A. Hanna. He promised that no expense would be spared in remodelling the block "to the comfort or convenience of the bank's customers."[9] Until the new building was completed, the branch relocated across the street. The new branch opened for business in 1920. The bank was rebuilt again in 1957.

Eleven managers served the Nanaimo branch during those years, the first being W.A. Spencer from 1898 to 1899. Many of the men remained in the position for only a year or two. Mr. C.C. MacRae's managerial tenure had longevity, as he served for six years from 1911 to 1917.

Royal Bank of Canada on the ground floor of the Vendome block.

Newspapers Reflect Vibrant Economy

The *Nanaimo Free Press*, founded in 1874 by George Norris, provided information and news of the day and reflected the tenor of the times. When George Sr. passed away on January 6, 1902, his sons George and William ably took over the operation. The partnership was dissolved in 1912 when George took over as manager. The weekly *Nanaimo Herald*, founded in 1899 and managed by editor Edward T. Searle, gave readers an alternative source of news. Merchants also took advantage of the newspaper to advertise their sales or promote their businesses.

Pioneer businessman John Hilbert retired from his business, John Hilbert & Son, Funeral Director & Embalmers, advertised as "graduates of The Oriental, The Eureka, The New York, and the Clark's School of Embalming," and sold to D.J. Jenkins Limited. Hilbert's son Albert, who had apprenticed under his father, continued on with the new owners. Mary Jane Hilbert, John's wife, opened a small confectionery store at Departure Bay, selling fruit, candy, and cigars during the summer months.

A.R. Johnston & Company store on Bastion Street, located under the Forester's Hall, offered everything from groceries and grain to general farm produce. The owners, A.R. Johnston and Thomas Watson Glaholm, were also the agents for the steamers operating to San Francisco and Portland, as well as for the east-coast steamers and B.C. Express Company.

F.J. Stannard's flour and grain store, operating out of the Hirst Warehouse at the corner of Front and Bastion Streets, was well positioned, with the stockyard next door and the slaughterhouse across the street.[10] Stannard was an agent for Ogilvie Flour Mills.

The Stannard family had been associated with Nanaimo since 1882 when John Spadget Stannard first opened a store selling dry goods and furnishings. He moved to Victoria as manager of Spencer's Department Store. His son, Francis John Stannard, returned to Nanaimo and began his feed business in 1902. It was the only feed store in Nanaimo at the time. The business eventually passed down to his sons, George and William, who expanded into farm machinery, dairy supplies, and poultry. The brothers moved the business to an old warehouse off Pine Street, in Chinatown, where there was a railway siding nearby. The business name was changed to Stannard's Flour and Feed.[11]

Nash Hardware on Commercial Street was another of the old pioneer stores whose original location was at the present site of the Coast Bastion Inn. William Alfred Nash opened the store in 1891 as a painting and decorating business. The business grew through several Nash generations to become a complete hardware store.

The Scotch Bakery was one of the oldest bakeries in town. Jerome Wilson and George Leask purchased the business from the Evans Brothers in December 1892. The bakery then relocated to Victoria Crescent next to the Crescent Hotel. Prior to that it

F.J. Stannard's flour and grain store in the Hirst warehouse on Front Street, now the home of the Nanaimo Port Authority.

View of Commercial Street before the turn of the twentieth century. Note the wooden buildings and that driving is on the left side of the street.

had been in operation for several years under James Ritchie of California in a building known as the "Westward Ho" Printing Office. The bakery gained a reputation for having the best bread in town, but it also offered a wide variety of baked goods.[12]

The bakery entered the modern age in 1916 when it announced it had purchased a Ford delivery automobile from Sampson Motor Company in Nanaimo: "It makes quite a difference to the old style of horse and wagon and long hours."[13]

Pimbury's Drug Store was still in business on Commercial Street. In business since 1882, Edwin Pimbury was now in semi-retirement, and his clerk, Charles Van Houten, operated the store. Pimbury Point near the B.C. Ferry dock is named in his honour.[14]

In 1893 George Fletcher began his business, Fletcher Brothers Store, in Nanaimo with a pony and wagon and two sewing machines. He moved around the community in his wagon, demonstrating the sewing machine. After saving enough money he opened the first Fletcher Bros. store on Haliburton Street, selling sewing machines, musical instruments, sheet music, and gramophones. In 1901 he moved Fletcher Bros. Music Store to Commercial Street in the *Free Press* block. Ten years later he moved again, this time to Church Street, and four years later, in 1915, he moved to a more permanent location on Commercial Street.[15]

Over the years, four generations of Fletchers, beginning with George, to be followed by Earl, then Alan, and finally Rob, have

135

Bryant's Harness Shop on Victoria Crescent, 1905.

introduced shoppers to the latest in technology as it developed.

Bryant's Harness Shop, established at Number 18 Victoria Crescent in 1902, was a unique harness and repair shop. Owner Charles F. Bryant came to Nanaimo in 1888 from Dudley, England. Bryant could create almost anything to do with leather or canvas. He repaired harnesses, made hay bags for the mules from the mines, and also made leather kneepads for miners. Although he had sewing machines, he sewed some of the harnesses by hand. The store sold canvas covers and sails for boaters, outdoor clothing for fishermen and loggers, store awnings, Venetian blinds, and trunks; Bryant even repaired suitcases.

The large store, with its distinctive leather smell, became a gathering place for visiting farmers who enjoyed sitting around the old coal-burning pot-bellied stove that heated the entire building.[16]

Rummings Bottling Works began on Bastion Street as the Pioneer Soda Works Manufactory. The plant supplied soda water of "a very superior quality." The plant passed successively into the hands of different owners: Mr. Phillips, John Mahrer, John Mitchell, and Edward Rumming. Under Mitchell, the plant moved to larger quarters at Wentworth and Wallace Streets, and in 1896 new equipment from England was installed. The company could now brag of an English connection; the bottles were imprinted with the name Riley Mnfg. Co. London, England.[17] Riley added a Nanaimo logo to the bottles—a crossed pick and shovel.

When Edward Rumming joined the company, he brought his experience in manufacturing soda and mineral water in England.

Pioneer Soda Works Manufactory, later Rummings Bottling Works. Stanley Sutton and Peter Wiggle. Circa 1900.

The company name was changed to Rumming & Mitchell, then changed again to just Rummings Bottling Works. Rumming was born in London, England, and came to Canada in 1889. He married a Victoria woman, Charlotte Mebius.

The Rummings Bottling Works specialty was ginger beer; however, the plant also made fruit syrups, bitters, and essences. Over the next two decades, the company expanded into Ladysmith and took over Courtenay's Gold Star Bottling Works.

Cigar-Rolling Davis

Perhaps one of the more unusual business enterprises in Nanaimo was the Cigar Factory. Albert Davis had visited the city previously with several stage shows before deciding to settle here in 1894. With his expertise in rolling cigars, he soon had a job with Phil Gable's Cigar Factory on Bastion Street, and not long after, he became a partner.

"Cigar Rolling Davis," as the locals nicknamed him, had had a very interesting career before settling in Nanaimo. He was born in 1836 in Somerset, England, and at age sixteen joined his uncle in Kalamazoo, Michigan, where his uncle taught him the art of cigar making. After completing his apprenticeship, he moved to Chicago,

Enterprise Cigar Factory staff, Bastion Street.

became active in the Cigar Makers Union, and was elected union president.

While in Chicago, Davis became interested in the theatre and liked it so much he quit his job with the union to join a travelling stage show which was visiting that city. He went with the troupe to California, where he learned of people getting rich digging for gold, so he quit the theatre to try his hand at prospecting for gold. He soon discovered he could make more money rolling cigars than digging for gold.

Davis paid his way to San Francisco by rolling cigars and acting in various shows. One show in 1880 brought him to Nanaimo, where he performed on the stage of the Institute Hall. He returned several times with other shows before deciding to bid farewell to the stage and settle here.

Davis left with the Nanaimo men for the Klondike in 1897, but soon discovered his knack for rolling cigars made him the most money. He returned home to work in the Cigar Factory.

Phil Gable sold his interest in the Cigar Factory to Davis and went on to operate faro and roulette games at the Opera House. Gable was respected by all and was never known to have cheated a customer.

In his spare time Davis teamed up with W.K. Leighton to sponsor a number of variety shows at the Nanaimo Opera House, owned then by John Mahrer. The team of Davis and Leighton sponsored picture shows, the performing arts, and visiting sports figures in the wrestling and boxing circuit, giving local fans a chance to see world champions.

Over the years Albert Davis became well known in the community under his trade name "Enterprise" for his hand-rolled cigars. Even after the introduction of cigar-making machines in 1908, he continued to hand roll them. When a new excise tax on imported tobacco leaves and imported cigar boxes was introduced, Davis limited his work to making a few cigars for selected patrons who did not mind paying a premium for his hand-rolled cigars.

Albert Davis never lost the art of rolling cigars by hand. On his 90th birthday, several Nanaimo organizations he had been involved with over the years presented him with tobacco leaves and the instrument required to prepare the leaves for hand rolling. Davis showed he still had the touch and rolled his last cigar. In 1902 he was a charter member of "The Ancient Order of Arabic Shriners," and the Loyal Order of Moose, Nanaimo Lodge Number 1052.[18]

Early Movie Theatres

The Opera House continued to serve the community, and as important as it was to Nanaimo, other theatres emerged with the development of the moving picture show. The *Nanaimo Free Press* gave lots of space to the promotion of these events.

On July 15, 1902, the Broscope Company presented a "moving pictures" show in the Opera House: "a series of scenes from the Coronation procession in London, England." This was the coronation of Edward VII, the eldest son of Queen Victoria and Prince Albert. According to the promotion, there were estimated to be 100,000 animated pictures in the show. The reviewer noted, "The coloured series were simply marvellous."

The first moving picture theatre was the Crown Theatre, built on Commercial Street, on the site of the former J.H. Good and Company.[19] Jack Warren learned his skill in the old Crown Theatre during the days of silent movies before he opened his own theatre in Port Alberni.[20] The silent moving pictures usually had live musical accompaniment.

The next place of entertainment was the Princess Theatre, on Selby Street. This building later became the Nanaimo Roller Rink and the home of several badminton clubs.

The Orpheum Theatre, at 22 Commercial Street, held its grand opening on February 4, 1914. Moving pictures were the main attraction. The name of the theatre was later changed to the Bijou, and under this name the proprietors installed a pipe organ and boasted of having a theatre orchestra. During the First World War, the theatre advertised moving pictures of the Vernon military camp: "See our boys in training."[21]

The Bijou was taken over by Famous Players in 1935, and the name was changed to the Strand Theatre. Later it became part of Fletcher Bros. Music Store.[22] In 1915 the Dominion Theatre opened on the corner of Bastion and Skinner Streets. It was billed as one of the finest theatres in Nanaimo to date. It showed first-run moving pictures while an orchestra played musical selections. Hundreds were turned away as the theatre featured Charlie Chaplin in *Shoulder Arms*, which had already played to three capacity houses.[23]

In 1924 talking picture equipment was installed in the theatre, and the name was changed to the Capitol Theatre. The opening feature was "Broadway Melody." All of the town's dignitaries were invited to attend. Bing Kee was invited to join the mayor's party. Chinese historian Dick Mah related the events concerning his grandfather.

> Upon entering the theatre the manager that was there to greet people said to Bing Kee, "You have to sit upstairs." The mayor said that was an insult because Mr. Bing Kee was with his party. "I'm sorry sir, but that's the theatre policy," said the manager. The mayor said, "We'll see about that." He threatened to go across the street (where City Hall was located) and hold a special meeting to revoke the theatre's licence.
>
> The manager and other theatre dignitaries that had come from other parts to attend the opening relented and said, "Mr. Bing Kee, you may sit downstairs anytime." Bing Kee retorted, "Not only me but all Chinese people." No Chinese people were ever segregated in any of the theatres. Bing Kee's regret was that he should have said, "All people regardless of race, culture or ethnic background." At the spur of the moment he only thought about himself and the Chinese people in Nanaimo.[24]

With the advent of talking pictures, the orchestra was not required. Both the Orpheum and the Dominion theatres were equipped with stages and dressing rooms. In 1939 the Capitol was renovated; it received a new floor, new seats, new carpet and drapes, and became one the finest theatres on Vancouver Island.

New Lines of Communication

The Nanaimo Telephone Company began in 1887 with twelve poles and twelve subscribers and laid the groundwork for the first telephone link with other communities. Nanaimo's telegraph operator, Mr. J.A. Callaghan, talked to a few leading citizens to see if there was any interest in establishing a telephone service. After hearing positive feedback, he ordered a dozen telephones with a Hubbard board. Victoria already had a telephone system in place, started by R.B. McMicking.

Among the leading citizens who subscribed to the first private telephone service were George Norris of the *Nanaimo Free Press*; Marshall Bray, government agent; J.E. Jenkins, owner of the Old Flag Inn; A.R. Johnston of A.R. Johnston and Co.; Edward Pimbury, druggist; John Please, hardware merchant; Peter Sabiston, former owner of the Commercial Hotel; W.L. Le Ballister, of IXL Stables; Thomas Hirst, merchant; and John Pawson, president of Nanaimo Hospital. Each paid $1.80 for the service. Callaghan described how things did not go quite as planned:

> "Doc" Le Ballister got the poles and we had a bee and set them up. I worked on the installation and Please on the wiring. The board was set up in George Cavalsky's store, but it did not work. We got the only known telephone expert in the country, R.B. McMicking up from Victoria, and on his recommendation we got a board similar to the one in use in his city. Mrs. Cavalsky was the first operator. After about a year the board was moved to a building on Front Street.[25]

George Cavalsky and Laura Gilbert were married in 1887. Laura was born in 1864 in Penzance, Cornwall, and came to Nanaimo in 1874 with her family to join their father, who worked in the mines. He died the following year. Soon after their arrival, the Gilbert family operated the Temperance Hotel on Bastion Street. Mrs. Gilbert re-opened the hotel after her husband's death. Laura and George were married in the Methodist Church. The couple had three daughters and one son, J. King Cavalsky.[26]

Each year the number of subscribers increased as Nanaimo residents recognized the value of the telephone system. Physician Emil Arnold Praeger, butcher Edward Quennell, James Dunsmuir, and livery stable owner Walter Thompson added their names to the roster. This early system was a complicated method when compared to today's technology. The old telephone system operated on the

"Hello" system, not telephone numbers. The number of rings determined who was being called and everyone on the line could listen in, which made for very interesting gossip.

Instructions on how to use the "instrument" were essential for subscribers to the Nanaimo Telephone Company exchange. Manager G.E.T. Pittendrigh gave explicit directions and a code of conduct:

> Take a position immediately in front of the instrument. Hold the telephone close to the ear. Speak in an ordinary but distinct tone of voice. Avoid shouting. Call Central by giving two short rings. Hang up your telephone and give one long ring. Take your telephone down at once and listen. When called up do not ring back, but take down your telephone and ascertain through the instrument who calls. When the conversation is ended, only the person who made the call should give one short ring as a signal to disconnect. Profane language strictly forbidden over the company lines. Address inquiries or complaints to the manager.[27]

On April 6, 1898, the first long-distance calls could be made when four lines were strung between new telegraph poles along the E & N Railway from Wellington to Victoria.[28] In December 1901 Mayor William Manson made Nanaimo's first long-distance telephone call to Victoria's Mayor Hayward. It was reported that "the working of the system was a great success. One might have been in the next block to one's conversation partner, so distinctly was every syllable heard."[29] At the same time, the SS *Tartar* laid a cable across the Strait of Georgia, connecting to Vancouver.

In February 1905 the Nanaimo Telephone Company merged with what was then the British Columbia Telephone Company Limited, later called B.C. Telephone.[30] King Cavalsky worked for the company for 38 years until his retirement in 1961. There were 350 customers listed at this time. In 1908 the exchange relocated to 76 Bastion Street where it remained for several decades.

Submarine Telephone Cable

Eleven years after the first cable was laid across the Strait of Georgia, B.C. Telephone decided to replace the old cable with a new one. A new record was established, as this was the longest submarine telephone cable in Canada at the time, and "with two exceptions it [was] the longest continuously loaded cable in existence."[31] The cable crossed the Strait of Georgia from Point Grey on the mainland to Newcastle Island. The length of the cable between terminals was 32.6 statute miles in one continuous piece, and was laid to a maximum depth of 1,380 feet.

Establishing a record was not the goal of the telephone company, which needed to provide better communication between the mainland and Vancouver Island as the population of the island had grown considerably since the last cable was laid. Prior to this direct route, the old line went via New Westminster to Bellingham, then to Lummi Island, Orcas Island, Shaw Island, San Juan Island, and across to Victoria with five sections of cable, the longest being ten miles. Transmission between Victoria, Nanaimo, and Vancouver suffered. Now the new line could go north to Courtenay and west into Alberni, opening up new lines of communication to those outlying districts.

Aerial construction included the highest telephone poles in the province erected at the Brechin Mine at Nanaimo and on Newcastle Island at Kanaka Bay. The two at the Brechin Mine were 118 feet in length, and two more on Newcastle Island were 70 feet. They carried the 1,000-foot span over the Newcastle Island Passage. The cost of the new route, including cable, was over $200,000. Pacific Coast Cable Company ably laid the cable under the direction of Captain A.B. Richardson.

Experts came from around the world to watch. Such was the interest in the event that a large flotilla of vessels met the cable ship several miles off the Vancouver Island coast to follow the action. Nanaimo Mayor John Shaw and other civic and public officials extended an official welcome. "Owing to the fine working condition of the cable they were able to communicate directly and for the first time with civic officials in Vancouver, and voiced their pleasure at being able to see personally the completion of the project."[32]

By June 16, 1913, the *Nanaimo Free Press* announced the completion of the project. By this time the old telephone magneto, or crank-type of system, had been replaced by a common battery operation, and a new switchboard and equipment were housed in a new telephone building.

Visit of the Princess Victoria

Over the years many ships visited the Nanaimo Harbour, but the arrival of the new passenger ship *Princess Victoria* in September 1903 gave the city fathers a chance to show the delegates of the Chamber of Commerce of the Empire the progress being made here. Mayor Manson welcomed the *Princess Victoria* to Nanaimo. This was the ferry's maiden visit here and was cause to celebrate.

The *Free Press* reported the ship was "the finest passenger boat plying the coast waters."[33] The ship was built in England in 1902 for the Canadian Pacific Railway's Victoria-to-Vancouver run. When she entered service the next year, she broke all records in the popular tri-cities run: Vancouver–Seattle–Victoria.

A busy itinerary had been laid out for chamber delegates. Some visited the Number 1 Mine, while Mary Ellen Smith, president of the Women's Auxiliary, gave a guided tour of the Nanaimo Hospital, now celebrating its 26th year. Other delegates visited the garden of Thomas Kitchen of Newcastle townsite; the garden was a prime attraction and reported to be "at its best." The Kitchen mansion was also an attraction. It had 4,000 square feet of living space, plus adjoining servants' quarters. It had been built "as a castle with a turret and flagstaff at one end and a low spire near the entrance at the other."[34] The house was barged to Parksville in the 1970s and is still used as a residence.

While the chamber delegates were wined and dined, local residents took the opportunity of touring the new ship. The *Princess Victoria* left the next day for Vancouver, a trip that reportedly took 1 hour and 50 minutes.

The Thomas Kitchen Garden, Newcastle townsite.

CHAPTER THIRTEEN

Women Serving Nanaimo

*U*ntil the early 1900s, women of the community had gone about their business of caring for their families. They could not vote, nor could they hold public office. Early historical records seldom give the first name of the woman, only the name of her husband; however, it is acknowledged that few churches or hospitals would have survived without the essential fundraising of the women in the community. The emergence of the Women's Auxiliary to Nanaimo Hospital showed women were taking steps to organize into groups.

As the population of Nanaimo grew, it soon became clear that the accommodation at the hospital was insufficient to meet the needs of the community. Several extensions had been made to the Franklyn Street Hospital, including the "Mary" ward for female patients, the John Pawson ward, a nurses' home, and a maternity patient building.

A short notice printed in the *Nanaimo Free Press* on January 24, 1900, noted: "The Ladies of Nanaimo are taking steps to organize a ladies auxiliary similar to the organization existing in Victoria, the object being to aid the Hospital." At the meeting, held on January 30, the women adopted bylaws similar to those of the Royal Jubilee Hospital Women's Auxiliary in Victoria. The first president was Mrs. Stanton and the vice-president was Mrs. (Mary Ellen) Smith. The executive consisted of fifteen members; patrons named were Mrs. Cooper, Kitchen, Pawson, and McKechnie. Membership dues were two dollars per year, in quarterly installments of 50 cents.[1]

The Nanaimo Hospital Auxiliary has given Nanaimo more than 100 years of service. This is an early photo of the auxiliary.

The auxiliary's stated policy was to supply such items for the hospital as requested by the matron. These included a wide variety of goods from chairs, water jugs, feather pillows, towels, blankets and sheets, and cups and saucers, to buckets and brooms.

Somehow the women always managed to raise enough money to meet the requirements. When the hospital experienced financial difficulties during the Big Strike, the auxiliary gave an interest-free loan of $800 to help pay accounts.

The arrival of the First World War did not diminish the enthusiasm for the annual ball that the auxiliary sponsored in January. Even in wartime, social events still made a profit. When two hospital staff members left for war, the auxiliary presented them with gifts. Miss Pauline Rose, the "Lady Superintendent," received a wristwatch, and the head nurse, Miss Eveleigh, was given a thermometer in a silver case.

During the Spanish influenza epidemic, hospital staff did not escape unscathed. Volunteer nurses were called in assist. After the illness had run its course and the community returned to normal, the volunteers at the hospital were presented with special pins in recognition of their service. (The pins can be seen in the Bastion collection at the Nanaimo District Museum.)

It would be difficult to imagine the hospital without the auxiliary workers who put in countless hours raising money to provide furnishings and equipment. To date, the Nanaimo Auxiliary has given over a century of service to the hospital.

Nanaimo Nurses' Training School

If you were young, strong, well educated and had good teeth, you could become a nurse.

The Nanaimo General Hospital Training School for Nurses that operated from 1906 to 1926 offered a three-year course in nursing. After twenty years, it was decided that the training of a fully competent nurse could be better done at hospitals: "Nanaimo needed trained nurses rather than nurses in training."[2]

The prospectus of the Nurses' Training School, now in the Nanaimo Community Archives, gives a peek into the qualifications and early training of nurses: "Women of superior education and cultivation will be given preference." The applicants had to be over eighteen and under 35 years of age and had to have a strong physique. They also had to "have their teeth in good order before entering school." The probation period for "nurse-pupils" was two months; during that time they were carefully observed. Pupils had to pass each course with a 75-percent mark.

> During the two months of probation the applicants receive board, lodging and laundry, and the instruction of the school, and will receive $7.50 per month for one

Nanaimo School of Nursing graduation class. The nurses' training school operated from 1905 to 1926.

147

year, $10.00 per month for the second year, and $15.00 per month for the last year, and must wear the uniform prescribed by the school.[3]

Any time lost by the student nurse due to illness had to be made up at the end of her term. She was allowed three weeks of vacation each year, as well as "two hours each day, one afternoon a week, and a part of Sunday" off duty. Nurses were expected to attend church every Sunday when possible. All students were under the control and management of the Lady Superintendent, who had the power to dismiss or suspend.

Junior Red Cross Club—Canadian Red Cross, Nanaimo Branch

The Junior Red Cross Club had been in existence for only two years when war was declared. Flora McGirr, wife of William, recalled the war effort made by wives, daughters, and sisters who belonged to what became the Nanaimo Branch of the Canadian Red Cross:

Red Cross Club fundraiser Carnival of the Allies, held September 20, 1916.

On September 20, 1912, Mrs. Arthur Randall called twelve young women together for the purpose of forming a junior auxiliary to the Nanaimo Hospital and also to bring these young people to the knowledge of their city's other needs. The names of the original group were some of our early pioneers: Mrs. MacGregor, Crawford, Mrs. Walter Thompson, Calderhead, McQuade, Stockett, Gibson, Planta, and Mrs. Arthur Yates. The chosen name of Junior Auxiliary to Nanaimo Hospital was changed immediately to the Red Cross Club to enable us to broaden our field of work. Fees were set at $2.00 a year. Meetings to be held at member's homes and open to our young women.[4]

Mrs. Charles Crawford was the first president. The club's initial mission was to raise money for the hospital. Dances and card parties were held and were an acceptable way of making money. The first year the club loaned the hospital $275, without interest; as well, members sewed and helped in the hospital in a variety of ways. Flora McGirr continues:

When labour troubles began in 1914 most social affairs were at a standstill. At this time I was on Gabriola Island, as a teacher. On August 4, war was declared and our first two years of the Red Cross Club came to an end. I still remember marching along the beach and singing, "Soldiers of the Queen," an old Boer War song. Our hilarious behaviour did not last long as September saw us back to work … everyone plunging into very serious war work as everything looked dark for world peace.

The declaration of war changed the focus for the young women. All money on hand was turned over to the hospital, and four wartime years of hard work began in earnest.

Kate Grieve established committees set up to buy, cut, sew, knit, and entertain. Six sewing machines were put to good use in the Oddfellows Hall dining room, which the club used until the end of the war. The workroom was open four afternoons and two evenings a week. Nanaimo women began sewing and knitting scarves, socks, and mittens to be sent overseas; even Snuneymuxw women helped with the knitting. Amanda Theresa (Gough) Norris was active with the group and taught many young women to knit socks. "After school Elva Hygh (Deno) ran many times to the apartment on Commercial Street 'to have a heel turned.'"[5]

A gathering at a Red Cross Club fundraising event.

The club raised money with tag days, military socials, moving pictures loaned from the Dominion Theatre, plays, and operas. On two special occasions members of the Vancouver Symphony came over to Nanaimo to help. One two-day carnival held in the Nanaimo Athletic Club raised enough money to donate $550 to the wounded soldiers, $500 to the Canadian Patriotic Fund, and $500 to the prisoners of war fund. Another successful carnival was held in the Agricultural Hall at Wentworth and Machleary Streets in 1917. Nanaimo residents also subscribed over $4,000 to the Victory Loan program.

The winters of 1916 and 1917 were very cold, but that did not stop the young women from their work. They packed their first shipment of knitted garments, pyjamas, and other items of clothing in boxes and mailed them overseas. Later that year the club became officially the Nanaimo branch of the Canadian Red Cross Society, and from that time on all orders came through the society.

Sisters of St. Ann Convent and Church

Two years before the Nurses' Training School commenced, the Sisters of St. Ann took a major step and enlarged the convent school on Wallace Street. Then in 1907 a new three-storey school with boarding accommodation was attached to the old school, which was 27 years old but still in good condition. The new building was estimated to cost $15,000, and the contractor was McRae and Elliott.

The three-storey building contained ten large rooms, several smaller ones, and a basement to house the heating system. The assembly room, playroom, and toilets were on the ground floor; there were two schoolrooms on the second floor, and the top floor contained three small and one large dormitory and toilets. The building also had an elevator.[6] After the building opened, 45 orphaned girls were transferred from Quamichan (near Duncan) to Nanaimo.[7]

Disaster Strikes Convent

The new convent had three good years before disaster struck on July 11, 1910, when a fire reduced the church and school to ashes. The Sisters of St. Ann, who had erected the original convent in 1877 and enlarged it at their own expense, still owed a debt of $8,000. They also supported the orphans financially and could not afford to rebuild the school. The fire was a terrible setback, but the goodwill of Nanaimo residents came through and donations poured in, enough to rebuild.

The convent fire headlined the *Nanaimo Free Press* on July 12, 1910. The alarm was turned in shortly after the *Joan* tied up at the wharf around 5:30 p.m. Prior to the fire, there had been three days of intense heat. Fire broke out in the laundry of the convent, and with everything tinder dry, particularly the roof, there was little the firemen could do to stop it.

St. Ann's Convent and Church.

Perhaps adding fuel to the fire were the remains of the old building that had been dismantled. The building had stood on the convent grounds at the corner of Wentworth and Wallace Streets. The debris was piled up at the end of the laundry. Confounding all efforts to save the building, there was also a shortage of water from several fire hydrants. The *Nanaimo Free Press* wrote about the valiant effort made by firemen to save the building:

It was simply painful to watch the efforts of the firemen at this stage of the fire. One hose was taken into the convent building itself the other was being worked by Billy Edmunds and Harry Freeman and others from the roof of the kitchen. Another hose was brought in and then it was seen that the firemen were driven to a pitiable expediency of using their thumbs to make the water spray. Neither hose was as good as the garden sprinkler with fair pressure.[8]

The Nanaimo fire chief was John Parkin. The fire engine had been pumping from the hydrant beside the Ladysmith Lumber Company office. The horse-drawn fire wagon was dragged into place in front of the building, the ladder raised, and the hose directed at the flames. The water had no effect whatsoever. The flames now reached in all directions and the church became totally engulfed. Fragments of shingles were blown for blocks, setting fire to several buildings on Commercial Street, including the Provincial Hotel on the Crescent. Things could have been worse; for once, the ravine became a blessing because it stopped the fire from spreading farther. Father W. Heymen's residence was ablaze as were the roof of the Young Men's Institute hall and the bell tower. Residents with homes in the vicinity were evacuated and wet blankets were spread over roofs. A number of people were recruited to save Captain Arthur Yates's home at the corner of Wallace and Fitzwilliam streets.

The Sisters of St. Ann put the unfortunate event behind them and looked to the future. A new building was erected in 1911, and the school continued to offer tuition from Grades One to Eight.

In fire chief John Parkin's report to the city for the year 1910, he noted that 2,000 feet of hose were used on the fire, twenty men had been called up, losses were $15,000, and the cause of the fire was unknown.[9]

Nanaimo Fire Department members with Ronald steam fire engine.

Tom and Jerry, the Fire-Wagon Horses

The days of horse-drawn wagons came to an end for the Nanaimo Fire Department in 1913 when two La France Fire trucks were purchased and the horses retired. Over the years teams of horses pulled the wagon to fires within the city. Tom and Jerry were purchased in 1901 and stabled on the ground floor of the fire department building.[15]

The stables were constructed in such a way as to allow the horses to move forward into their special harnesses that hung clear. The driver on duty led the pair into the stall, tripped a lever, and the harnesses came down onto the backs of the horses to be buckled up. This was the routine procedure.

On one occasion, the fire alarm sounded and the driver went to the stables only to find Tom and Jerry standing, already harnessed and waiting to be buckled up. This puzzled him. Later the mystery was solved when the driver accidentally tripped the alarm and was amazed to see Tom and Jerry move forward, trip the lever, and down came the harnesses. The two gallant four-legged firefighters were ready to race to another fire.

CHAPTER FOURTEEN

The Changing Face of Nanaimo

N anaimo miners had a strong sense of community, and family ties were strong. Many descendants of the first miners still worked underground and made a comfortable living for their families. They valued their British identity. When Queen Victoria died on January 22, 1901, Nanaimo City Council declared an official day of mourning. The Dominion Post Office building on Front Street was draped in black, reflecting the sadness felt in the community. However, the cultural identity of the town had changed with the arrival of the Chinese, Japanese, Norwegians, Italians, Finns, Croatians, and other European workers. These newcomers gave the community a decidedly multicultural look; it was, in many ways, a microcosm of the future face of Canada.

Kalevan Kansa Colonization Company Limited—Finns

The Finns who came to Nanaimo and worked in the Western Fuel Company mines settled around Milton Street in an area that became known as Finn Town. Others made their homes in Wellington and worked for the Wellington Colliery, while some cleared farms in the Cedar District and became farmers. The Nanaimo Finn miners built a church at the corner of Milton Street and Victoria Road, a building that still stands today.

The Wellington Finn miners founded the Kalevan Kansa Colonization Company Limited, whose sole purpose was to organize colonies and bring immigrants from Finland to B.C. They regarded the president of the company, Kurrika, as a prophet, someone who believed in the inherent goodness of man. He was described as "a real handsome man, tall [with] a good personality."[1]

Kurrika and fellow Finn Matti Halminen searched up and down the coast for a location to organize a Finn colony. Malcolm Island was chosen and named Sointula—"The Land of Harmony." On November 27, 1901, a contract was signed with the provincial government giving the company immediate control of Malcolm Island and promising ownership after seven years if the population increased and improvements were made.

On December 6, 1901, the first of the Nanaimo Finns left for Malcolm Island, where logging began almost immediately, providing lumber for building homes. By March 1902 fourteen people had settled on the island. Slowly their numbers increased as more countrymen arrived from the prairies and from Finland. In June 1902 the steamer *Capilano* was chartered from Nanaimo to take a load of supplies and more settlers to the colony at Sointula, thus increasing the number of shareholders in the Colonization Company to 127.

Unfortunately the colony got buried under a huge load of debt. Creditors seized timber, the Dominion Trust took possession of the sawmill, and the government took all lands in exchange for a loan to cover the colony's debts. Dominion Trust sold all the property and forests that had come into its possession for $5 an acre. The dream of a Finnish paradise never materialized.

The Felice Cavallotti Society—Italians

The first Italians to settle here in 1865 were Bartolomeo Corso, Joe Vazzo, and Joe Cuffalo. Corso divided his time between fishing and farming, and occasionally did some logging. Cuffalo worked in the mines and managed to save enough money to build the Wellington Hotel in South Wellington. When this burned down, he built the Italian Hotel (Columbus Hotel) on Haliburton Street in 1885.[2]

On November 4, 1900, the Felice Cavallotti Mutual Relief Society was formed at Extension, named after a nineteenth-century poet and politician who was known for his efforts to bring democracy to Italy. There were 54 founding members of the society, all male. (Women were admitted to membership in 1946.) The first president was John Giovando. Other chapters of the society were soon formed in Nanaimo and Cumberland. The society's mission was to help Italian coal miners and their families. Since there were no social programs in existence at that time, injured miners or sick

155

people relied on family and friends for aid until a group of miners banded together to help each other. To be eligible to join you had to be of Italian ancestry, and dues were one dollar per month—the going rate for room and board at the time. The benefits in the event of an injury or sickness were one dollar per day up to 100 days, then $15 per month for a further twelve months.[3]

The National Croatian Society, St. Nicholas Lodge—Croatians

The communities of Nanaimo, Ladysmith, and Extension were home to a number of Croatian families who worked in the mines in the district. They brought a distinctly European flavour to the communities, particularly during celebrations, with their traditional dress and music.

In 1903 the National Croatian Society, St. Nicholas Lodge, was formed in Ladysmith; it was the first Canadian branch of the society whose origin was in Pittsburgh, Pennsylvania. The first meeting was held October 21 in the home of William (Bill) Keserich. Eighteen members voted unanimously to elect Keserich as the first president.[4] The society offered cultural and social activities as well as insurance protection.

James Dunsmuir had lured the young Croatian men with promises of work in his mines at Wellington and Extension. Some came from the U.S., others came directly from the old country, and all were in search of a better life. However, before they could go underground in the mines, they had to learn mining techniques and pass government examinations for a miner's ticket. They worked as trip or rope riders, miners' helpers, loaders, chunkers, muckers, pushers, cagers, sprag men, and mule drivers. Some with little education never became miners but spent most of their working lives at jobs learned from experience.

The Croatian orchestra or "tamburitza" with Jack Djuric as first musical director, staged many musical concerts in all the neighbouring communities. The twelve-piece orchestra entertained at dances, churches, and special events. It was most in demand during Christmas and New Year celebrations. Dressed in their national costumes, the tamburitza musicians went from house to house, singing special Christmas songs, wishing good health and happiness to households, and receiving food and gifts for their performances. Zelimir Juricic of the Croatian community described the mood at Christmas:

There was a special bond of understanding between miners at Christmas, which transcended language and cultural boundaries. We were of different nationalities, the Croatians, the English, and others, but at Christmas we all got together because coal miners, they all had the same job. They all had the same worries and the same way of life.[5]

Ilija Badovinac was born in 1873 in Zumberak, Croatia. At sixteen, he came to Nanaimo, working first in the mine at Diver's Lake then later at the Wellington-Extension Collieries. Later his wife Martha and a young son, George, joined him from Croatia. Ilija joined the Croatian lodge in 1907, and for the next two decades he served in various positions. His fifteen-year-old son George also started work in the mines, although his father had warned him it was dangerous work. George also joined the society.

Ilija narrowly escaped being killed in an explosion at the No. 2 West Mine on October 5, 1909, when 32 men were killed, including six Croatian miners. The first president of the Croatian society, William Keserich, was among the dead miners.[6] For the wives of the Croatian miners, many of whom had just arrived from the old country and didn't speak or understand English, it was an agonizing wait to find out if their loved ones had survived.

Ilija Badovinac survived another twenty years in the mines, but in 1929 he was killed working in the No. 1 section of the Extension Mine. He was 55 years old and was survived by three sons and one daughter.[7]

When the Extension mine closed in 1931, the National Croatian Society, St. Nicholas Lodge, moved to Nanaimo.

The Extension Mine Explosion

On Tuesday morning, October 5, 1909, 32 men were killed in an explosion in the No. 2 West Mine at Extension, which was operated by the Wellington Collieries Company. A number of men managed to escape or were rescued. Of those killed, 27 died from the explosion; the remaining five were overtaken by gas while trying to escape.[8] The force of the explosion was so powerful it blew doors from their hinges, tore up rails, flattened posts and stringers on the floor, and blew out air stoppings. This last damage caused difficulty in reaching the miners, as there was no ventilation.[9]

The small town of Ladysmith awoke to the news there had been an explosion in the mine where most of the Ladysmith miners worked. Anxious relatives waited on the railway station platform to find out details of the tragedy. In the afternoon, searchers brought out the first five bodies. Joseph Mullin, the colliery doctor, identified the bodies as they came from the mine. That evening the first train arrived at Ladysmith, carrying the bodies on the floor of the caboose. As each was lifted from the stretcher, the name was called, and relatives claimed the body and took it home. The stretchers were returned so they could be taken back immediately to the mine.

The rescue work continued on through the night. One reporter present when the bodies of two men were placed on stretchers noted: "The faces were unrecognizable except to their nearest friends."[10] By Thursday, all had been recovered.

Ladysmith lost a number of its prominent citizens: James Molyneaux, 36, was a popular young tenor who sang with the Welsh Glee Club and was a presiding officer of the Ladysmith Aerie of Eagles; 40-year-old Robert White was the father of six and a member of the local school board; and his brother-in-law, Thomas O'Connell, was a well-known fullback who played in the Ladysmith football club.[11] Thirteen of the men were married, leaving 38 orphan children. Widows received $300 from the miners' sick-and-burial fund, and under the Workmen's Compensation Act each family was also entitled to the sum of $1,500 from the company.[12]

The chief inspector of mines, Francis H. Shepherd, in his annual report stated that dangers could exist in the mine atmosphere that were not apparent to the ordinary mine official, and that mine management should determine "the condition of the mine atmosphere regarding marsh-gas, and take necessary precautions."

The inquest attached no blame to Wellington Collieries Company. The combination of gas, coal dust, a poorly set shot, and an open-flame lamp caused the explosion. Miners were not all required to use safety lamps. The Big Strike in 1912 was triggered by a report of gas in this same mine. It was not until 1918 that open-flame lamps were banned from the mines.

CHAPTER FIFTEEN

Mayors and Aldermen, 1901–1920

Six mayors served the city during the period of the next two decades, which included the "Big Strike," the troubling two-year strike by miners, and the four years of the First World War, plus the Spanish influenza epidemic of 1918–1919. The city may have felt beseiged on all fronts as it tried to cope with one crisis after another. Somehow the administration kept the business of the city on a steady course, and Nanaimo emerged in the 1920s as a much stronger community. Samuel Gough continued to hold the position of city clerk, as he had since 1880, and all councils valued his experience and knowledge of city affairs.

William R. Manson held the position of mayor for four years, from 1901 to 1904. He was knowledgeable on city affairs, having been involved in municipal politics for three years under the esteemed first mayor, Mark Bate, who held the position for sixteen years.

Bate considered his years on council as rewarding, as was his community, business, and political career. He loved the province and looked upon Nanaimo with special pride. When his wife Sarah died in 1897,[1] he took an extended vacation to England to visit his home town of Birmingham. He returned with a new bride, a widow, Mrs. Hannah Harrison.

During William Manson's tenure as mayor, Western Fuel Company purchased the New Vancouver Coal Company. Mine employees and the city said farewell to their friend Sam Robins,

The Amazing Mansons

William Manson's family became known throughout B.C. One astute observer noted there were more Mansons (three in the House) than there were members of the opposition. Premier Richard McBride's Conservative party had made a clean sweep of the province in 1903 and would hold power until the Liberals gained office in 1916. All three Mansons would serve under his administration.

The Manson family trek to Vancouver Island started with Michael, William's cousin, who came here in 1875 from the Shetland Islands in Scotland. He drove a locomotive, hauling coal from Chase River Mine to the loading wharf at Nanaimo. In letters home to his brother Lawrence, he bragged about how easy it was to get work in Nanaimo and how the living conditions here were so much better than in Scotland. Here, he said, he could have meat in his meals as often as he wanted, even twice a day, whereas once a week was a luxury back home in Shetland.[16]

Michael built a home on Haliburton Street that he shared first with three other bachelors until he married Jenny Renwick. The lot had a ready supply of water from a good well, an added bonus in early Nanaimo. He also built and operated Manson's General Store at the corner of Haliburton and Farquhar streets. The store, which lasted 40 years, carried every line of goods for the home, including groceries, dry goods, and clothing. Michael also served the city briefly as clerk in 1880. He qualified for his captain's papers and bought a tug for towing barges, and he finally settled on Cortez Island, where he was elected MLA in the McBride government.

Lawrence took his brother's advice and arrived here in 1877. His first job was with the Vancouver Coal Company. Later he bought the Manson Store from Michael. He married Catherine Duncan, who joined him from the Shetland Islands in 1880. They had six children. Another brother, John, also settled on Cortez Island, as a rancher. The youngest brother, William J., was the next to arrive. William worked for a time in the Manson Store before moving to the Mainland to continue in business. Later, he too was elected, in the Dewdney District, for the McBride government.

Yet another Manson joined the family, cousin William R., and it was he who became mayor of Nanaimo. William later served as mayor of Prince Rupert, and he too was elected as an MLA.[17]

the company manager, who had maintained labour peace in the mines and had given the city the Five Acres development. The city purchased the water works, and telephone communication was established with Victoria. Manson did not leave politics behind; instead, he directed his attention to provincial politics and joined other family members in the Conservative McBride government.

Manson's Shop on Haliburton Street. Pictured here are Lawrence Manson (left) and Ernie Manson.

Albert Edward Planta was the next to fill the mayor's chair. He served eight terms as mayor: 1905–1908; 1910, 1911, and 1914 and 1915. Before he was elected mayor, he had already served eight years as alderman.

A son of the former magistrate, Joseph P. Planta, he came with his parents from Australia in 1879. Planta was educated in Nanaimo and began his working life in a drugstore at age fifteen. After two years he took a position with Dr. Cluness, the colliery surgeon. Following the death of the doctor, he entered the insurance and real estate business and headed a large thriving business. In 1911 he sold his interest in the business to Dominion Trust Company, and he became manager.[2] He married Amy Gordon on June 3, 1890; she was the daughter of Member of Parliament David William Gordon. The couple had five sons: Gordon, Edward, Clive, Murray, and Ranelaugh.

Politically, Planta was a Conservative and took an active interest in local affairs, particularly the water system of the city. During his years as mayor, the E & N Railway was sold to the Canadian Pacific Railway, Planta welcomed the Governor General Earl Grey and Lady Grey to the city, and major improvements were made, including the sewer system installation and the paving of more streets. Nearly five acres of the ravine was partially filled in to a depth of almost six feet.[3] The mayor also negotiated with Western Fuel Company to extend the waterfront roadway along Front Street to Comox Road.[4]

Mayor A.E. Planta (centre) and City Council of 1914.

Among Planta's other credits in public life were his service as chairman of the Nanaimo School Board and, in 1910, president of the B.C. School Trustees Association. He also presided over the Union of B.C. Municipalities for two years. He was appointed senator in 1917.

Thomas Hodgson was a one-term mayor who beat out Planta in another bid for re-election in 1909. Hodgson also had a number of years under his belt as alderman, from 1904 to 1908.

Hodgson was born in England and came to Nanaimo in 1892 from Victoria, where he had learned the trade of stonemason. When he heard that Alex Henderson was hiring experienced stonemasons in Nanaimo, he came here and started working for him. The job was physically demanding, so after several years he resigned and entered the general insurance and broker business.

As a founding member of the Agricultural Society in 1894, Hodgson successfully negotiated a deal between the society and the school board for a building the society could no longer afford. The community needed another elementary school, and the society had a building it could not manage. "Without official approval Hodgson risked his career and on his own accord, set aside $15,000 toward renovating the building, eliminating a lot of red tape; the work was billed to the city."[5] In the fall term of 1921, the old agricultural hall opened as an elementary school and was named the Thomas Hodgson Elementary School in his honour.

The agricultural hall at the corner of Wentworth and Machleary streets became the Thomas Hodgson Elementary School in 1921.

John Shaw stepped into the mayor's chair in 1912, beating out Planta by a majority of 43; he was re-elected in 1913. Shaw is remembered as the mayor who requested Attorney General William Bowser call in the militia to keep the peace during the early days of the Big Strike. The militia never left. Despite the troubling labour situation during his two years of administration, the city was in the midst of a real-estate boom.[6]

Born in Manchester, England, in 1863, John emigrated with his parents, Mr. And Mrs. Alexander Shaw. The family settled on Gabriola Island, where his father educated himself and his children, including John. In 1884 he and John became teachers. John was appointed principal of the Boy's School, then later became the first principal of Central High School in 1896. He resigned this position in 1908 to join the Inland Revenue Board as a collector of revenue, a position he held until 1921 when the Department of Customs and Inland Revenue amalgamated.[7]

John Shaw was an advocate for education, and he served as a member of the school board for twelve years. He was honoured on January 21, 1931, for his 50 years of devotion to education in Nanaimo. Central High School was renamed the John Shaw High School in his honour.[8]

Frederick A. Busby served only one term, in 1916, during these two decades; however, he had already served seven years as alderman. After a lapse of a few years Busby returned to the mayor's chair from 1921 to 1924, and again from 1927 to 1929.

Born in Oakville, Ontario, in 1872, he came to Nanaimo in 1892 and began working for Hemans & Walmsley. He stayed with the company as manager after it was taken over by Pat Burns & Company in 1912.[9]

Like other mayors, Busby served on the school board for a total of 25 years, two of those as chairman. He was a Rotarian, president of the Pioneer Society, and a member of the Foresters.

Henry McKenzie had only served two terms as alderman before being elected mayor in 1917. He was re-elected in 1918, 1919, and 1920. McKenzie saw the community through the final days of the First World War and the Spanish influenza epidemic. He saw the first airplane visit Nanaimo in August 1919. He also welcomed two royal figures in the autumn of 1919: the Prince of Wales in September and the Governor General of Canada and his wife, the Duke and Duchess of Devonshire, in October.

Mayor Frederick A. Busby (centre) and City Council of 1916.
Members of council are listed in Appendix I.

McKenzie defeated J.R. McKinnell in the mayoralty race in January 1920. The following month he officially opened the Nanaimo Public Library on the second floor of the Athletic Club.[10] He died two months later, and Frederick Busby was re-elected to fill the vacancy.

165

Aldermen With Longevity

The mayor is only as good as his council. Several aldermen became mayors while others were happy just serving on council. Charles Wilson served seven years; John W. Graham and W.J. Ferguson served six years each.

Edward C. Barnes served nine years as alderman between 1902 and 1918. Born in England, he came to Nanaimo via Australia in 1891. For a time he worked for the New Vancouver Coal Company as a carpenter, but he left to start a contracting business. His company was known as Barnes and Wilson. His interest in public life extended to the school board, the licence board, and the hospital board.

Alexander Forrester served eight years as alderman between 1907 and 1918. He was born in Kingskettle, Fifeshire, Scotland, and came to Nanaimo in 1891 from Utah. Later in life he recalled his arrival here when the Silver Cornet Band played on the wharf to welcome American visitors.[11] Forrester was a champion soccer player and a welcome addition to the local soccer club. As a building contractor he had to his credit the Royal Bank (Vendome Block), the Dominion Post Office Customs House addition, Balmoral Hotel, Globe Hotel, Crown Theatre, Oddfellows Block, and the Shades Saloon, which became part of the Windsor Hotel. Forrester was a Klondiker and in his later years enjoyed telling stories of his experience as a sourdough taking the Yukon Trail. He also served on the school board and the hospital board. His wife Rose (Rhoda) was a Malpass descendant.

Edward George Cavalsky served as alderman for six years between 1909 and 1916. Cavalsky had a reputation as "a prudent and careful guardian of the city purse strings." He was repeatedly appointed finance chairman.[12] Born in Denmark, Cavalsky came to Vancouver Island in 1880 and worked for the Canadian Pacific Navigation Company on the Victoria to New Westminster run before being transferred to the SS *Amelia*, which operated between Nanaimo and Comox. In 1886 he left the steamship service and opened Cavalsky's grocery store on Victoria Crescent in Nanaimo.[13] He was a partner for five years with A.R. Johnston, then ten years with Lawrence Manson, and he also worked for James Hirst. Later he opened his own insurance and accounting business. The first telephone system was installed in his store, and his wife Laura became the first telephone operator.

In 1888 Cavalsky became a volunteer fireman with the Black Diamond Fire Company. He was paid $1.50 per trip regardless of the hours worked. In 1895, he became secretary, a position he held for 35 years until his retirement.

Henry Shepherd also served six years as alderman between 1909 and 1915. He came to Nanaimo in 1887 from County Durham, England. He opened up and operated the Shepherd Mine at Wellington and the brickworks at East Wellington.

James Young was alderman for seven years. He was first elected in 1910, then re-elected in 1912 through 1916, and again in 1919. However, it is not his city record that is of note, but the fact he was expelled from the Nanaimo local of the Social Democratic Party in January 1913. The stated reason for his expulsion was "on general principles for working against the interests of the other candidates nominated." The party asked all Socialists of the South Ward to withdraw their support from James Young.[14] According to the party statement, he had been asked twice to attend a special meeting but refused. Young explained that the SS *Oscar* explosion had wrecked his house, greenhouse, and barn, and he had to stay home and repair the damage. In his own defence, Young wrote a letter to the editor asking his friends in the South Ward "to answer this cowardly, treacherous malicious vindictive attack by returning me at the head of the poll." He vented his anger toward individuals in the party:

> I am not sure how many were present but judging from the previous campaign meetings I fancy the lot present consisted of Hodgkinson, Jordan, Temple, Pettigrew and possibly two or three others. I leave it to all men to say what brand of justice could be expected from that tribunal even had I been present. But I could not possibly be there, and even the worst Capitalist Court would have postponed action under the circumstances.
>
> I have given years of my life to the movement, a pile of money and a great amount of labor. I flatter myself I have done more real work for Socialism than all of them ever have or ever will.[15]

Young's constituents returned him for another year and several more.

CHAPTER SIXTEEN

Nanaimo Fishery— Herring and Whales

*H*erring were caught almost everywhere along the coast, but Nanaimo became the principal centre of the industry. Although the Snuneymuxw had traded herring for blankets during the early years of their contact with white men, the commercial herring fishing industry started here in 1896 when James Brown caught 100 tons of fish. These fish were cured in the form of bloaters and kippers and sold to markets in Vancouver, Victoria, and Seattle. The following year Brown was shipping herring to Australia, but this venture was not a success and was discontinued. In 1900 he sold out his business to J. Foreman, who in turn sold to Jarvis. By this time, except for a small demand for local markets, the resource was underutilized; herring were used only for halibut fishing bait and the guano was used as fertilizer.

Japanese in the Herring Industry

Japanese began arriving in B.C. toward the turn of the twentieth century. Whites generally viewed them as just another "Oriental menace," and like the Chinese they were disenfranchised. Japanese fishermen settled in Steveston, at the mouth of the Fraser River, as early as 1885. They were so successful at fishing that others joined them, until the village had a population of about 2,000, consisting almost entirely of male Japanese. The seasonal nature of the industry caused them to migrate to other fishing grounds, so other Japanese colonies were gradually established. In places like Ucluelet on the west coast of Vancouver Island, they became a dominant part of the industry. In 1896 there were 452 fishing licences issued to Japanese. By 1901 they held over 2,000.

While James Brown was fishing herring, a number of Japanese families had established small salteries on Newcastle Island, on the Departure Bay side, now known as Saltery Beach. There was a market for salted pickled herring, using the "dry salt" method favoured by Japanese and Chinese. In 1903 Mr. Makino became the first to take advantage of what would become a lucrative herring fishery, when he exported 793 tons to Japan.

Ikeda & Co. had operated in Nanaimo for a number of years and had a plant at Departure Bay. All Ikeda employees were Japanese. The output of this small company took one-sixth of the total herring catch. All of the fish processed were shipped to Formosa, Shanghai, or Manchuria. Manager M. Ikeda said he found the Chinese market offered a better field than the Japanese, so he prepared and shipped exclusively for China, where he got a better price. In 1907 he said the demand for Nanaimo herring was unlimited, and he planned to hire more men and increase production.[1]

Japanese did not operate the entire Nanaimo herring fishery, but they were dominant. A Japanese employment office managed by S. Harada established an office at the Japanese Boarding House on Comox Road, next door to the Newcastle Hotel.[2] Other companies had a "white only" policy that excluded all Japanese labour.

Other Fishing Companies

One white company, the Nanaimo Fisheries Company, formerly known as the Nanaimo Fishery Co. Limited, was owned by a local businessman and managed by Mr. J.E.T. Powers. In March 1905 the company purchased a torpedo boat from the admiralty, hoping that the speed of the boat would ensure fast trips with its fresh fish. The torpedo boat Number 40 was 100 feet long; it had a fourteen-foot beam, a speed of seventeen knots, and a capacity of over 22 tons. Captain A.H. Mace and chief engineer McNiven commanded it.[3]

The Bell Irving Company of Vancouver purchased the company on October 16, 1906.[4] The deal included boats, nets, fishing gear, and the plant. Bell Irving's entry into the local fishery boded well for the future. Bell Irving was well known, particularly in the salmon fishery. The company planned to increase herring production in Nanaimo on a much larger scale.

The Nanaimo herring fishery grew rapidly. The herring were so plentiful "that large numbers were washed up on the beaches by the waves of a passing steamer."[5] In 1905 and 1906 there were six companies employing 150 engaged in herring processing. The total catch for the season of over 2 million pounds was either "dry" salted, made into kippers or bloaters, or sold as bait to halibut fishermen.

In the 1907–1908 season the number of companies working in the industry increased from 13 to 19, employing 500. The greatest catch of all happened in the season 1908-1909, when the total doubled that of the previous year from 18,870,000 to 43,300,000 pounds. This brought more companies into the industry and increased employment opportunities. The major markets were in Shanghai and Kobe. The *Nanaimo Free Press* reported as follows:

> With each year the value of the fisheries of Nanaimo increases. Inspector Taylor predicts that the business this year [1908] will be conducted on a larger scale than ever with probably 500 men.
>
> Last year fifteen drag seine licenses were issued and twenty gill net licenses. Each of the drag seines will employ on an average of 8 to 10 men. The Japanese companies employ many more to each seine, as high as 16 to 18. The gill nets will engage about two men to a seine. Besides those actively engaged in fishing other men are employed in the curing establishments and in other ways.[6]

The Nanaimo harbour was alive with fishing vessels preparing for another season. In 1908 Fisheries Inspector Edward G. Taylor predicted the whole "fisheries business was enjoying a healthy development."

Steveston may have been home to the first saltery, but Nanaimo rapidly became dubbed "herring town."[7] The extraordinary success of the previous year brought more companies into the industry. In the early part of December 1909, 43 companies were in operation, employing 1,500. Wooden canneries crowded the waterways all along the shoreline of Departure Bay, Newcastle Island, and along Newcastle Passage,.

One magazine writer assessed the herring fishery in 1908:

> Nanaimo Harbour is yearly the scene of the most remarkable herring run on the Pacific Coast. For several months in the year the harbour fairly teems with herring, at times the run being so remarkable that the herring pile up on the beach several feet deep. The fish are so thick on occasions that they actually smother themselves and float to the surface.[8]

The cost of constructing a saltery was estimated at $3,000, including the driving of piles and the cost of lumber and tanks. The cost of seines, fishing boats, launches, scows, and salt brought the average cost of a camp to $5,000; a total for the 43 camps came to $215,000.[9]

Fire Danger

One of the biggest fears for owners of the canneries was the ever-present danger of fire. There were a number of fires that totally destroyed the plants, two of them only weeks apart in 1910.

On July 21, 1910, smoke and sparks filled the night air from a point between Brechin and the Red Fir Lumber Company's mill. Sparks flew everywhere; the whistle sounding the alarm brought crowds to the area adjacent to the provincial jail on Stewart Avenue. The *Nanaimo Free Press* speculated the fire had brought men from the farthest corners of the city "influenced no doubt by the fear that the premises of the Nanaimo Herring Packing & Canning Co., in which so many local people have shares,"[10] was on fire. The company employed 30 people. It had formerly conducted business on a barge that was towed from place to place.

The fire that consumed the waterfront canneries was said to have started in a vacant building connected to the home of a Japanese man named Wakesah. It spread quickly to another cannery owned by another Japanese man named Fujawara, and then progressed south to the building owned by Green and Murray.

The Japanese canneries were totally destroyed by the time the spectators arrived. The firemen did everything to try and save the Green and Murray building, but it was too late to stop the flames spreading. This company suffered the greatest loss for it had just stocked up on supplies.

Another fire on September 23, 1910, burned four cannery buildings: three owned by Japanese and one by Benson and Graham of the North Pacific Fish Company. An odd note to this fire was the fact that Green and Murray, the company that had suffered in the previous fire, had stored their supplies at the Benson and Graham plant.[11]

This fire was suspected of starting in a shack behind the Makagawa cannery, where a Japanese family lived. Makagawa owned one cannery; two others belonged to Korenaga, and the fourth was owned by Benson and Graham. The fire was almost in the same location as the July fire "down by the provincial jail" on Stewart Avenue. The damage estimated at $20,000 was partly covered by insurance.

New Herring Fishing Licence Regulations

In 1910 the federal government implemented new regulations for the herring fishing industry. For years white men purchased licences but never fished under them. Instead, they sold them to those who wanted to fish, generally Japanese men. The government charged $50 for the licences, which were then resold for $500 to $1,500. Under the new system, herring fishing licences were not transferable. Another regulation prohibited seining in the harbour and established properly regulated hours for fishing.[12] Until this time, it was not uncommon to see seiners at work in Nanaimo Harbour.

A *Nanaimo Free Press* editorial called attention to the "ghastly muddle" in which the herring industry in Nanaimo operated; in particular, the newspaper cited, "the incompetent or careless administration. Twenty licenses had been issued for 1910, and that was five more than recommended by city council or the Citizens' League." The challenge of managing the Nanaimo fishery (District 3) was under Fisheries Inspector Edward G. Taylor, a former Presbyterian minister from Port Alberni. The newspaper put the fault clearly at the feet of Taylor, claiming it to be the "result of maladministration."

One of several herring canneries on the waterfront. For several months each year, Nanaimo Harbour teemed with herring. The town was dubbed "herring town."

Scotch Curing Herring

In November 1905 James Cowie, a Scotch-curing herring expert, brought Mr. Cumming, a Scottish cooper, and three "lassies" to Nanaimo to demonstrate their skill in handling fish, packing, and curing. Within a month the Nanaimo Fisheries Company shipped a carload of its pickled herring to New York. The first shipment of 150 barrels, or approximately 50,000 pounds, was taken by ship to Vancouver and loaded on trains for the eastern market.[18] "Gratifying and complimentary" letters were received from agents in New York and Chicago who handled the product. One New York firm was so pleased with the fish that it ordered 10,000 barrels, or 60 train carloads, of Nanaimo-cured herring, enough to keep the company operating for the entire season.

When the herring industry in Nanaimo started, only fourteen licences had been issued and that number remained stable for a number of years. In 1909, 42 were issued, and that meant a boom in business for Nanaimo. These companies built salteries and put in equipment worth thousands of dollars. Now the licences were being reduced; fear grew that some companies would go out of business, and ultimately, Nanaimo would suffer.

Between 1911 and 1912 there were 36 smoke and fish houses and a clam cannery employing 400 workers.[13] The First World War created a heavy demand for canned herring, pilchards, and salmon.

The herring fishery, Nanaimo.

The Nanaimo Fish and Bait Company in Newcastle townsite was an amalgamation of Robinson & Stanall and Johnston & Rudd, two companies that were involved in the herring industry from its inception. The company supplied bait for fishermen engaged in halibut fishing and also dry-salted fish for the Orient.

The company holds strong views on the question of Oriental labour, and although the fishing industry is one in which Japanese are almost exclusively employed, the employees of the company are all white men.[14]

John Rudd, a partner in the firm of Johnston & Rudd, was the managing director of the company.

Page's Lagoon Whaling Station

Attempts to establish a whaling industry in B.C. were made as early as 1868, but it was not until 1905 that commercial whaling really began in earnest when the Pacific Whaling Company, formed in Victoria, built the first whaling station at Sechart in Barkley Sound.[15] The company chose four sites for its whaling stations; one was at Page's Lagoon, on the southeast end of Hammond Bay near

For a brief time—1907 and 1908—Pacific Whaling Company operated a whaling station at Page's Lagoon.

Departure Bay, where the company owned 132 acres of waterfront property. (The site is now known as Piper's Lagoon.) The other two sites were Fitzhugh Sound and Rose Harbour.

Three sealing skippers were credited with starting the first west-coast whaling fleet. They were Captains Reuben and Sprott Balcom, and Captain William Grant. The Balcom brothers were from Nova Scotia, and Captain Grant lived in Victoria. At a time when the sealing industry was approaching extinction, they started whaling, using Sprott Balcom's experience gained while whaling in Newfoundland.[16]

With great anticipation, Page's Lagoon Whaling Station began operations on November 8, 1907. The company had constructed docks and concrete ramps, installed a donkey engine, drilled for fresh water, and built bunkhouses for the 125 employees, who were predominantly Oriental.[17] The first shipment of 400 barrels of whale oil from Page's Lagoon was delivered to Vancouver via the Canadian Pacific Railway's steamship *Otter*.

Whaling stations were notoriously smelly places. The smell from the tanks full of whale oil left many gagging. Fortunately the plants were usually located in isolated places.

In 1908 the Victoria *Colonist* reported that the Pacific Whaling Company had brought in three to five whales per day during the season, taking a total of 500 between April and August. The oil was shipped to Glasgow and the fertilizer to Honolulu. Whales were valued between $400 and $800 each.

There were a few prosperous weeks of whaling at Page's Lagoon, then suddenly the operation ceased on January 25, 1908. There were rumours that complaints had been lodged against hunting whales in the Strait of Georgia, where the Terminal Steamship Company operated whale-watching boats. However, it was more likely there was a shortage of whales in the strait. The whale catcher, the *St. Lawrence*, which had been brought out from eastern Canada to begin operations at Nanaimo, was diverted to the Sechart station.

For a short time the company tried to operate the facility as a plant for converting dogfish to fertilizer. By March 1910 the company finally wrote off Page's Lagoon Whaling Station, dismantled it, and sent the machinery north to Rose Harbour. The Nanaimo location was abandoned for good, and in 1912 O.H. Burt & Company sold the property to a Mr. Clelland for $50,000. Clelland had no interest in whaling and only wanted the property for land speculation.[18]

CHAPTER SEVENTEEN

Dunsmuir's Interests

Premier James Dunsmuir now controlled the E & N Railway, but it had never been a paying concern. The railway's terminus was at Wellington, a town that had prided itself on this fact; it had a roundhouse, five engine stalls, turntables, a repair shop, and storehouses. The town had once been the centre of the Dunsmuir coal enterprise, and in the early 1890s the population had equalled that of Nanaimo. Once Dunsmuir's Wellington coal seam was played out, the town was reduced to almost village status because he had relocated most of its buildings to Ladysmith, where he resumed mining operations.

The Dunsmuir Mansions

The Dunsmuir family had amassed a fortune from its mining interests and from the E & N Railway Land Grant. Joan Dunsmuir and her eight daughters led a privileged life in Craigdarroch, the family mansion in Victoria, while James and Laura and their children lived a more modest life in Ardoon, at Departure Bay, which had been a gift from his father in 1884. However, this was still considered a mansion by Nanaimo's standards. Laura liked the thirteen-room southern-style estate located on the hillside, overlooking the company's wharves.

After Joan decreed that James and Laura move to Victoria, James built a fine new mansion on twenty acres of waterfront in Victoria; he named it "Burleith" after Robert Dunsmuir's Scottish birthplace. James found a buyer who was willing to pay a good price for Ardoon. Mr. C.H. Babbington, a carpenter, purchased the mansion with the understanding that he would maintain it in a dignified manner. He grew strawberries there, which netted him a good income until ill health forced him to sell in 1907 to C.J. Keighley, who lived there for another 50 years.[1]

Preoccupation With Railways

James Dunsmuir's term as premier from 1900 to 1902 was turbulent. The provincial government still operated without party affiliation. Somehow he managed to stay in office during that time with only a slim majority of supporters. In the 1901 session one of Dunsmuir's principal measures was an act authorizing a loan of $5 million to help in the construction of railways and other public works.

Railways were on everyone's mind at the time. In a province where rugged mountains and cascading rivers had to be crossed, rail was the obvious solution. Past history showed B.C. had great mineral wealth just for the taking if only speculators could get easy access. Rail construction costs would have been prohibitive without government help. This was something Dunsmuir understood and sympathized with. According to the E & N Railway charter and early maps of Vancouver Island, the Dunsmuirs had always intended to continue the E & N Railway to the northern end of Vancouver Island to Cape Scott, and James wanted that line built.

The provincial railway subsidy was contingent on the railway receiving matching grants from the federal government and would be

Some of James and Laura Dunsmuir's children. The couple had eight daughters and two sons.

limited to $5,000 a mile. In return, the province would expect to receive 2 percent of the railway profits until the grants had been repaid; freight rates would be government-controlled; and after twenty years, the province would have the option to purchase any line it had subsidized.

There were several interested railways who submitted proposals to the legislature. One in particular caught the eye of the premier. It was that of the Canadian Northern Railway (CNR) whose transcontinental scheme would bring the railway into Victoria. The CNR proposal followed the earlier route rejected years before by the Canadian Pacific Railway, to cross Seymour Narrows and run south to Victoria. Dunsmuir was only moderately interested until he learned that the CNR was prepared to pay him $8 million for the E & N Railway along with $1.7 million for the "worthless" acres of the land grant remaining.[2] This offer was one he could not refuse.

Now Dunsmuir faced a dilemma: He was not the sole owner of the E & N Railway Company. Almost half the shares were still owned by his father's American partners. The obvious answer was to buy them out. Fortunately for Dunsmuir the partners were not too happy with the money-losing E & N Railway and were as eager as he to sell, but they wanted $4 million for their shares. He calculated this would still be a good deal for him. It was time to take his money and run and get out of politics; after all, he had given the province two years' service as promised.

He sent a telegram to General Thomas Hubbard, the partners' representative:

> Can sell the roadbed to Canadian Northern for two million dollars, they giving three per cent first mortgage bond. I am willing, are you? An answer by noon tomorrow, the eighth, is very important.

Hubbard replied that he could not decide without more information. He received another telegram from Dunsmuir, advising this was the final offer: "Two million dollars, three per cent first mortgage bonds, fifty years, quarter of a million cash in two years, and another quarter of a million in three years." Of course, the sale depended on the bill passing in the House.

The deal with CNR was too good to be true. The railway company had second thoughts and decided instead to buy only the roadbed; it was not interested in the land holdings. The CNR reduced the offer to $2 million. Dunsmuir weighed his options and considered the only solution was to renege on his offer to buy out his American partners. Telegrams went back and forth between Dunsmuir and his partners, but they refused to move. If Dunsmuir seemed rushed there was a reason. Rumours circulated in Victoria he had made a private deal with the CNR. The newspaper headlined, "A Deal or a Steal. Is Dunsmuir selling his railway for the good of the country, or his country for the good of his railway?"[3]

The railway became an issue in the Victoria by-election where his friend Edward Prior sought office. Prior, a former resident of Nanaimo and former inspector of mines, was an old friend of the Dunsmuir family and was regarded as an excellent businessman and a careful administrator. The two men stood side by side on the election platform and defended the government's position on the railway. They assumed people would be pleased with any plan to bring a transcontinental railway into the city. Prior's opponent, E.V. Bodwell, was determined to bring down the government. He had been the chief lobbyist for the Coast-Kootenay Railway and was one of the most prominent lawyers in the province. Bodwell charged that Dunsmuir had a monopoly and was squeezing out competing railways.

The public dislike for Dunsmuir was such that in the midst of the election fever his wife Laura received a warning to keep her husband home from an election rally or else he would be shot.[4] He attended anyway, and Prior won the election by a narrow vote. A week later, opposition members accused Dunsmuir of corruption and forced him to agree to a provincial inquiry. Charges against him were not proven, but Dunsmuir had had enough of politics. On November 21, 1902, he resigned, and Prior was invited to form

What Conflict Of Interest?

Prior's term as premier was short. He came under attack when it was discovered that while he was premier his company, E.G. Prior and Company, had received a government contract to supply wire cable to be used in the construction of the Chimney Creek Bridge over the Fraser River. Prior failed to see the conflict of interest and hoped to brazen it out. When presented with the facts from an investigative committee, Lieutenant-Governor Sir Henri Joly de Lotbinière decided he had no confidence in Prior's judgement and dismissed him. On June 1, 1903, Richard McBride, who had been the recognized leader of the opposition, formed the next government.

The next election would be fought along party lines. McBride said, "The step was not only desirable but necessary."[19] The old system had failed. There had been five governments in five years, and that alone was a good argument in favour of the new system.

a new government. The CNR contract had been conditional on federal subsidies, but these were not forthcoming so the proposal faded away.

On October 17, 1902, Dunsmuir bought out his partners for $1 million, becoming the sole owner of the E & N Railway. He was now free to negotiate a sale without the impediment of partners, but it would take three years before another buyer was in sight.

CHAPTER EIGHTEEN

Labour Unions and Politics

W hen James Dunsmuir returned to private life in 1903, there were two mining companies operating in the Nanaimo District: the Western Fuel Company (WFC) and the Wellington Colliery Company. Thomas Russell had replaced Samuel Robins as the manager of the WFC's Nanaimo colliery, with Joseph Randle in charge of the No. 1 Shaft, Esplanade, and Thomas Mills in charge of the Protection Island Shaft. There were attempts to make the old Harewood Mine operational, but by 1903 it had been idle for months.

James Dunsmuir's Wellington Colliery Company Limited now focussed south of Nanaimo, in Extension and Ladysmith, and in the Comox-Cumberland area. His general manager was F.D. Little, with Andrew Bryden managing the Extension's No. 1, 2, and 3 slope mines and the tunnel mine, and John Matthews managing the Comox operation.[1] The old Wellington Mine had been sealed off a few years before.

There had been relative labour peace within the Western Fuel Company colliery thanks to the employee associations formed under manager Samuel Robins years before. Each mine had a committee made up of staff and employees that managed to hammer out grievances. The same could not be said for the Wellington Colliery. Unlike Robins, James Dunsmuir had not endeared himself to his workers; his company was in a perfect position for the Western Federation of Miners to move into Canada.

James Baker, a union organizer, arrived on Vancouver Island in 1903 to sell the miners on the merits of an international union.

At a mass meeting held in Ladysmith in March, workers voted to join the union. Two days later, an angry Dunsmuir advised that the Extension Mine would be closed down and that miners were to turn in their tools to the storekeeper. He had decided he would rather close the mine than recognize the union.[2] Workers like Samuel Mottishaw and James Pritchard were dismissed for attending organizational meetings.[3]

Baker then took aim at Dunsmuir in his Cumberland Mine. The meeting with the miners there was stormy and only partially successful. Of the 600 miners who attended, only 100 signed up.[4] Dunsmuir was encouraged; he felt he had paid good wages and had gained loyalty from the men who had worked for him for years. Still, he threatened, "If there is a strike, I will close the mine down, just as I did at Extension, and keep them closed—for ten years if need be—before I will submit to this tyranny." Between November 1902 and March 1903, 2,000 miners joined the union.[5]

Provincial Labour Unrest

The Dominion Labour Commission's report presented a rather grim picture of B.C. in 1903. It stated that the province had been "threatened with a breakdown of morality."[20] Not only was there trouble in the mines, but a labour dispute with the United Brotherhood of Railway Unions had brought the Canadian Pacific Railway to a standstill, and longshoremen, teamsters, and members of other unions had walked off the job in sympathy. Also, a strike by fishermen on the Fraser River had tied up that industry, but this dispute was resolved when the white fishermen agreed to follow the lead of the Japanese and accept the canners' terms.[21]

What the commission did find out—to its surprise—was that the American Labor Union (ALU), the Western Federation of Miners (WFM), and the United Brotherhood of Railroad Employees (UBRE) conspired to stop all transportation and mining when it suited their cause. George Este of the UBRE sent this telegram to Clarence Smith, secretary of the ALU at Butte, Montana:

Strike spreading. Revelstoke out: Longshoremen struck today. Please have WFM refuse to allow coal loaded on cars; steamboats ships, or bulks at Ladysmith, Union (Cumberland) or other points on Vancouver Island for Vancouver. This is to prevent the Canadian Pacific getting coal. Rush orders by wire. Don't fail—fight for life.[22]

B.C.'s labour troubles had investors wondering if they should place their money elsewhere. Everyone hoped the new premier of the province, Richard McBride, could put the economy back on track.

Dominion Labour Commission Visits Nanaimo

Cumberland miners had only to look at the effect of the closure at Ladysmith to see how serious the situation would be should Dunsmuir make good on his threat. The entire Vancouver Island economy could be in jeopardy. It seemed the union had gained a foothold and only the intervention of Mackenzie King could help. Not yet prime minister, King was appointed secretary to a royal commission sent by Ottawa to report on the labour trouble in B.C. On May 20, 1903, King and the Dominion Labour Commission met in Nanaimo.[6] It was obvious the sympathy of King and the other two commissioners, Chief Justice Hunter and the Reverend Dr. Rowe, lay with the miners.

One of the first people to address the commission was James Baker. He so impressed the inquiry that King began to dislike the "millionaire monopolist" who had shut down the mines. Even Hunter thought Dunsmuir's treatment of his men was a "damnable outrage."

The commission was prepared to dislike James Dunsmuir, but they found instead a businessman who clearly expressed his views about unions. He said he would have nothing to do with them and he would hire whomever he liked and would treat his men just as he pleased. He was asked if he thought great wealth carried with it an obligation to the community. He said it did not. And what about the ownership of large works to the workmen? No, sir. "Do you mean to say you have a right to close your works regardless of the interest of the workmen or the community?" "I have. It is my property."[7] He questioned the commission, "Haven't I as much right to refuse to recognize a union among my men as Baker has to tell them if they do not join the union, they will be blacklisted all over the North American continent?"

"King Jamie," as Dunsmuir was nicknamed by his workers, found he had little to worry about from the Dominion Labour Commission's final report. So-called revolutionary socialists such as the Western Federation of Miners were to be outlawed and employee associations encouraged. James Dunsmuir had won round one in the fight for union representation.

Richard McBride—"Glad-hand Dick"

Richard McBride, the sixteenth premier of the province, was a young lawyer from New Westminster. He was the first premier born west of the Rockies, and he served for twelve years instead of the usual two.

McBride was first elected to the provincial legislature in 1898. Two years before, he had married a young woman from New Westminster, Christina Margaret McGillivrary. Blessed with an outgoing personality, McBride could charm everyone; he was as much at home with the social elite of Victoria as he was with the working people of the province. Somehow it had not mattered to him when he was appointed minister of mines under Dunsmuir and that his boss was the biggest mine owner in the province. The Dunsmuirs had welcomed the young couple to parties at their mansion Burleith.

McBride became premier in 1903 under the banner of the Conservative party. He was returned with a slim majority of 22 members out of 42, but he hoped to win the support of the two Socialists from Nanaimo, James Hawthornthwaite and Parker Williams.

The new premier faced a tremendous challenge, as the province was close to bankruptcy. McBride promised to restore fiscal responsibility. The public debt stood at $12.5 million; financial guarantees to railways amounted to more than $1 million, and the credit of the government was exhausted. The new finance minister, Robert G. Tatlow, could not obtain a bank loan of $1 million until he promised that all work on highways and other projects would be suspended. Dunsmuir and Prior had left the finances of the province in a dreadful mess.[8]

Nowhere else in Canada were working people considered more radical than in B.C., and the hotbed of discontent was Nanaimo, where Ralph Smith, former president of the Trades and Labour Congress of Canada, had been elected federally and was now closely affiliated with the Liberals.

Big Jim Hawthornthwaite and Parker Williams Enter Politics

Those miners in Nanaimo District who had advocated joining a union turned their attention to the ballot box in the October 3, 1903, provincial election. There was a redistribution of seats in Nanaimo from three to two. The miners found kindred spirits in James Hurst "Big Jim" Hawthornthwaite and Parker Williams.

Hawthornthwaite's Legacies

Hawthornthwaite, an Irishman, represented the Socialist Party of B.C. (SPBC). He had been dismissed from the Vancouver Coal Company, some felt, because he was connected to a disagreement with Member of Parliament Ralph Smith, whom miners regarded as "a Company man running under Labour colours." Dunsmuir had supported Smith in prior elections.[9] Hawthornthwaite had been acclaimed in the 1900 election when Ralph Smith resigned to seek a federal seat. The MLA was well liked and was handily re-elected in Nanaimo City, running against former mayor, Conservative candidate Edward Quennell, and Liberal-Labour candidate Harry Shepherd, a former president of the Nanaimo Miners' Union and a Nanaimo Board of Trade member.

Williams, a Welsh miner, also represented the SPBC and was elected in the newly formed Newcastle riding of Extension, Ladysmith, Old and South Wellington, and Northfield. His opponents were Conservative Andrew Bryden and Liberal David W. Murray. Bryden was the manager of the Extension Mine.[10]

McBride hoped to win the support of Hawthornthwaite and Williams by making compromises such as shorter working hours in the mines and the introduction of government safety regulations. The two Nanaimo socialists came through for him and gave him their support.

During a debate on the amendment to the Coal Mines Regulation Act for shorter working hours, Hawthornthwaite explained that he wanted to "relieve men from merciless and deadly exploitation." The gallery, packed with miners, broke into applause. McBride once complained that Hawthornthwaite took

The Parker Williams family at their farm in Cedar. Back row: Kate, Parker Williams, wife Eleanor, Parker, Baden, daughter Frances, David. Front row: Clifford, daughter Eleanor.

up too much time of the House on his labour legislation. He is credited with the passing of the first Workmen's Compensation Act in Canada in 1902, and he also introduced a bill in 1906 that would have given women the vote. But it would be over another decade before that became reality.

Orator-Comrade Parker Williams

A former Welsh coal miner and now Socialist politician, Parker Williams was one of the first politicians who gave a voice to the grievances suffered by B.C. miners. He was the son of a farmer, but early in his life he began work in the Clydath Vale Colliery. He married Eleanor Price in 1891, and the following year the couple immigrated to Canada. They settled first in the Ottawa Valley, where he worked in logging camps and where his first two children, David and Catherine, were born.

Leaving Eleanor and the children in Pembroke, he headed west, working at harvesting grain in the prairies, coal mining in Alberta, and on railway construction in eastern B.C. He arrived in Nanaimo in January 1898 and decided this was the place where he could settle down with his family. Two more children were born here, Baden and Parker.

It was while he was employed with the Western Fuel Company mines that he became active in union affairs. His first venture into politics was in 1902 when he ran unsuccessfully in a by-election for Nanaimo North (Wellington) as a Socialist candidate. Encouraged by a strong showing, he ran again in the 1903 election, for the riding of Newcastle, and this time he was successful. He was described as "a decent plug, but no socialist" and was a down-to-earth type of individual.

The Williams family moved to Chase River where four more children were born: Clifford, Frances, Eleanor, and Rose. Williams established Northwood Farm, in the Oyster District, and took a keen interest in the North Oyster School Board from 1907 to 1912.

Parker Williams won four more provincial elections in 1906, 1909, 1912, and 1916 and gained a reputation as an eloquent speaker in the legislature. One newspaper report of 1907 noted he had addressed the House for over an hour "at the rate of 100 words a minute":

For a ready tongue, Mr. Williams easily beats the house. It is almost as easy to record what Mr. Williams didn't say as what he did. He travelled all over the earth as well as all over Webster's Unabridged Dictionary. And by and by, Mr. Williams resumed his seat to the feeble applause of his smiling colleagues, [Hawthornthwaite and McInnes] which alone broke the silence of the obviously disinterested House [Conservatives and Liberals].[11]

In 1909 he presented a bill to "Revise all the Statutes, all legal terms couched in Latin, and other foreign languages, be translated into plain everyday English." Williams claimed that the mystifying terms of the written law were responsible for what he called a "horde of social parasites"—lawyers.

After the election of 1912 the opposition's ranks were reduced to two—Parker Williams and Jack Place of Nanaimo. Parker became leader of the opposition. It was a frustrating time for the two members, as they were totally ignored, especially since this was during the coal miners' strike on Vancouver Island.

Parker Williams.

After the 1916 election, there was a change of government—the Liberals defeated the Conservatives. Parker Williams was the only Socialist elected and was expected to support the Liberals. He resigned to accept an appointment as one of the founding commissioners of the Workmen's Compensation Board (WCB).

Later the WCB was given the responsibility of administering the Mothers' Pension and the Old Age Pension. Parker Williams had the honour of signing the first Old Age Pension cheque that was presented on October 16, 1927, by MP A.W. Neill to Alberni senior Bill Derby. Williams retired in 1943 to his family farm.

CHAPTER NINETEEN

The Sale of E & N Railway

*T*he Canadian Pacific Railway (CPR), which had snubbed the province twenty years before when the province was attempting to have the E & N Railway built, now seemed interested in purchasing the railway. The CPR was already a major player on the West Coast. In 1901 it purchased the Canadian Pacific Navigation Company fleet, part of the old Hudson's Bay Company fleet, and renamed it the British Columbia Coast Steamship Service. This move into shipping was good business. The new service would be like railway branch lines reaching into communities and industries along the coast. The CPR headed the calls for improved steamship service. Victoria was already an important port of call for the *Princess* ships that had established connections with Vancouver, Seattle, and Victoria, and in 1903 the CPR announced plans to build a tourist hotel in Victoria. The Empress Hotel would become a city landmark. There was little opposition to the prospect of the CPR purchasing the E & N Railway.

The deal with the CPR was not as lucrative as that proposed earlier by the Canadian Northern Railway (CNR). The final agreement signed on June 5, 1905, netted Dunsmuir $2.33 million and gave the CPR all of the 25,000 E & N Railway shares. In turn, the CPR conveyed to Dunsmuir's Wellington Colliery Company all the lands and rights of way needed for the operation of the mines at Alexandra, Extension, and Cumberland, plus all the coal rights under the land within the railway belt. Dunsmuir received $1,075,000 after the share transfer was completed. The CPR had the option of paying the remaining $1,225,000 in the form of 4 percent debentures with a 25-year maturity.[1]

Dunsmuir Appointed Lieutenant-Governor

In 1906 James Dunsmuir was appointed lieutenant-governor, succeeding Sir Henri Joly de Lotbinière. He would be the first British Columbian to hold this office. Why he accepted such a position is unknown, for he disliked the social aspect of being in public office. Perhaps the social ambitions of his wife Laura and those of their eight daughters influenced his decision. On May 26 he became the eighth representative of the Crown in the province.

His first year in office seemed to be quite successful. With Laura as the perfect hostess at Government House, the couple managed to fulfil public engagements with some degree of interest and grace. Dunsmuir's down-to-earth approach and "his ruddy outdoorsy appearance and obvious nervousness" endeared him to many.[23] But the honeymoon with the public did not last long.

Along with the purchase, the CPR acquired the E & N Railway's steamships *Joan*, which operated between Nanaimo and Vancouver; the *City of Nanaimo*, used along the east coast of Vancouver Island; and the tug *Czar*. All became part of the CPR fleet. The tug was soon replaced by a new tug, christened the *Nanoose* after the bay north of Nanaimo. She was painted the familiar CPR colours with black hull, white bridge and upperworks, and a yellow- and black-topped funnel.

The deal with the CPR did not make James Dunsmuir a wealthy man. The cash he had received barely covered the sales commission and other expenses. The debentures provided him with an income of $50,000 a year, but it was not the wealth he had hoped for. However, he was now out of the business of running the railway and had managed to keep his coal mines. He returned to private life and turned his attention to the business of mining coal.

The Natal Act

In 1907 the provincial government passed "An Act to Regulate Immigration into British Columbia," sometimes referred to as the "Natal Act." It required that all immigrants, namely Orientals, were required to have an educational test. The federal government hoped it had appeased British Columbians in 1904 when it instituted a $500 head tax on Chinese immigration, a tax that effectively slowed the number to a trickle. Now the threat came from an increasing number of Japanese entering the province, this at a time when Dunsmuir wanted to bring in cheap labour to work in his mines. Premier McBride supported the Act, mainly to pacify the unions and small businessmen who opposed the importation of the Japanese. The premier's support was merely a gesture, as he knew that in this matter federal jurisdiction would prevail. Lieutenant-Governor Dunsmuir sent a letter to McBride serving notice he would not give assent to this bill. Did a lieutenant-governor have the power to prevent legislation from coming into effect? This was the constitutional question debated at the time.

Vancouver was rife with rumours that thousands of Japanese were on the way and would soon constitute one-third of the population in the province. Once again Mackenzie King was sent to B.C. to investigate the situation. To his amazement he discovered the Canadian Nippon Supply Company had a contract with Dunsmuir to bring 500 Japanese men to work in his mines. The Vancouver-based company acted as a contractor, arranging for recruitment of labour in Japan.

At a meeting of the Asiatic League and its Socialist allies in January 1908, Parker Williams—with tongue in cheek—stated the following:

This is a commercial age and the Lieutenant Governor should be permitted to enjoy the full benefit of what he has bought and paid for. In his enmity to labor, the Lieutenant Governor is at least consistent, and he is no worse now than when he got his present job.[2]

Hawthornthwaite concluded that impeachment of Dunsmuir was essential, and he did everything he could to rally support for Dunsmuir's removal. He described Dunsmuir as "a brute," "an inhuman monster," "a champion union-smasher," "an honorable scallawag," and "a human Hyena."[3] No doubt Big Jim's action further endeared him to his constituents, but it did not remove Dunsmuir.

The Socialist Party did not support the "yellow peril" and warned workers not to be drawn into such rhetoric as it only diverted energy from the real issues. The two Nanaimo MLAs listened only to the people who had voted for them; however, when a bill that would change the Elections Act and prevent Hindus from voting was introduced in 1907, both Hawthornthwaite and Williams supported it. The bill passed. Williams thought all the discussion on this issue was a waste of time, as he would much rather be talking about an eight-hour day or his bill for fortnightly wages.

James Dunsmuir survived the Opposition's motion of censure, but this may have been the beginning of his end as lieutenant-governor. Normally the position is held for five years, which would have meant he would stay in office until 1911. This latest controversy caused him to prepare for a graceful way out. His consistent refusal to recognize unions and his support of cheap Chinese labour made him an easy target for criticism. Dunsmuir seemed indifferent to public opinion and somehow managed to stay on until 1909 as the Crown's representative in B.C.

Canadian Collieries (Dunsmuir) Ltd.

Sir William Mackenzie, president of the CNR, had turned away from purchasing the E & N Railway in 1902, and three years later it became the property of the CPR. Mackenzie had failed to get federal support for his earlier plan, so he had abandoned the idea. But times change, as do governments, and now Mackenzie had another plan for which, this time, federal subsidies were already in place. He proposed building another transcontinental railway that would compete with the CPR, and he planned to start construction in B.C. in January 1910 and have the line completed by July 1914.

In 1910 Premier McBride signed the contract with Mackenzie and Donald Mann to build a railway paralleling the CPR line through the province, but there arose a problem with the E & N Railway line on Vancouver Island.

When the CPR purchased the E & N Railway line it failed to exercise its option to purchase the Dunsmuir coal mines. Mackenzie discovered this fact and approached the now-retired Lieutenant-Governor Dunsmuir with a view to buying the mines. Dunsmuir liked the proposal, but once again he found himself in a conflict-of-interest position. He was a CPR director and received interest on the million dollars in CPR debentures he had accepted as partial payment for the sale of the E & N Railway. An arm's-length approach was needed to keep the sale above reproach. Dunsmuir therefore transferred all his shares in the Wellington Colliery to his lawyer, Richard Elliott, and nine days later Elliott assigned those shares to William Mackenzie, who in turn transferred them to a newly chartered company, Canadian Collieries (Dunsmuir) Limited. Dunsmuir was a happy man for he had made a good deal. When the offer had come in 1902, he would have sold both the railway and mines for $8 million. Now for the mines alone he was offered $11 million.[4]

The bill of sale was not very explicit. There was no listing of inventory or assets and no legal description given of the land. The agreement of sale was dated January 3, 1910. It assigned and transferred all shares of the Wellington Colliery Co. Limited, and R. Dunsmuir Sons Co. (California) and Dunsmuir's right under the agreement with the CPR dated June 5, 1905, under which he had sold the E & N Railway to the CPR.[5] Mackenzie could be forgiven for wondering just what he had purchased. Did the sale include the coal ships? Not according to Dunsmuir: They were his personal property. He also declared ownership of the farm located near the Wellington Mine, whose earnings were also entered into company books. Condescendingly, he offered an eight-acre property on Hornby Island; Mackenzie could have that if he wanted it!

Mackenzie also discovered the company had no operating money. Just two weeks before the sale was final, Dunsmuir, then the only shareholder of the Wellington Colliery, called a shareholders' meeting and declared a $700,000 dividend be paid to him. He easily shrugged off any criticism: "I used the colliery books as my private account. When I felt like it, I would declare a dividend to balance it. I owned all the shares."[6] Mackenzie launched a legal action, but the Supreme Court decided in Dunsmuir's favour. Mackenzie appealed the decision, but again the court decided in favour of Dunsmuir.

While Mackenzie was busily securing the collieries, the E & N (CPR) extended the railway into Port Alberni on December 20, 1911. Now the CNR indicated it planned to build a railway from Victoria to Port Alberni via Cowichan Lake and the Alberni Canal and then on to Seymour Narrows. The topography of the terrain must have been overlooked.

Canadian Collieries (Dunsmuir) Ltd.'s head office was in Victoria. The two main officers of the company included Mackenzie as president and Alexander Duncan McRae, later known as colonel, as vice-president. The two were powerful financiers with interests in CNR, forestry, and fishing. The new company had a labour force of 2,079 employed at the Union Colliery in Comox and at the No. 2, 3, and 4 mines in Extension. The company was by far the largest mining operation in the province.

The End of the Dunsmuir Dynasty

In 1908 Dunsmuir had moved his residence from Burleith to Hatley Park. Architect Samuel Maclure received the important commission—to design a castle-like stone mansion on the 800 acres of the estate.[7] Like his father Robert, James was now the lord of the manor. There, he and Laura became the social leaders in Victoria.

The Dunsmuirs had a large family of eight daughters and two sons. The young women fascinated and scandalized the capital city. Robin, his elder son, left Vancouver Island and made his home in various parts of the world; he died in 1929 in Singapore at age 51. The second son, James or "Boy" as he was nicknamed, joined the army at the outbreak of the First World War. He was aboard the *Lusitania* when it was torpedoed on May 7, 1915. The death of Boy greatly disturbed Dunsmuir, and it is said he listened for hours to the gramophone recording of John McCormick singing "Where, Oh Where, Is My Wandering Boy Tonight?"

James Dunsmuir may have been a millionaire, but money gave him no real happiness. He died on June 6, 1920, in Cowichan, where he had been on a fishing trip. During the night he suffered a stroke and died of a massive cerebral hemorrhage. His estate, estimated to be over $3 million, was left to his wife Laura.

Coast Steamship Service Brings New Ferries

Now that the CPR owned the old E & N steamships, the *City of Nanaimo* and the *Joan*, the public expected improvements. Captain James W. Troup became superintendent of the British Columbia Coast Steamship Service and he moved from Nelson to Victoria to take over the service. Under his management the fleet was upgraded and enlarged.

The visit of the *Princess Victoria* to Nanaimo in 1903 gave Nanaimo residents a hint of things to come in passenger ferry service to the mainland. The old ferries had provided a valuable link between Nanaimo and the mainland and other communities along the east coast of Vancouver Island, but the years had taken their toll. They could not compare to the grand *Princess Victoria* with its 78 cabins, staterooms, and beautifully decorated dining saloon.

The *Princess Mary* Ferry

The *City of Nanaimo* was replaced with the *Princess Mary*, a small vessel by *Princess Victoria* standards, but nevertheless sturdy. She arrived in Victoria on February 15, 1911, after a rough voyage from Scotland, and following refitting was ready for service on the Nanaimo-Comox-Vancouver run. Captain Douglas Brown commanded her maiden visit to Nanaimo. The *Nanaimo Free Press* described the ship as follows:

> [She is] lavishly and luxuriously fitted up with every modern convenience, and there was general agreement that she was far and away superior to any passenger boat on the Nanaimo run [and] it is significant of the foresight of the management of the coast service in providing a vessel of such pretensions.[8]

The *Princess Mary* could seat 64 in the dining room; it had a central social hall on the awning deck above, a second-class smoking room and bar forward under the pilothouse, and a first-class smoking room aft on the boat deck. Staterooms had hot and cold running water, steam heat, and reading lights. She could carry between 500 and 600 passengers and had sleeping accommodations for 160. Four special rooms called "bridal suites" had private shower baths for a price of $4 overnight or $3 for a day trip. Typical staterooms with single upper and double lower berths cost $2.50 to $3.00, although a few rooms were just $2 per night or $1 for a day trip.[9]

The *Princess Mary* was built to carry everything that people needed; even 90 head of cattle could be accommodated easily. However, she was not built to carry cars. On the rare occasion an early motorist could sometimes squeeze the vehicle onto the freight deck.

After only three years on the Nanaimo run, the *Princess Mary* had another 24 staterooms and a new social hall added. After reconstruction she was assigned to the Alaska and North Coast services.

Collision of the Charmer and the Quadra

The old steamer SS *Charmer* still served the Vancouver–Nanaimo route. The Union Iron Works had built the iron- and steel-hulled steamer in San Francisco in 1887. Marine author-historian Ruth Greene called her "a romantic little outlaw," but she was also considered a "happy ship," as she was better in fair weather than in storms.[10]

She was not a happy ship when on a foggy day, February 26, 1917, at Gallows Point by the entrance to Nanaimo Harbour, she collided with the government lighthouse tender *Quadra*, one of the most venerated vessels on the coast. The *Quadra* had already completed two decades of service when the accident happened. The lady of the lights was towed to shallow waters in Nanaimo Harbour, where she sank with only a portion of her funnel and masts showing above the water. Britannia Mines purchased her and

First Ferry to Carry Cars

The first ferry to carry cars was the SS *Joan*. She crossed the Strait of Georgia in 1907 with two cars belonging to George A. Fletcher and Dr. Hogle lashed on her foredeck.[24] Loading cars on the *Joan* was so complex that two days' notice had to be given before they came aboard.[25] Another early car owner in Nanaimo was Guy J. Burnham, the works manager at the Canadian Explosive Company.[26]

formed the Quadra Steamship Company. During prohibition, the *Quadra* played another role in the history of B.C. The *Charmer* was not badly damaged by the collision and after some repairs was able to resume service.

Introducing the *Princess Patricia*

In 1912 the Coast Steamship Service added the *Princess Patricia* to the Vancouver-Nanaimo route. Originally called the *Queen Alexandra*, she was a fast pioneering turbine-powered passenger vessel that had attained a speed of 21.63 knots on her trials. Captain Troup purchased her from the Clyde Passenger Service in Scotland, where the ship had been a day-passenger steamer, operating on the two longest runs of the Clyde.[11] The ship had been damaged in a fire, so Troup was sceptical about buying her. However, Leslie Denny of Wm. Denny & Bros., Dumbarton, had built her and reassured Troup of her capabilities.[12]

The arrival of the *Princess Patricia* in the spring of 1912 was a red-letter day for Nanaimo. Sirens screamed and whistles blew in welcome as small boats escorted the new ferry into the harbour for the first time. Mayor John Shaw welcomed the ship's Captain Ritchie and Captain Troup and other CPR officials. In Shaw's welcoming speech he reminisced about the steam packet *Ada*, a small vessel that had once crossed the Strait every two weeks at eight knots an hour: "Now the crossing could be made in just two hours." Ritchie expressed the hope that thousands of tourists would come to Nanaimo on the *Princess Patricia*.[13]

The *Princess Patricia* became an important timing device for the men working the No. 1 mine at Protection Island. So precise was the ship's schedule that the miners almost timed their work day to the throb of the ship's engines overhead as she left the harbour.

The traffic between Vancouver and Nanaimo grew from just over 11,000 passengers in 1917 to nearly 147,000 in 1923. Automobile revenues increased from just over $500 to over $33,000 in the same period.[14] The *Princess Patricia* had done yeoman service with passengers, but there were complaints about the difficulty boarding cars. Some owners had to lower their car tops because of the low clearance on the ferry. The need for a car ferry became obvious.

CHAPTER TWENTY

Three Explosive Years in Nanaimo, 1912–1914

There were two black powder plants in Nanaimo: the first one built at Northfield in 1890 and known as the Hamilton Powder Company, and the other at Departure Bay, in the area today known as Cilaire. When the Bowen Island plant of the Western Explosives Company was moved to Nanaimo, the company changed its name to the Canadian Explosives Company. The first shipment from the Departure Bay company wharf was made on December 15, 1897. Mr. W.A. Young managed both plants until his death in 1900; then Guy J. Burnham replaced him as works manager.[1]

The Departure Bay complex covered more than 100 acres. The innocent-looking manufacturing plant had a series of what were termed "danger" buildings. Shoes with nails or hard metal of any kind in the soles were forbidden in the danger houses; matches were considered high treason, and even hairpins were frowned upon. Nothing was allowed to enter these buildings that would cause a spark. The floors and walls were all lined with lead or rubberoid. No movable article of iron or other hard metal was permitted.[2]

The first building housed nitroglycerine, "an explosive ten times more violent than gunpowder, and a hundred times more sensitive to shock or friction." At the sign of any danger, a warning whistle blew outside, and everyone raced for cover.

Other buildings included the separating house, the washhouse, and the mixing house. The buildings were located some distance from each other so that an explosion in one would not involve the others. Cartridges were made in another building. The Nanaimo plant boasted of producing more dynamite cartridges than any other plant on the continent.

In a province rich in natural resources, the Nanaimo plant was a profitable venture, as blasting agents were needed in mining work, especially in the coal mines, to dislodge the coal, and in railway work, blasting through rocks in rugged country.

Working with explosive materials was a delicate operation and required the utmost caution. The work force was made up of white men, young women, and Chinese labourers. On January 4, 1903, ten Chinese and two white men were killed while making gelignite. The *Nanaimo Free Press* reported the workers "were launched into eternity."[3] This explosion was heard in Parksville and Ladysmith, and windows all over Nanaimo were shattered. The explosive gases blew away a stretch of railway track; it was found wrapped in a graceful spiral around a tree some distance away. "The biggest piece we found was one man's arm. Everybody went around with buckets and pails and sticks to pick up the flesh and bits of hair."[4]

On May 19, 1910, another five men were killed when the separator building blew up. The explosion was felt as far away as Duncan. Debris fell more than half a mile away. The sound of the explosion reverberated like a thunderclap, as a mass of debris and smoke blew out over the harbour. Five minutes elapsed before anyone dared to venture near the plant for fear of another explosion. A number of men on the road leading to the entrance were blown into the bush. Others dived for cover. Shreds of debris hung from treetops.

The five men killed were Herbert W. Hygh, George Preston, William Baldwin, G.L.L. Wager, and Harry Meredith. Hygh, the master mechanic, was a young married man with three children. The body of William Baldwin was the only one recovered. The men were doing repair work in the separator building, a wooden shed about 22 by 30 feet long. Only a large hole remained where the building had stood.[5] The local coroner, Dr. Davis, convened a jury of six men, and together they viewed the scene of the explosion, but the actual cause would never be known, as little remained after the blast.

There were other explosions. Two occurred in 1911: one at the Northfield plant in October, and another at Departure Bay on December 22. This latter blast killed three men when the gelignite room exploded. Those killed were Joe Depries, Willy Day, and Mr. Wilcox. Nanaimo residents demanded action be taken to protect everyone. However, it wasn't until the biggest explosion of all,

*The Hamilton Powder
Company staff at
Northfield in 1890.*

*Giant boilers in the
Canadian Explosives
Company plant.*

two years later, that a clear message was sent for something to be done.

The SS Oscar Incident—1913

It was a wintry afternoon in Nanaimo on January 15, 1913, with snow falling and poor visibility. Bing Kee had just sat down at the dinner table. For some reason, perhaps a premonition, he got up from his chair and went into the kitchen. Suddenly a terrific explosion was heard coming from the area of Protection Island. A pane of glass shot across the room that Bing Kee had just vacated. If he had not moved, he would have been decapitated.[6]

The explosion came from the 82-foot SS *Oscar* that had been carrying explosives from the Canadian Explosives Limited plant at Departure Bay to Vancouver. Unknown to the Nanaimo harbour master, the ship had crept in during the night to take on bunker coal at the Western Fuel Company's loading dock. She carried 1,910 cases of Giant Powder in her hold that had been loaded at Telegraph Bay, Victoria. More cargo had been loaded at Departure Bay from the explosives plant there: another 1,880 cases of dynamite (50 tons) and 50 bags of black powder were secured under canvas on her foredeck.

Weather conditions were poor; the storm battered the ship as it rolled in heavy seas. When close to Entrance Island Lighthouse on her way to Vancouver, Captain Alexander McDonald decided to turn around and seek safe harbour in Nanaimo until the weather improved. On the way back, to the horror of everyone on board, a fire was discovered near the boilers. The crew tried unsuccessfully to control the fire as it threatened to engulf the ship. Captain McDonald put the ship on full speed in the hope of running ashore.[7] As she neared Protection Island, the crew abandoned ship and swam to shore on the island, afraid to look back at the blazing vessel. It was a chilly and frightening swim for the captain and his mate Albert Edge, engineer George Donaldson, fireman Thomas Rankin, deck hand George Leighton, and cook Charlie Wong.[8]

The Western Fuel Company's Protection Island Mine was nearby, so the men raced through the bush, falling over slag heaps, in an attempt to reach safety. Along the way they encountered a bewildered Native woman and without explanation, scooped her up, taking her with them as they continued their desperate run. They had just reached the boiler room of the mine building when there was a blinding flash followed by a tremendous explosion that hurled everyone off their feet.

The explosion was heard and felt all over Nanaimo. "Big Frank," the clock at the post office on Front Street, stopped at precisely 1:55 p.m. The scene on Protection Island was one of havoc and destruction, as tops of houses were blown away and the machinery at the mine was left in grotesque twisted shapes. In the city, the blast shattered all the windows in the downtown area and cracked the plaster on a house on Skinner Street. Some bricks were dislodged from a portion of the wall at the rear of the Opera House. All around town windows were shattered. People took to the streets in panic to escape flying glass; horses broke loose from their harnesses and galloped along the streets. Hardly a store escaped damage.

The Windsor Hotel, now the Dorchester Hotel, lost most of its windows, and some of its doors were blown right off their hinges. Damage was estimated at $4,000, with $1,000 being for glass alone.[9] The courthouse suffered $2,000 in damage, and the Oddfellows Hall lost all its skylights and glass on the roof.

Mayor John Shaw's face was badly cut. He was taken for emergency medical treatment to a doctor on Commercial Street. John McMillan, working in the drugstore of J.B. Hodgins, narrowly escaped injury when glass bottles and cases flew from their shelves.

At the Middle Ward School, children panicked as glass from the windows shattered in the classrooms. The young students huddled together in terror as teachers tried to calm them. The old Central School had to close as every window was without a pane of glass. At the Quennell School, scores of children were slightly injured.

Dallas Square with Windsor Hotel and St. Paul's Church.

Witnesses would always remember exactly where they were when the explosion occurred. William Lewis recalled the event many years later in an interview with William Barraclough. The experience remained most clear in the elderly gentleman's memory:

> The *Oscar* was carrying a cargo of dynamite and black powder and when fire broke out on her the crew abandoned ship. Thirteen windows were broken in my home and two chimneys damaged. Most citizens sustained similar damage, and only those who took very prompt action were able to get early replacements for their windows. Miraculously no one was killed and most injuries were minor.[10]

Big Frank—The Post Office Clock

The Dominion Post Office clock that stopped precisely at 1:55 p.m. on the day of the *Oscar* explosion was nicknamed "Big Frank" in honour of Frank H. Shepherd, the Conservative Member of Parliament.[27]

Shepherd, from Castleford, Yorkshire, began working for the Vancouver Coal Company in 1879 as assistant manager under John Bryden. One of his jobs was to assist mining engineer James Beaumont in sinking the Esplanade No. 1 Mine shaft. When Beaumont became ill before the shaft was completed, it was Shepherd who completed the job in 1884. Beaumont returned to England, where he died two years later.[28]

Shepherd became manager of the South Prairie Coal Company in Washington State in 1882. After ten years he moved on to New Zealand and Australia, then returned to B.C. in 1893. He explored Vancouver Island and Alaska before taking the position as chief inspector of mines for B.C.[29] He was first elected MP for Nanaimo in 1911. During his first year in office he acquired a four-faced clock for the tower of the Dominion Post Office building.

After the installation, Nanaimo residents who had relied on the No. 1 Mine whistle to mark the start and the end of shifts now had a clarion of chimes from Big Frank to indicate the passing of time. Local clockmaker Joseph M. Brown maintained the clock, kept the moving parts oiled, wound it up every week, and kept it clean. Brown had his own watchmaker store on Commercial Street, established in 1882.

For many years the clock dictated the pace of life in Nanaimo. When the first memorial services were held after the First World War, Big Frank signalled the two minutes of silence.

Frank Shepherd served Nanaimo as MP until 1917, when he was appointed inspector of dredging in Vancouver, a position he held until retirement in 1923.

On Protection Island a large crater marked the spot where the ship had beached. The undersea workings of the Protection Island Mine, located below the shattered seabed, developed serious flooding problems that closed certain areas of the mine forever.[11] However, the top workings of the mine received the full blast of the explosion. A beach boulder weighing 100 pounds was hurled 300 yards in the direction of the pithead, embedding itself to a depth of three feet, then bounding another twenty feet, before finally coming to rest. Damage on the island was estimated at $25,000.

Don Gray, a blacksmith on the island, was injured and taken to Vancouver for medical treatment with the hope of saving an eye. Mine engineer Mr. Woodman narrowly escaped death while informing Captain Yates that the *Oscar* was in flames and the powder might ignite.

Carpenters, glaziers, and doctors worked around the clock. Some schoolchildren were given a holiday so school windows could be replaced, and saloonkeepers helped calm the nerves of jittery customers. The *Free Press* exercised a little journalistic humour: "Many visitors to saloons were so scared that they forgot to pay for their 'drops.' Some were blown into the next hotel afterwards."[12]

A week later the Princess Theatre on Selby Street advertised in the *Nanaimo Free Press* a "big scoop" by showing pictures of the big explosion. "As the home of moving pictures, the Princess sets the pace with big crowds attending nightly."[13]

In the aftermath of the explosion, Nanaimo residents began to question why a dynamite plant should be located at their doorstep. On August 8, 1913, Canadian Explosives Limited announced it planned to move to James Island, Victoria, not because of public pressure, but because the Departure Bay plant could not expand. Under the Explosives Act, a plant had to be 1.5 miles from a dwelling not owned by the company.[14]

The Big Strike, 1912–1914

The Vancouver Island collieries gained a reputation for being the most dangerous in the province, but they also produced high-quality coal. In the 28 years prior to 1912, 373 men were killed in the mines, many as a result of coal gas explosions. Wellington had 83 deaths, Extension 50, Cumberland 69, and Nanaimo 180.[15] On October 5, 1909, an explosion at the Extension No 2. West Mine killed 25 miners.[16]

Attempts to unionize the coal mines had failed in the past, and with only two Socialist MLAs in the legislature to look after workers' interests, the combative United Mine Workers of America (UMW) was invited to try again.

The Coal Mines Regulation Act, amended in 1911, gave miners the right to appoint one or two representatives to inspect the mine periodically and to report on dangerous conditions—in particular, gas—in any part of the mine. Unfortunately, when the "gas committee" found danger, the company somehow found ways of getting rid of the men. It was this action that precipitated one of the longest strikes in B.C. history, which involved all the mines on Vancouver Island. By this time the UMW had a membership of 900 in the three mining communities of Nanaimo, Extension, and Cumberland.

Within the Canadian Collieries, miners had several grievances, including low wages, which ran from $1.35 to $2.86 per day. They also thought that giving certificates of competence to illiterate Chinese made working conditions dangerous for all.

The beginning of the strike can be traced back to the Extension Mine when Isaac Portrey and Oscar Mottishaw reported on June 15, 1912, that they had found gas in several places in the No. 2 Mine. The inspector of mines verified their report.[17] The two men returned to work, but the location where Mottishaw had worked subsequently ran out, and management seemed to have difficulty finding another place for him to work. He went to Cumberland to work, but after a short period of time there he was fired.

Oscar Mottishaw was considered a skilled young miner but also a troublemaker and agitator. His co-workers protested by declaring a general holiday for September 16 at all the mines in Cumberland. When they returned to work, they found they had been locked out. They could only get back to work if they signed individual work contracts for two years under the old non-union conditions. Miners were evicted from company-owned houses. White miners were furious the next day when Chinese and Japanese workers signed on for the two-year contract. The department of labour's report on strikes and lockouts in Canada, published in Ottawa in 1912, noted that the reason for the strike of September 1912 was "discharge of employees."[18] This simplistic terse statement told little of the turmoil and labour unrest brewing on Vancouver Island.

At the Extension mines, workers took a one-day holiday to discuss the situation as it applied to them, and on their return to work were met with the same notice used at Cumberland. By the beginning of October all men employed by the Canadian Collieries had been locked out. A few weeks later provincial Attorney General William J. Bowser sent a special contingent of police, 100 on foot and 20 mounted, to Cumberland.

Miners' General Strike

The miners decided to stage a general strike at all the mines on Vancouver Island in an attempt to influence Premier Richard McBride's government to investigate the circumstances surrounding the lockout. MLA Parker Williams had asked for a committee of inquiry to investigate the lockout, with one member being MLA Jack Place of Nanaimo. The resolution was overwhelmingly defeated. Miners celebrated May 1 as Labour Day, so it was decided to issue the strike call on the evening of April 30, 1913. At a mass meeting of miners held in the Princess Theatre in Nanaimo on May 1, the feeling was overwhelmingly in favour of a strike. The big strike had begun.

Western Fuel Company manager Thomas Stockett decided to close the mines on May 2 and 3 to allow his employees to vote on the question of a strike. He obviously thought enough workers would vote to return to work and the strike would be broken. Another meeting was held on May 2, again in the Princess Theatre, and the strike question was put to the meeting. Only 85 of the 900 present stood up in favour of returning to work. The chairman declared an adjournment and said a regular ballot would be taken at the courthouse the next day.

On May 3, 478 of the 2,000 men employed at Nanaimo, South Wellington, and Jingle Pot voted on the question, and only 33 voted against going back to work. Those voting were company officials, clerks, carpenters, and men working around the top of the mines. Only a small percentage of voters were miners.

Within a week, 95 percent of the men who were not in the union on May 1 had joined. The Pacific Coast Coal Company's mines at South Wellington were left without a man, and the shutdown in the Nanaimo district was complete.

The federal minister of labour, T.W. Crothers, visited the mining camps with the hope of finding a solution to the strike. In Nanaimo he chided miners for going on strike; in his opinion they had acted too hastily. The rest of his speech was devoted to praising Nanaimo MP Frank Shepherd. Crothers did not believe anything the miners told him. It was obvious that he had come to the meeting with a closed mind on the subject.

As the strike dragged on, pockets of violence broke out in Cumberland and Ladysmith, but Nanaimo so far had escaped the turmoil. Most of the Nanaimo miners worked for Western Fuel Company, and they had a good relationship with the company. Many owned their own homes, so they could not be evicted as the

Cumberland miners were, and the Chinese posed no threat for they had not worked underground since the explosion of 1887.

Company Pressures

The Western Fuel Company visited strikers who seemed to be wavering and might return to work. News spread that over 200 had decided to do so. On August 11, 1913, miners turned out in large numbers in the hope of stopping anyone from beginning work and breaking the strike. Eleven men were escorted to and from work. Strikers tried to dissuade firebosses from working. On August 12, MP Frank Shepherd and company manager Thomas Stockett warned of the danger of the mine being destroyed by fire. The miners consented to having 50 men work the next day, provided the company would recognize the union. Stockett agreed to meet a committee of his miners. A committee was struck, but it included Frank Farrington, the UMW official in charge of the strike. Stockett objected to Farrington as a member. If he had agreed to the union member, he would have been more or less recognizing the union.

Events deteriorated from that point on. At South Wellington a disturbance ensued when miners annoyed at the Nanaimo situation approached the bullpen in the mining camp, where a number of strikebreakers had been housed, to try to get them to quit. One of the strikebreakers, who introduced an axe into the argument, received a sound beating. The bullpen was approached on another occasion, only this time the camp strikebreakers were armed and they fired bullets. Again the rumour mill got into high gear; on hearing someone had been shot, miners in Nanaimo decided to go to the scene of the trouble.

Hundreds of miners headed for Extension. That evening, their targets apparently picked out in advance, the crowd ransacked and set alight homes and buildings belonging to the company, the strikebreakers, and the Chinese, driving their inhabitants into the woods.[19]

News spread quickly, as it does in a small town, that 23 special policemen were on their way to Nanaimo from Vancouver. When the policemen landed, the miners escorted them back to the boat. One policeman drew his gun. The miners realized the dangerous situation the young policeman had brought about and tried to get him back on the boat without incident. He fought off all efforts by the miners, and in return he received two black eyes.

Women in the mining communities joined their husbands and sons on the picket line, harassing strikebreakers and special constables, and supporting their loved ones during the most difficult days. There was a wonderful fighting spirit amongst the women. Some were fined because being in a crowd meant that they were part of a riot. They were also confronted with the dilemma of feeding and clothing their children on a small strike pay. Strikers received $4 per week strike pay. If they were married, they received another $2 plus $1 for each child. The average wage for skilled miners was $4 per day.[20]

Some women found jobs outside the home and even managed to help families in need in an attempt to preserve striker solidarity. Early in the strike women began to associate the coal miners' labour protest with reform of the suffrage laws. The women's vote had long been on the political agenda in Nanaimo, a cause championed by Big Jim Hawthornthwaite in 1906 and Jack Place in 1912.[21] Seventy-two delegates of the Women's Suffrage Movement had, on February 1913, presented Premier McBride with a petition signed by 10,000 women. The women were brusquely told that it would not be in the public interest to endorse their proposal.

Military Keeps the Peace

In August 1913 Mayor John Shaw sent a message to Attorney General William Bowser, requesting the militia be assigned to keep the peace in Nanaimo. In turn, the miners also sent a message to Bowser with what they thought was a reasonable suggestion: They would keep the peace if the special police were withdrawn. The hard-line reply from Bowser became famous in labour history:

> When day broke this morning there were nearly 1,000 men in the strike zone, wearing the uniform of His Majesty and prepared to quell the disturbances. This is my answer to the proposition of the strikers that they will preserve the peace if they are left unmolested by the special Police. If the men will not obey the Police, they must have the military, and now that we are in the field, we intend to stay to the bitter end.[22]

On the morning of August 14, 300 fully armed and uniformed members of the 72nd Regiment of the Seaforth Highlanders landed at Departure Bay. They moved into Nanaimo and camped at Dallas Square. Later in the day a detachment went out to Extension. The presence of the military resulted in a great deal of animosity in the community. A story that trouble had broken out in Cumberland caused more troops to be dispatched there, even though the town already had special police in force. Troops were everywhere.[23] Bob Mill composed the words and the music to a skit on the Seaforth Highlanders. The following is a sample verse from "Bowser's Seventy-Twa":

> Oh, did you see the kiltie boys,
> Well, laugh 'twould nearly kilt you, boys,
> That day they came to kill both great and sma,
> With bayonet, shot and shell.
> To blow you all to hell,
> A dandy squad was Bowser's Seventy-twa.
>
> Then, Hurrah boys, Hurrah,
> For the Bowser's Seventy-twa
> The handy, candy, dandy Seventy-twa!
> "Twill make the world look sma,
> Led on by Colonel Hall
> And Bowser and his gallant Seventy-twa.

Militia arrive to keep the peace. The military remained in Nanaimo until the outbreak of the First World War.

The militia was paid $1 a day for its effort. By the end of August, 179 miners had been arrested and imprisoned without bail; among them was MLA Jack Place, who was charged with being in possession of a gun taken from a policeman. Union leaders Joe Taylor and Sam Guthrie were also jailed; Guthrie was arrested at his home in the middle of the night. The militia remained on duty for a year in Nanaimo, escorting non-striking miners to and from the mines and maintaining order, until August 1914. The B.C. Miners' Liberation League published a booklet, written by J. Kavanagh, which describes the strike:

> Martial law had not been proclaimed, yet Russia was never more militarized than was Vancouver Island. Soldiers armed with rifles and bayonets searched the trains, looked under all the seats, and subjected all passengers to an inquisition as to their business. All persons travelling to Nanaimo by boat had to pass an examination at the hand of special police, reinforced by a file of soldiers. It was impossible to send telephone or telegraph messages out of the city without the military knowing the text of such messages.[24]

Militia parade in front of St. Paul's Church, 1913.

On August 18, 1913, a notice was issued that a meeting would be held in the Nanaimo Athletic Club to consider an agreement between the Vancouver and Nanaimo Coal Company (Jingle Pot Mine) and the union. About 1,200 men attended. Shortly afterward, the hall was surrounded by troops under the command of Lieutenant-Colonel A.J. Hall, who gave them one hour to finish their business. Later he asked to address the meeting; he said they could go ahead and finish the meeting, but he was tired and was going to bed. Everyone suspected the colonel had had too much red wine.[25]

The meeting ended when the miners voted to accept the agreement with the Jingle Pot Mine management. Special police marched them out single file in groups of ten, attended by a guard of soldiers with bayonets fixed on either side, and escorted them to the courthouse. There, each man was searched, his name recorded, and, if he wanted, placed in detention. The remaining men were then taken out to the grounds in front of the courthouse and kept there under guard. Forty-three men were detained; the rest were kept under guard until 2:00 a.m. before being allowed free. J. Kavanagh described the tense situation:

> Nanaimo and the surrounding districts experienced an epidemic of military imbecility that is scarcely equalled in history. The floor of the Athletic Club was torn up in an effort to discover armories of rifles. Hardware stores were raided and their stock of sporting ammunition confiscated. Every store that was so raided was said to be for the purpose of frustrating the strikers.[26]

The Canadian Collieries (Dunsmuir) Limited annual report for 1913 gave the company viewpoint on the strike. The strike had cost the company in sales and output, and it was predicted that "until the Mine Workers' organization determines to abandon the struggle," expenses would be high.[27]

After making an agreement with the union, the Jingle Pot Mine's manager Harry Freeman resumed operations August 19.[28] That same day, 100 striking miners were arrested on various charges.

In Nanaimo, Chief of Police Jacob Neen's report for the year ending 1913 stated there were 532 cases disposed of in court and $3,501 collected in fines and cost; 98 had been arrested for rioting, 12 for intimidation, and 117 for drunk and disorderly conduct.[29] The chief noted the work of his department had increased owing to the labour trouble, as they had been called on to do extra duty.

A Personal Account of the Strike

David Williams, the eldest son of MLA Parker Williams, wrote an account of his experiences during the labour unrest of mid-August 1913. His family lived on the family farm in the Oyster district, north of Ladysmith. The weather had been hot and dry, and his mother was a patient in the Ladysmith Hospital. On the night of August 13 David visited his mother in hospital, then he went down to 1st Avenue. His story follows:

> During the day a number of special policemen had been brought into Ladysmith, some mounted. Feelings were quite stirred as one of the mounted policemen was accused of being under the influence of liquor, and in riding his horse on the sidewalk, injured a woman. In the course of the evening there was a lot of milling about. I spent most of the evening and night on the steps of the Canadian Bank of Commerce, corner of 1st Avenue and High Street.
>
> In the evening a blast went off at the rear of the Temperance Hotel, across the corner from the bank. It was a boarding place for strikebreakers. It was said no one was injured. Later a blast was heard at the south end of the village. We were told that a bomb had been thrown into Mr. McKinnon's house and in throwing it out, he sustained severe injury to himself but was successful in saving his wife and children from injury.
>
> Ladysmith was the shipping point for Extension coal, also the bedroom for the Extension miners. Early on the morning of the 14th of August, a number of strikebreakers were dissuaded forcibly from going to work at the Extension mine. A number of them had their houses damaged by rocks thrown through the windows. Militia was brought into Ladysmith and Nanaimo area. The "kilties" were dubbed "Bowser's seventy twa's," Colonel Currie of First World War fame in charge of the Ladysmith detachment, Colonel Hall of the Nanaimo group.
>
> On August 19 mass arrests were made in Ladysmith, South Wellington and Nanaimo. Over 1,200 men were under arms in the strike zone. Two-hundred-and-fifty men were arrested, including MLA Jack Place, the president of the B.C. Federation of Labour J.J. Taylor, UMW leader Joe Naylor, and Sam Guthrie, president of the UMW of Ladysmith. One-hundred-and-sixty-four were committed for trial.

In October, Judge Howay of New Westminster was brought over to try the cases. He sentenced three men and two boys to two years in the pen; 23 to one year in jail and $100.00 fine; 11 to jail for three months and $50.00 fine; 11 more were tried and jailed in New Westminster; in December. J.J. Taylor and Sam Guthrie received two-year terms.

Sixty-five arrested in Ladysmith were taken by the E & N to Nanaimo and lodged in the provincial jail in Newcastle Townsite north of Nanaimo. Bail was not entertained for any of the prisoners.

On entry to jail, prisoners were stripped, weighed, measured and fingerprinted. The Ladysmith group had preliminary hearings held in Ladysmith [and were] escorted to and from the train by militia with drawn bayonets. The charge was rioting and unlawful assembly. No food could be brought from outside. There were three men to a cell; the cells were about six by ten by about 8 feet high, three bunks on top of each other. A bucket in the cell [was provided] for sanitary purposes [and] was emptied once daily. There were two floors of cells, back to back, and no tobacco [was allowed]. At first visitors were allowed to shake hands. Money was passed to the prisoners and used to bribe guards and to buy sugar. [After that] no contact was allowed. All mail [was] opened and [prisoners] were allowed to write one letter a week, one side of one sheet, left open. [They were allowed] two hours daily in the exercise court. The walls were 30' high on two sides and building on the other two sides. Prisoners were given magazines to read.

Personally I was a guest of George V for 52 days. I spent my 20th birthday there and had a tough time securing enough to eat. Food could not be brought in from outside. When going to court in Ladysmith, relatives tried to pass food in, if possible. The militia would knock it down and trample it into the road. I saw that happen more than once.

It was suggested to the accused that should they plead guilty they would be discharged forthwith. Some fell for this and were penalized accordingly. At my trial, three police testified to seeing me in Ladysmith that evening. When they saw me, I was not doing anything wrong. The third witness was night watchman Tom O'Connell, who recognized me and said I was not doing anything while he observed me. I was discharged for lack of evidence. Later

I visited some of my friends in Oakalla. They stated both food and general conditions were superior to Nanaimo.[30]

The long strike ended just prior to the beginning of the First World War. Included in the terms of settlement was the statement: "The companies will employ all men in their employ at the beginning of the trouble, without discrimination and as rapidly as physical conditions of the mines will permit."[31]

A Martyr to the Cause—Joseph Mairs Jr.

The last of the jailed miners was released on September 25, 1914. Only one never regained his freedom—Joseph Mairs Jr., who became sick, died in jail, and was buried in Ladysmith. The inscription of his headstone reads: "A martyr to the noble cause— the emancipation of his fellow man. Erected by his brothers of District 28, United Mine Workers of America."

Joseph Mairs.

Inspector of Mines Thomas Morgan retired June 1, 1913, and was replaced by John Newton. The mining reports from both men do not tell the troubling story of the two most difficult years in labour history on Vancouver Island. The 1913 report noted: "Labour troubles greatly reduced coal production on the Island."[32] The 1914 report showed production had partially improved: "first half favourable for mining in the province." However, the second half of that year was "shattered by the unprecedented conditions ... by the great European War."

The Big Strike was felt for many years. Many of the striking miners were blacklisted and never worked in the mines again. The men scattered all over the province and organized new Socialist locals. Before long, mine owners forgot about their agreement as markets declined and the country prepared for war.

CHAPTER TWENTY-ONE

The War Years, 1914–1918

War came to Canada on August 4, 1914, with the unexpectedness of a lightning strike. It left everyone dazed and bewildered. Canada was still a very young country and totally unprepared for war. The Canadian army consisted of only 3,000 men and 600 horses. The navy had a modest force of 103 men, and the air force consisted of two canvas planes, still packed in crates, and twelve regular officers.[1] However, Canada did have 10,000 reservists, the majority of whom were called to service immediately with only 24 hours' notice.

On August 6 came the announcement that Canada's first contingent would consist of 25,000. When the call to enlist went out across B.C., Victoria was flooded with men eager to serve their country and willing to fight for a dollar a day. Three days later a Nanaimo contingent left for Esquimalt, including K. Cavalsky, Brownles, R. Beckley, H. Brown, A. Brown*, P. Brown, Arch. Brown, A. Davidson*, G. Davidson, Ol Peto*, Lionel Beever-Potts, C. Stevens, J. Whitehead, H.E. Hickling*, H. Greaves, Mesher, and A.D. Corker.[2] (The * indicates men killed in action as listed on the Nanaimo Cenotaph.)

Another contingent left on August 21, including Lionel Potts, Keighley, R. Brown, N. Waddington*, and D. Cocker, who all left for Valcartier Camp. Lionel Potts received the military medal for valour.[3]

Within two months the First Division, Canadian Expeditionary Force, headed across the Atlantic escorted by ten warships.

During the first few months of the war, a sense of imminent danger spread throughout Vancouver Island. There were stories, fuelled by fear, that German cruisers would attack the coast. Premier McBride took steps to protect Esquimalt by purchasing two Chilean submarines built in Seattle for $1 million. For three days of the First World War, there was a B.C. navy. The federal government eventually took them over and reimbursed Victoria.

Canadian soldiers waited impatiently through a long cold winter in Britain before the call to the front came in 1915. As eager as they were, nothing could have prepared them for what lay ahead: poison gas, the killing ground of the Somme in 1916, and the heroic victory of Vimy Ridge. The place names and campaigns of battles won and lost are now part of history.

In the meantime Nanaimo prepared for war. Prior to the First World War Nanaimo men trained to be soldiers on any property they could use, sometimes at the old Jingle Pot Mine. In 1904 the Nanaimo Independent Company of Infantry—with its cap badge being a replica of the Bastion—was formed, and it took part in the First World War. One oddity of this period was the local recruitment of a "Bantam Battalion" made up of men 5 feet 2 inches and shorter. The unit distinguished itself in the war.[4]

The Nanaimo Internment Camp

Many Germans, Austrians, and Croatians lived in Vancouver Island communities. Rumours of espionage and suspicion soon fell on workers of foreign birth or name. On September 20, 1914, the Nanaimo Internment Camp officially opened in the Newcastle Townsite's jail building on Stewart Avenue near the intersection with Townsite Road. This was the same building that had housed David Williams and other miners during the Big Strike. The jail, overlooking beautiful Newcastle Island Channel, was enclosed by strong wire fencing and described as "a stockade-style compound of heavy lumber, logs and wire, some 14 feet in height."[5]

Guards and sentries were on duty at all times. The militia band played at the changing of the guard. The guards were billeted in the old Agricultural Hall on Machleary Street, about a mile southwest of the internment camp. During warm summer weather, tents were also used for shelter. The commandant of the facility was Major A. Rowan, 6th Regiment Duke of Connaught's Own Rifles, a Vancouver militia unit.[6] David Stephenson, Nanaimo's chief constable, apprehended all aliens with the help of special constables and, occasionally, the Royal North West Mounted Police.

Under the War Measures Act of August 1914, the government received sweeping powers to override the rights of individuals; no one was free from arrest and imprisonment for even the slightest breach of the law. A history of internment operations records that "enemy aliens are not prisoners in the civil sense, but are 'prisoners of war' and entitled to the privileges of such under the Hague Convention of October, 1907."[7]

Only days after it opened, the camp received the first fourteen prisoners. The Austrians, who could have been Serbs, Croatians, Hungarians, or Ukrainians, had been rounded up by police and military authorities in Victoria and escorted under guard to Nanaimo.[8] Germans and Turks, by virtue of birth, were also arrested and placed under guard. They came from across Vancouver Island. Sixty miners, both single and married, were removed from the coal mines in Bevan, Cumberland, Extension, Ladysmith, South Wellington, Union Bay, and Nanaimo areas and locked up.

The 125 detainees were kept busy planting decorative trees on the boulevards of the townsite area, as well as doing other jobs around town. They were allowed to attend local concerts and church services, and in the summer they swam or played sports; soccer was popular with the men.

A total of 8,579 enemy aliens across Canada were registered by June 1915. Some were interned, some paroled, and others given permission for temporary absence.

Due to overcrowding at the Nanaimo camp, by mid-September 1915, Major Rowan redistributed the overflow of Vancouver Island prisoners—some 115 alien miners—to jails and detention camps in Victoria, Vernon, and Revelstoke. Vernon became the central permanent camp for the province, and the Nanaimo facility was closed permanently on September 17. Another 120 prisoners were transferred to the B.C. interior.

Attorney General William Bowser pleaded with the coal and railway companies to rehire some of the unemployed miners. About 30 were hired at Canadian Collieries in Extension while others moved to Winnipeg to work for the Canadian Pacific Railway. Still, there were others who, rather than face an uncertain future in Canada, decided to return home. Sixty miners from Ladysmith and Cumberland joined a group of more than 200 people in Vancouver for the trip home to Europe.

McBride Resigns—Bowser becomes Premier

Just before Christmas in 1915, Premier Richard McBride resigned and headed for his new job as the B.C. agent general in London.

He left the province with a debt of $10 million and with promises of $80 million earmarked for railways. Thousands of men were unemployed, exports had dried up, and even the real-estate boom had come to an end. As young men left their communities to serve in the war, small businesses suffered. Of the 435,000 people who called B.C. home, 55,000 men enlisted in the armed forces, and of this number 43,000 served overseas. It was a tremendous effort by a young province.

On Vancouver Island the Big Strike plus the First World War had serious repercussions on the economy. Canadian Collieries reported in 1915 that depressed business conditions on the coast, which were accentuated by war, had continued throughout the year with the result that the use of coal and the prices received for it had decreased. "The decline has resulted in great hardships to the people, forcing the Provincial Government to establish relief committees in various parts of the province, more particularly along the coast, to provide food for those who were unemployed. This depression affected all classes."[9]

It could be assumed that following Premier McBride's abrupt departure from the political scene in B.C. an election or convention might be called to choose a new leader. Instead, the deputy Premier William Bowser, or "the little Kaiser," or "Napoleon of British Columbia," went ahead and announced a new cabinet. Bowser was by far the smallest man ever to be premier, but he was a scrapper, tough-minded, clever, cold, and ruthless.[10]

Premier Bowser was a lawyer from New Brunswick, whose interests had always been politics. He liked power and enjoyed electioneering and all the activity associated with it. Under McBride he had served in various ministries, including finance and attorney general, so he had knowledge of the province and the issues of the day.

He disapproved of "the drink trade" and felt a kindred spirit with the demands of the temperance societies for prohibition. In Nanaimo, where the number of hotels, bars, and saloons had dominated the cityscape for many decades, the issue of prohibition was not exactly favoured by the electorate. He also had to address the women in the province who persisted in their attempt to get the vote. Bowser plunged right into both issues by promising plebiscites on prohibition and women's suffrage, hoping to gain votes in the next election to be held September 1916.

Canadian Patriotic Fund
—Nanaimo Branch

From the beginning of the war it was evident that some assistance would have to be provided for soldiers' families, and to that purpose the Canadian Patriotic Fund was formed. Married soldiers normally assigned a portion of their pay to their wives, but it was usually less than $15 a month and occasionally $20. Under the fund, a woman would receive $30 per month, plus $7.50 per month for children between ten and fifteen years, $4.50 for those between five and ten, and $3 for a child under five years of age.[11]

The Nanaimo Branch was formed on September 24, 1914, with Mayor A.E. Planta as chairman, John Shaw as vice-chairman, and John M. Rudd as honorary secretary-treasurer. Following Planta's appointment to the senate in 1917, Mayor Henry McKenzie took on the role as chairman. John Rudd remained in office throughout the war, supported by a committee of twenty. Rudd had his own real estate and insurance business.[12] His record of community service was long, and it included service on the local Building Society and Hospital Board.

The Nanaimo Branch record was one of the best in the province. Up to March 31, 1919, the branch fell short of being self-supporting by only $6,000. The employees of local industries gave much of the subscribed money. The Women's Auxiliary also helped, with a special fund established to meet the expenses of all soldiers' dependants who were treated at the local hospital during the war. Nearly a thousand families were assisted by it. The total money disbursed was $107,697. The success of the effort has been credited largely to the personal energy and generosity of John Rudd.

Until all the soldiers were discharged, either with or without a pension, their families continued to receive assistance. If the men were hospitalized or sent to convalescent homes, their families continued to receive the same separation allowance.

Campaigning for Prohibition
and Women's Suffrage

Bowser's visit to Nanaimo in August 1916 was a big success. The Opera House was packed with citizens wanting to hear speeches by the premier and the Conservative candidate, Albert E. Planta, as well as Miss Helena Gutteridge—who spoke on the subject of women's suffrage.[13] Planta's opponent in this election was William Sloan, who ran as a Liberal candidate under leader Harlan Carey Brewster.

Following his return from the Klondike, William Sloan attempted to enter political life in the 1900 federal election, but he was defeated. He tried again in 1904 and was elected by acclamation in the Comox–Atlin riding. In the next election of 1908 he was once more acclaimed as member for the district. However, in this election the Honourable William Templeman, minister of mines and inland revenue in the Sir Wilfrid Laurier cabinet, was defeated in Victoria. Laurier pleaded with Sloan to give up his seat to make way for Templeman. The prime minister claimed this was best for B.C., so Sloan gave up his seat, believing he had acted in the best interests of his constituents.[14]

Nanaimo was on the speaking circuit of women's suffrage organizer Mrs. MacLachlan from Victoria. She spoke in the Oddfellows' Hall prior to the September 1916 vote. MacLachlan said it was her mission to interest people of Vancouver Island in the movement. She did not hold the view that a "woman's proper place, according to the fundamental laws of nature, was in the home rearing children," and she made compelling arguments for women's voting rights, concluding with the following statement:

> Women in the state today were on the same plane as the stokers in the engine room of a battleship going into action. They were not allowed to fight but they had to run an equal risk with the fighters, and were it not for their work neither the state nor the ship could keep going. In British Columbia today, men and women were alike interested in the prosperity of the province and therefore equally entitled to a voice in the shaping of its destiny.[15]

William Sloan handily trounced Planta in the September 14, 1916, election and was appointed minister of mines. In that position he led attempts to restrict Oriental immigration and continually tried to improve the safety of miners.

The soldiers' vote, cast in Canadian military camps, the base hospitals in England, and at the war's front, played an important role in this election. When the votes were counted, the Conservatives had been soundly beaten and left with only nine seats. Even Parker Williams, the lone Socialist elected, was expected to support the Liberals. Bowser resigned and Liberal leader Harlan Carey Brewster became premier.

In this election the following question was put to the electorate: Are you in favour of bringing the British Columbia Prohibition Act into force? Nanaimo voted 867 in favour and 864 against. The civilian vote was 838 in favour and 832 against, and the soldiers overseas' vote was 29 yes and 32 no. However, the overseas vote defeated the province-wide referendum and caused a great deal of controversy. A commission of inquiry was set up to investigate. It recommended that the entire overseas vote be disregarded, giving the yes vote the majority.[16] The Prohibition Act came into force on October 1, 1917.

The bill banned the sale of liquor except for medicinal, sacramental, and industrial purposes; however, the bill was difficult to enforce. Medical doctors freely prescribed liquor, bootlegging flourished, and alcohol could still be imported for personal use from outside the province. Bars remained open, legally selling a low-alcohol beer known as "near-beer." In the 1920 provincial election, voters got a chance to toss out the old legislation by approving a system of government control. The Nanaimo vote was 879 for prohibition and 1,998 for government control.[17]

On the subject of women's suffrage, this question was asked: Are you in favour of the extension of the electoral franchise to women? There was no trouble with this vote. The civilian vote was 1,278 in favour and 393 against. The soldiers vote was 44 for and 18 against.[18]

Premier Brewster gave women the vote, and for this the Conservatives labelled him the victim of a "petticoat government." The new government set to work cleaning up the financial situation of the Bowser government. Premier Brewster had started with such high hopes, but he did not endear himself to fellow Liberals when he refused to grant patronage to those out of office for some time. The death of his minister of finance Ralph Smith added an additional burden, as he had to take on the portfolio until John Hart assumed the post. Adding to his troubles, the war in Europe was making little progress, and its casualty list was climbing. In the summer of 1917 the federal government considered conscription.

Ralph Smith had represented Nanaimo federally from 1900 to 1911, when he and Mary Ellen left the community to join their sons living in Vancouver. There, he ran in a Vancouver riding for the provincial Liberals in 1912 and was defeated, but four years later he topped the polls in the Brewster government. Brewster's victory in 1916 for the provincial Liberal party was a cause the Smiths could both celebrate; Ralph became the new minister of finance and women got the vote—something Mary Ellen had advocated for many years.

Harlan Carey Brewster

Like Bowser, Brewster was from New Brunswick, but unlike the former premier, he had a passion for the sea. He became a sailor, acquiring a mate's ticket in deep-sea navigation. His first job in B.C. was as a purser, working for the Canadian Pacific Navigation Company. He became part owner in the Clayoquot Sound Canning Company. There he accomplished what had been believed to be impossible: All the company's fishing and canning was done by white or Native labour—no Orientals were employed in any job.

He entered politics in 1907, topping the polls in Alberni and defeating William Manson. In the election of 1912 he took on McBride in his own riding of Victoria. His platform supported women's suffrage and public ownership of certain utilities. Although defeated at the polls, Brewster was chosen to head the Liberal Party at a convention in Revelstoke in 1913. When he became premier on November 23, 1916, he had three men in his cabinet who would also eventually become premier: John Oliver, John Duncan MacLean, and Thomas Dufferin Pattullo.

Mary Ellen Smith Seeks Election

The *Nanaimo Free Press* announced Ralph Smith's death on February 12, 1917, in Victoria. He had been ill for only a short period of time when his condition took a turn for the worse. His passing prompted a by-election in the Vancouver riding. Women could now run for office, so Mary Ellen decided to seek her husband's seat. She received an overwhelming mandate from the Vancouver electorate to represent them in the Victoria legislature.

Mary Ellen Smith became the first female MLA in B.C., and the first woman cabinet minister in the British Empire. Although she no longer lived in Nanaimo, her former home town was very proud of her accomplishment. As Mary Ellen was seeking election, her son John was fighting in Europe with the 72nd Seaforth Highlanders.

Brewster's term as premier did not last long. He had been in Ottawa, conferring with Prime Minister Borden. On his journey back to Victoria by train he became ill and had to be taken off at Calgary where he died of pneumonia on March 1, 1918. His successor was John Oliver, a pig farmer from Delta.

Conscription

The war continued unabated, and the U.S. finally got into the fight. The federal government ordered conscription, enlisting all men up to age 45. Acting Sergeant C.A. Phillips was appointed the registration officer in Nanaimo in September 1916. He canvassed the city, going house to house, looking for all eligible men. Only those who could show good reason for not serving in the war were exempt.[19]

In December a crowd gathered at the CPR wharf in Nanaimo to say goodbye to 40 recruits for the forestry battalion. Forest workers were needed as fallers, haulers and sawyers. Trench warfare and bridge building required large quantities of lumber. Forest owners in England and Scotland had provided the logs, so now skilled workers were needed to cut them into lumber for bridge, road, and railway building. The men were allowed a few minutes with family and friends before being marched aboard the ship. The *Nanaimo Free Press* reported on the farewell:

> Once on board, they lined the ship's rail and joined with the crowd on the wharf in singing popular and patriotic songs. Then as the good ship moved off those left behind gave three hearty cheers. Every whistle in the harbour shrieked its farewell, and in a few minutes Nanaimo's contribution was well on its way to do their share for King and country.[20]

Arthur Leighton Goes to War

There were many stories from the First World War of families split apart when husbands, sons, brothers, and uncles left for the front. There are a few documented experiences, like those recorded by Alice and Arthur Leighton of Nanaimo. A collection of letters, war diaries, and field books tells the story of their lives during the years 1916–1918.

Arthur Leighton was born to schoolteacher parents in 1899 in Wakefield, Yorkshire, England. He first came to Canada as a young man to work on a farm in Manitoba. The Boer War was in full swing when Britain sent out the call to the Empire for help in South Africa. In 1902 Leighton enlisted in the 2nd Canadian Mounted Rifles, a mounted rifle unit raised and paid for by the Canadian Pacific Railway magnate Donald Smith. The unit was dubbed Lord Strathcona's Horse, and was led by the famed Colonel Samuel Benfield Steele of the Mounties. The unit earned a reputation for raw courage.

After the war Leighton returned to Manitoba and worked on the Wesley Wright farm where he met Alice, one of Wright's daughters. They were married in 1908 in Brampton, Ontario, and eventually settled in Nanaimo on Machleary Street in 1910. Arthur established a law practice at 275 Skinner Street. When he was not practising law he enjoyed playing cricket with the Nanaimo Cricket Club.[21]

Arthur Leighton, assigned to the 72nd Battalion, Seaforth Highlanders, left Vancouver on April 16, 1916, via the CPR to Halifax. Alice planned to follow him to England. He wrote to her almost daily. Their letters speak of the love they had for each other and how difficult it was to be apart. Other letters from family and friends tried to keep a cheerful note in the face of difficult circumstances. Arthur's parents lived in Victoria.

Arthur and Alice Leighton.

At a stopover in Ottawa, the Duke of Connaught inspected Arthur's regiment. When the duke learned Leighton had served in South Africa, he told him he hoped he would "come as safely through in this one." Upon arrival in Halifax on April 23, Easter Sunday, his regiment boarded the *Empress of Britain* for the voyage to England. He cautioned Alice not to reveal the name of the ship, which had been well prepared for its new role in the war.

> The whole boat has been disemboweled and altered so that every available inch is in use. All frills have been eliminated. The only relics of her former glory are some comfortable chairs and card tables and a piano.[22]

Arthur's mother wrote to him: "Wherever you are you are never very long absent from my thoughts and prayers."

Arthur's voyage across the Atlantic was unpleasant, as most of the men and officers were seasick. As the ship neared Britain he served guard duty for submarine attacks. On May 4, 1916, Arthur wrote that mail was being censored, and he wondered where his battalion might end up. "We are in the zone of a real war now."

Alice Goes to England

Alice followed Arthur; with three women friends she boarded the *New Amsterdam* on May 27, departing from New York to Falmouth,

England. She observed the New York scene: "It seems strange not to see anyone in Khaki here—about as strange as it is in Canada to see them everywhere." On her journey she saw two airplanes flying near Toronto. "They were my first and I thought they were huge hawks until they turned and I could see the shape. They are wonderful."

Alice stayed in the Hotel Cecil, in the Strand district of London. On a visit to the "aerodrome" at Oxford she was still in awe of airplanes. She wrote about them:

> I had never seen them so close before and I particularly like the way they skip along the ground after they came down. This war has evolved some remarkable things. I suppose you have heard of the "toad tanks" which are doing such extraordinary things on the Somme.

She registered at the Canadian offices in London and met a man there who knew Nanaimo. She liked London and was pleased

Alice Leighton with airplane in England.

with the way everyone welcomed the wounded home at Charing Cross. The war became very real when Germany attacked England with Zeppelin airships. She wrote about these raids:

> The city experienced three Zep raids—two were brought down. Everything in London is guarded including Westminster Abbey and some of the tombs have sandbags heaped over them.

Alice volunteered for two years at St. Dunstan's Hostel for Blind Soldiers and Sailors. The top floor of the Hotel Cecil was turned into government offices, as was the Grand Hotel in Trafalgar Square. Residents who had lived in the hotels, some for twenty years, were forced to leave. Alice noticed the large number of Australian soldiers, "who are always arm-and-arm with at least one girl, very often two. That feather they wear in their hats is very fetching no doubt."

There were more Zep raids on London in October and another airship was brought down.

> We hear reports from Germany of Zep crews resigning, but it's hard to know what is true. The crew who came down in Essex and gave themselves up without a dash for the sea, rather look as though they flunked their first job.

News from Nanaimo

In December Arthur received news from Elizabeth Waugh from his law office in Nanaimo. She mentioned that the Beck and John Dick estates had been settled and that MLA William Sloan had been appointed minister of mines. She wrote about him and the Nanaimo scene:

> He (Sloan) has made quite a record for himself since he received his appointment; the South Wellington Mines came out on strike again, and he settled it for them within one week. Some record eh!
>
> Things in Nanaimo were very quiet this Xmas. It did not seem at all as it used to. Two days before Xmas about 70 Nanaimo boys who had enlisted left for overseas and I have a feeling that perhaps that accounted for the dullness.
>
> George Ritchie has enlisted with the 103rd and [is] now with the 29th Battalion (Vancouver) known as Tobins

Tigers, as a sniper. [The Tobin Tigers were named after its commander Henry Tobin and were formed with drafts of men from the 11th Irish Fusiliers.]

Elizabeth also expressed sorrow about the death of three Nanaimo men: Donald Planta, Jamie Caldwell, and James Pender. "I am sure that the war has come right home to Nanaimo now," she wrote.

On Leave in London

Arthur got leave in January 1917 and joined Alice in London. They attended a Harry Lauder concert on January 20. "Very good indeed, and both Alice and I like him immediately. His son had been killed in action about 10 days previously, which gave a very tragic note to his singing of a war song, 'When the boys come home again.'" They visited friends and did some sightseeing, before returning to duty on January 31.

Back in the Trenches

By February spring had come to London. Alice kept a keen eye on the war news. She hoped it would dry up the trenches and keep Arthur from "sinking miles into France. The Germans seem to be finding the area all together too hot for them for they are moving back at a rate."

Arthur wrote on February 4: "Many Huns killed and dugout blown up. Two prisoners and MG captured. Five men caught out in shell hole by MG fire unable to get in and came in after dark. An unfortunate accident cost 5 men wounded." One of the soldiers tried to remove a shell from a gun when it jammed and exploded, injuring the men.

He wrote a few days later: "February 7: The USA has broken off relations with Germany, though has not yet declared war." U.S. President Woodrow Wilson declared war on April 6, 1917.

On February 19 Arthur's battalion came under attack, but it managed to escape without casualties in spite of being hit by heavy trench mortars and artillery. He speculated that the Germans might have had foreknowledge of the raid: "There is no doubt that the phone is too much used, and higher officers are the worst offenders. Brigade staff do not observe rules they set for others in this regard."

Arthur was slightly wounded in a shell blast on February 23. Two days later he had his knee bandaged and was advised to "lie up as much as possible." Resting in a war zone was highly unlikely.

> ### Bloody Gas Attack
>
> The details of the March 1, 1917, attack are now known. This was to be the largest attempt by Canadians to damage German defences on the hill of Vimy Ridge, five weeks before the major attack; the casualties were appalling and the raid a terrible failure. The plan was to release clouds of poisonous gas in two waves—phosgene first, followed by chlorine—into the German lines. The first cloud hung over the battlefield; the second was blown back in the faces of the advancing troops. The Germans were ready for the assault; they had heard the clanking of the gas cylinders and knew the details of the plan from two prisoners who had escaped and made their way back to their own lines. The Kootenay Battalion was mowed down by machine guns, and only a few survived. Of the 420 members, more than 200 were casualties, including thirteen officers. The Mississauga 75th Battalion lost men, and the Seaforth Highlanders were also badly hit.
>
> The dying and wounded lay waiting for help that never came. It took another two days for the gas to dissipate, and when it cleared the Germans offered a truce to allow the Canadians to bury their dead. Both sides met under a Red Cross flag. The Germans carried the Canadian dead and wounded halfway, then handed them over. The losses in the raid were staggering: 687 casualties out of a total of 1,700 attackers, including the very serious loss of 2 seasoned battalion commanders.[30] The press regarded the raid as a victory.

Later in his diary he refers to his condition as "water on the knee." On February 28 he received word there would be an attack made in the morning. His diary gave the terse details of the outcome:

> Heavy bombardment early in the morning: By 11 o'clock the air is full of rumours as to the results of the attack—mostly of a pessimistic kind. This is perhaps due to the fact that first reports come in from men wounded early. It is reported that Major Johnson, Colquhoun are killed and Lumsden missing, and that the Colonel of the 75th is killed. 1 p.m. No word received yet from my men. Phoned Capt. Paulin and asked how things went and got a brief reply "rotten."

Later he confirmed the grim news: The Seaforth Highlanders 72nd Battalion had suffered 60 casualties.

Grim Statistics

On Sunday, March 4, Arthur went to the cemetery to make arrangements for the funeral of his men:

Found that the 54th Kootenay Battalion and the 75th Mississauga Battalion were also burying their dead and needed all the graves that were ready. The mortuary was full, with about 40 bodies, and as many more were lying in rows outside and more being brought in. Apparently there was an arranged Armistice this morning from 7-8 to collect the dead and wounded.

A raid by the 44th Winnipeg Battalion and 46th Regina and Moose Jaw Battalion on March 15 resulted in 15 killed, 30 wounded, and 20 missing, but no prisoners were taken. Arthur could not find out if Harry Jepson from Nanaimo had survived the raid or not. Jepson had been with the 47th Battalion, a reserve battalion of Japanese Canadians from B.C. Nanaimo had raised $1,000 as part of the war effort to buy a machine gun. The city requested it be donated to Lieutenant H.R. Jepson's regiment.[23]

In March Alice heard that all Canadian women were to be sent back to Canada, but nothing came of it. "Now no one would be allowed home until the submarine warfare is somewhat reduced, except under the most vital circumstances." She questioned Arthur about a raid he had mentioned in his letter, and she wondered who scored, suggesting that perhaps it had not been as successful as it might have been.

By this time all correspondence was being censored. Alice received her first censored letter on March 12, 1917, and she thought it strange after having a letter daily for months. The taking of Baghdad and the crushing of the Turkish army cheered them both. Meanwhile, Arthur's men were sick with trench fever, dysentery, and pneumonia. The abdication of Russian Czar Nicholas II was big news. This event capped months of turmoil in Russia. The Russian offensive on the German front had resulted in two million casualties during 1915 alone.

Alice visited family in Wakefield, Yorkshire, discovering her husband's birthplace and getting to know his Aunts Emily, Edie, Ethel, Florrie, and Dolly. Arthur's knee injury continued to give him trouble. Alice urged him to rest: "Take two or three weeks off now [rather] than keep on doing more damage to it till you might make yourself permanently lame." He finally had someone re-examine it and immobilized it with a splint. He was ordered to the base hospital for further treatment. The Duchess of Westminster Hospital, run by the Red Cross Society, was formerly a grand casino building with magnificent rooms. Arthur described these as, "not unlike the dining room and ballrooms of the Vancouver Hotel." Fifty men occupied the ward with Arthur.

The fighting continued in the trenches. New troops filled the gaps left by the casualties. The battle edged closer to Vimy Ridge. On Easter Monday, 1917, all four divisions of the Canadian Corps attacked and triumphed together. Canadians suffered 10,602 casualties in six days. But Arthur was not there to share in the victory. He was back in England having his knee treated.

Voluntary Food Rationing

Alice told Arthur not to fret, "as there [would] be lots of war left" even if he were laid up for a month, and then she wrote about food rationing:

> Lord Davenport gave out what he considered fair quantities of meat, flour, bread and sugar, and we have been sticking to it and find that we get quite enough to eat. Don't be anxious for I think things will work out all right.

A Charing Cross Reception for Soldiers

The medical officer ordered Arthur home to Blighty "as a stretcher case." He sailed on the hospital ship *Brighton* from Calais to Dover, then travelled by train to London. Arthur experienced first-hand that wonderful reception at Charing Cross Station where crowds waved and threw flowers at the injured men. He was taken to the Royal Free Hospital.

Alice expressed delight Arthur was home to "Blinkin' Blighty." Three weeks convalescent leave was prescribed, and they spent that time together. On May 12 the medical board passed him as "fit for service," enabling Arthur to return to his battalion and finish out his service. One of his last entries is dated June 16, 1918:

> The Hun attacked the night before last on a 50-mile front towards Paris. He crossed the Marne but was driven back by a counter attack and nowhere had penetrated beyond front line positions, up to last evening.

Peace Declared—Returning Home

Peace was declared November 11, 1918. Arthur and Alice returned to Nanaimo in 1919 where Arthur continued in his law practice of Leighton, Meakin & Weir. Alice became a Nanaimo School Board trustee in 1922, only the second woman to be chosen for the board, the first being Mrs. Fanny Skinner. She also assisted with the organization of the Local Council of Women.[24]

Raymond Collishaw— First World War Flying Ace

Raymond Collishaw has earned his place in history as one of Canada's foremost flying aces during two world wars. The airport to the south of Nanaimo is named in his honour. It was during the First World War that he first gained a reputation as a fearless flyer.

Collishaw was born in Nanaimo on November 22, 1893. As a young boy he played on the docks in Nanaimo, learning all he could about the ships that visited the city to take on coal, deliver goods, or pick up passengers. His summers were spent fishing. At the age of twelve, he announced to his family that he wanted to be a sailor; however, his family could not afford to send him to study navigation, so he vowed to learn as much as he could on his own. He sent for books on the subject and got some old charts from seamen.

Collishaw had remarkable eyesight and could spot distant objects that his friends could only see through binoculars. This gift would see him through many difficult battles in the air. At fifteen, he left school and became a seaman on the Victoria-Alaska run. He was made second officer at age seventeen, then spent three years on the Alaska run. From years of self-study he became a skilled navigator and could scan the stars in the night sky and draw charts giving an accurate location. Collishaw was

First World War, RNAS Squadron. Raymond Collishaw is in middle row, fourth from left.

aboard the Canadian Fisheries Protection Service ship the *Alcedo* when it sailed into the Arctic Circle in search of the Canadian Arctic Expedition under Vilhajalmur Stefansson, aboard the expedition flagship *Karluk*. However, help came too late; some members of the expedition crew were dead and the *Karluk* had been crushed by ice. Stefansson survived.[25] Collishaw served a total of seven years on the west coast; his final posting was as first officer aboard the *Fispa*.

Enlisted in the Royal Naval Air Service

When war broke out in Europe, he was 21 years old, but like many others, he didn't think the war would last long. When he realized he was wrong, he sailed for England in 1915 with the idea he would enlist in the Grand Fleet. However, it occurred to him that flying would be a new experience, so he enlisted in the Royal Naval Air Service, which had not yet merged with the Royal Flying Corps.

In January 1916 he qualified as a pilot and began patrolling the English Channel. On hearing stories of the daring Richthofen, "the Red Knight of Germany," he wondered if he had joined the right outfit. In August he transferred to the Number 3 Wing of "the Silent Service," as the naval unit was called. The unit's job was long-range bombing. Collishaw scouted with the bombers as they took off for flights into German territory. Scouts rarely left the bigger ships except to fight off attackers; therefore, he did not get into any wing-to-wing scraps for several months.[26]

His first kill came on October 12, 1916, when he escorted bombers over a rifle factory at Oberndorf. Along the way they were attacked; Collishaw picked off one fighter and shot him down. Thirteen days later he was attacked near home base by six enemy planes. He shot down two more and for this attack was awarded the Croix de Guerre. On his way back from a bombing party two days before Christmas, his plane crashed, but he managed to walk away from the wreckage before it blew up in flames.

Collishaw was restricted to scouting again until February 1917, when he joined the Number 3 Naval Squadron, operating near Cambrai. His next encounter was with three enemy aircraft. During this battle a bullet ricocheted off his instrument board, taking the glass out of his goggles. Splinters of glass almost blinded him. He saw a landing field and landed only to discover it was a German airfield. Fortunately the Germans were all in the mess hall at the time. By the time they discovered what had happened, Collishaw was taxiing off with ground gunners swinging into action. He made it back and somehow managed to escape permanent blindness by not rubbing his eyes. Later he learned that in that excursion he had chalked up his fourth kill. After being temporarily blinded, he had somehow careened around and fired his machine gun. His bullets had brought down another German plane.

The Black Death Flight

In April 1917 Collishaw transferred to Number 10 Naval Squadron, operating out of Dunkirk, and in late May he was transferred to the Number 10 Squadron, Eleventh Wing of the Royal Flying Corps. He was promoted to lieutenant and so began the "Black Death Flight." His flight crew included four Canadians who had been similarly transferred because they had distinguished themselves. Their five triplanes were painted black except for small white letters spelling out their names and their pilots. They were *Black Maria*, Collishaw; *Black Roger*, Ellis Reid of Toronto; *Black Death*, J.E. Sharman of Winnipeg; *Black Sheep*, J.E. Nash of Hamilton; and *Black Prince*, Martin Alexander of Toronto.

The Black Death flyers had charmed lives; they were constantly in German territory, getting into dogfights and wing-to-wing combat. Collishaw's score rose from 15 to 23 enemy planes, and he was not yet finished. On June 26, 1917, the Black Death Flight battled with Richthofen and a dozen of his planes. Besides the Red Knight, another plane caught Collishaw's attention; it was painted brilliant green, and Collishaw knew Lieutenant Karl Allmenroeder piloted it. He was next only to Richthofen in German victories. In the battle, one of his pilots went missing; it was Nash. The four remaining triplanes, with their Black Death crew, went on the hunt for the green fighter. He was spotted over Lille, in France, and the Canadians went after him.

Next day, in a German prison camp, a badly injured man on a cot heard church bells ring. His guard, who spoke English, told him they were ringing for the funeral of a great German fighter, Lieutenant Allmenroeder who was killed over Lille, France, the day before by the leader of what they called the Black Death Flight. The prisoner asked if he could have a drink to give a toast. He lifted the glass and toasted Allmenroeder and Collishaw. Then the prisoner, Lieutenant Nash, drained his glass.

The *Nanaimo Free Press* headlines on December 26, 1918, read: "Col. Collishaw on way home":

> Among the returned soldiers arriving on two steamers docked at St. John was Lt. Col. R. Collishaw of Nanaimo

who commanded an air squadron in France.

He is one of Britain's foremost aces, some authorities crediting him with the first place. He brought down sixty German machines, but he accords the position of Canada's premier airman to Lt. Col. Bishop, V.C.

Collishaw had accumulated many decorations. Among them were the Distinguished Conduct Medal bar, the Distinguished Service Order, the Flying Corps, the Croix de Guerre, and the Mons medals. He was welcomed back home to Nanaimo as a war hero. He did not remain at home for long but continued flying in war zones. Serving first with the White Army in Russia; in Persia in 1920; in Mesopotamia against the Arabs; and in Palestine during the Arab-Jewish trouble. He became a wing commander and alternated between the Royal Flying Corps headquarters and posts in Egypt.

Great War Veterans' Association

Returning soldiers formed a Nanaimo branch of the Great War Veterans' Association (GWVA) in April 1918. The president was D.R. Bell, the vice-president was A.R. Tair, and the secretary-treasurer was P.W. Brown. Committee members included J.W. Wagstaff, S. Davies, Thomas Wallace, E.J. O'Hara, and J. Sumption.[27]

The first objective was to secure a suitable meeting place and headquarters for the men. At first the Athletic Club seemed the ideal place, but Senator Planta, owner of the Assembly Hall, offered the group his building "on generous terms." The hall was a big enough room for dances or concerts and had space for a library reading room and a canteen. It was similar to that enjoyed by the Vancouver branch.[28]

The Governor General, the Duke of Devonshire, and Lady Dorothy Cavendish officially opened the club in October 1919. Lady Cavendish's father, the Marquis of Lansdown, had visited Nanaimo in 1885. The Imperial Order Daughters of the Empire, Collishaw Chapter, presented the couple with a model airplane. In presenting the gift, the regent of the chapter, Louise Caldwell, spoke of Nanaimo's pride in its young flying ace:

Nanaimo has the distinction of having sent to the war an airman who has won high honours in the fight for the world's liberty. Lieutenant Colonel Collishaw, whose name our chapter has the honour to bear has accounted for sixty of the enemy planes and as commandant of the Canadian

Royal Air Force did exceptional service along with his splendid band of flyers in bringing fear and defeat during the latter days of the war.[29]

The GWVA's headquarters was one of the busiest places in the city as local soldiers returned from war. The venue provided a meeting place, a social centre, reading room, canteen, and a comfortable home for returning vets as they began the road back to normality. A grand smoking concert was held on opening night.

Protection Island Mine Cage Disaster

September 10, 1918, began like any other day in Nanaimo. Miners working the morning shift in the Canadian Western Fuel Company's Protection Island Mine boarded a scow being pushed by a tug, to take them across the harbour to work on the island. The mine shaft was situated on the southern end of the island and was formerly used to hoist coal from what was then known as the Newcastle seam. The shipping wharves were also located at this point. Some years before, the hoisting of coal out of this shaft had been abandoned and all the coal mined in the Protection Mine was hauled to the No. 1 mine, creating one central screening and shipping plant. However, after the passing of the eight-hour law in 1904, the shaft was used for lowering and raising men from the north side of the No. 1 mine.[30]

Six cages, each loaded with sixteen men to work the morning shift, had already been safely lowered, while the night shift had been brought to the surface. As usual, the seventh cage loaded another sixteen men and began its descent. Suddenly, the cable broke, sending the cage with its human cargo crashing 150 feet down through heavy twelve-inch lumber at the bottom, cutting through it like matchwood and taking all the miners to their deaths. Miners already at the bottom heard the roar and feared the roof of the mine had caved in. They learned the truth by telephone. Of the sixteen victims of the accident, ten were British, five were Italian, and one was Russian. Fourteen were married, and 40 children were left orphans.[31]

John Hunt, mine manager, and D. Brown, underground manager, made their way through the underground workings of the No. 1 mine, at the Nanaimo side, to reach the crash site in the neighbouring mine. Volunteers rushed quickly to the scene. They included Jack McGregor and Mr. Bonner from Pacific Coast Collieries and H.N. Freeman of Jingle Pot Mine. MLA William Sloan, the minister of mines, arrived that evening and promised an investigation into the accident.

The people of Nanaimo once again prepared to bury their dead as they had done so many times before. People lined the route of the funeral procession up Bastion Street to the cemetery. The Silver Cornet Band led the way, accompanied by city council and fellow miners.

The investigation into the accident was thorough. It focussed on the defective cable. It had been installed on March 6, 1915, and had been in use for only three years, six months, and nine days. This was a "Lang's lay" cable that was used in 416 mines out of 427, so was considered a first-class cable. William Fleet Robertson, a provincial mineralogist, was sent to Montreal with a piece of the cable for testing to determine the cause of the failure. He gave his findings at the coroner's inquest convened on December 16, 1918, and January 14, 1919. The report concluded that the men came to their death by "descending on a defective cable which broke owing entirely to the oxidizing of the wires, chiefly caused by lack of any external lubrication, leaving the wire exposed to the corrosive action of water and the humid atmosphere."[32]

A month after the tragedy there were more deaths, but this time due to another cause.

CHAPTER TWENTY-TWO

Influenza Epidemic, End of War, and a Royal Visit

The autumn of 1918 should have been a joyous time as soldiers were returning home. The war was almost over, but another killer was loose in the world, and it would claim millions of lives worldwide. The Spanish influenza had swept across Europe before reaching North America and finally Vancouver Island; it crept in like a silent ship coming ashore.

The first alert came on October 9, when two people in Victoria died of it. The provincial capital began taking drastic steps to stop the flu from spreading. A special order-in-council closed all public places of assembly. Other communities on the island were alerted to the danger and warned to take all steps necessary to stamp out the illness. Nanaimo received a telegram from the provincial secretary on October 8, 1918, empowering the city to close all public meeting places to prevent the spread of Spanish influenza.[1] Large department stores and theatres in Vancouver—where over one hundred cases had surfaced—issued notices describing the symptoms. This information alert came from the U.S. Public Health Service:

> It is characterized by sudden onset, people are [stricken] on the street, while at work, in factories, shipyards, offices or elsewhere. First there is a chill, then fever with temperature from 101 to 103, headache, backache, reddening and running of the eyes, pains and aches all over the body and general prostration. Persons so attacked should go to their homes at once, get to bed without delay, and immediately call a physician.

The Nanaimo Medical Health Officer, W.F. Drysdale, met with city council on October 14, 1918, and he reported there were at least half a dozen cases in the Chase River District and Five Acres, but only two reported in Nanaimo. There were also a few cases among the Snuneymuxw.[2] The local board of health met on October 15, 1918, with Mayor Henry McKenzie. They decided to close all schools, churches, fraternal lodges, theatres, moving picture theatres, pool rooms, and clubs in the city until further notice.[3]

First Flu Death Reported In Nanaimo

On October 17, 1918, Mrs. Phillip Frenchie, a resident of the Snuneymuxw Reserve, became Nanaimo's first recorded victim.[4] The flu spread so rapidly that by October 18 there were 135 cases in the city. A special meeting was held with the mayor and aldermen, the medical health officer, and Doctors Ingham, Wilks, and McPhee, the directors of the Nanaimo Hospital, and Mr. Fraser and Mr. Powell of the Granby Consolidated Company, at Cassidy's Siding, south of Nanaimo.

Dr. Ingham told of a family in which the father and mother and two children were critically ill. A nine-year-old girl was looking after all her family. Neighbours were fearful of entering the house, and the local hospital could not accommodate more patients.[5] It was essential another emergency hospital be found. A committee was appointed to secure a building for the expected overflow of patients from the hospital. The Nanaimo Athletic Club building became the emergency hospital. Members of the Canadian Red Cross went on duty there.[6] Women in the community made sheets and pillowcases and other articles for patients in the emergency hospital. As nurses in the main hospital also became sick, volunteer workers courageously filled their positions.

Hundreds Infected

By October 20 it was reported there were 20 cases at the emergency hospital and 88 at the Nanaimo Hospital—47 from outside the city. Five people had been discharged and two had died.[7] Approximately 700 people were infected with the illness.

Further measures were taken to keep the disease from spreading. The city pound keeper posted notices on the doors of the infected families, and people who came in contact with others were required to wear a mask. Dr. Ingham noted there was a shortage of serum in the community. Patients required three or four injections daily, and there had been a number of cases that had not received attention. Not everyone trusted the serum! Mah Bing Kee believed Chinese herbal remedies might be the answer:

> Chinatown was also infected and many were ill. Moaning and groaning could be heard day and night from Bing Kee's house on Skinner Street. Many people died. Bing Kee's family came down with it. The local doctor couldn't help his family or others that died. Bing Kee went to Vancouver and brought back Chinese herbs as well as a prescription that could be refilled at Nanaimo's Chinatown Herbal Shop. It did cure their ailment. In later years his family liked to talk about it and wonder if it was luck, or coincidence, or was there something in the herbal remedy.[8]

On October 21, 1918, the city received a letter from James N. Jemson of the Western Fuel Company. He and George Yarrow were asked by Dr. Ingham to volunteer to go to Chase River and transport the serious cases to Nanaimo. George Yarrow was experienced in first-aid. In 1904 he was one of the first people to join a first aid class, and now he was in charge of the first mine rescue station of the Western Fuel Company. The two men did as asked and continued to transport patients for several days, bringing in a total of fifteen. Jemson wrote a letter to city council, requesting remuneration for the loss of his clothing that needed to be destroyed:

> I found it necessary to disinfect our clothing, which of course ruined it, and today I burned the clothes to avoid infecting myself and the members of my family. I am asking you to grant me $15 toward buying other clothes.[9]

It is unknown if Jemson received any compensation.

Emergency Hospital Adapts Well

The number of victims kept mounting. The old Athletic Club building adapted well to its new role as emergency hospital. There seemed to be no end to the number of funerals being held. More Snuneymuxw died; a husband and wife married only a year died within days of each other, and children who should have been playing were laid to rest.[10] The *Daily Herald* made this report:

Among the many homes in our district which have been the scene of death's invasion, is that of Mrs. M.L. Duggan, the postmistress of Northfield. First her son-in-law Thomas Scott Ketchin, and on the day of his funeral, his wife Annie, the second daughter of Mrs. Duggan, died also.[11]

At the end of October there were fourteen cases in the men's ward and seven in the women's ward. Many of the patients had come from the Granby Mine at Cassidy. The acting superintendent of the hospital, Miss Pearson, was assisted by Helen Daily and Olive Green on night duty, Ethel Rogers and Miss Carroll on day duty, and Misses Grace Morgan, Blendell, Kenyon, and Murphy in the ward. Blanche McDonald looked after the office during the day while Eva Coombs answered the telephone at night. The kitchen was under the capable hands of Mrs. McIndoo, and Misses Calbeck and Woodman. All the orderlies were employees of the Western Fuel Company. The call went out for more people to help in the kitchen as well as in the wards.[12]

Doctors worked themselves to exhaustion, but there was always someone to carry on. Doctor McPhee and Doctor Wilks were infected, but they recovered enough to return to work.

Conflicting News Reports

Although the news was grim concerning the influenza epidemic, it was interspersed with encouraging news that the war in Europe might soon end: "The allied spirit is not wavering; German Navy under discussion; Hindenburg sends message to army." Many soldiers had died, but the news on October 26 of the death of the head nurse from the Nanaimo Hospital added more sorrow: "Nursing Sister Henriette Millett lost her life in the torpedoing of the *Leinster* ... a victim of the murderous Hun, she being one of several hundred persons who lost their lives when the passenger steamer *Leinster* was sunk."[13]

In November the influenza epidemic abated. The *Nanaimo Free Press* reported, "The number of new cases are not keeping up with the recoveries."[14] Although the hospitals were still busy, they were not overcrowded or as rushed as when the illness first appeared.

There were still a few cases being recorded in February 1919, but it was clear the epidemic had waned. City clerk Samuel Gough wrote to the provincial health officer, H.E. Young, asking if he could remove the ban on dancing in the city. Young advised the city to keep the ban in place, but indicated it could be removed shortly. By the end of February it was business as usual at all public places in Nanaimo.

How Nanaimo handled the influenza epidemic was the topic of the annual city report for 1918 by medical health officer W.F. Drysdale:

> The epidemic of influenza, which visited this city, as well as almost every part of America, was the worst and most disastrous of any similar epidemic within the memory of man and caused an enormous loss of lives. Those between 15 and 45 years being most frequently attacked. October and November being the worst months, while December was almost free in our locality. Fifty-six deaths took place in the general and emergency hospitals during the seven weeks when it was most prevalent.[15]

Drysdale praised the work and heroism of the nurses and volunteers of both hospitals, and he said the people of Nanaimo should be proud and their efforts should not be forgotten. He offered advice should another epidemic arise:

> We should remember—this is a crowd disease and the ban should be applied at once. Vaccine should be used freely as in our experience, not one case occurred where it had been properly used. All infected homes should be placarded. An isolation building, or an emergency hospital, should be arranged for so that it could be ready for use on short notice and working staff provided.

For a number of years the need for an isolation hospital was brought to city council's attention, but it was the need for a larger hospital to serve the growing community that soon took precedent.

The Spanish influenza epidemic of 1918–1919 that swept around the world in a few brief months carried at least twenty million people to an early grave. The war of 1914–1918, long recognized as one of the greatest disasters, took ten million lives.[16]

Armistice Declared—Nanaimo Celebrates

There had been false expectations for weeks that the war was ending; then finally the good news came that Germany had accepted the Allies' terms for surrender. It had agreed to withdraw from all invaded territory and surrender all military equipment. Submarines and destroyers were to be surrendered as well as 5,000 locomotives, wagons, motor lorries, and railways; as well, all Black Sea ports were evacuated. The news of Germany's submission reached Nanaimo at midnight when most residents were asleep.

The next morning, November 11, 1918, at about 7:00 a.m., horns, whistles, and sirens in the district spread the good news the war had at last ended. It was a glorious morning to awaken to. Miners who were preparing for the morning shift turned back from work, and an unofficial holiday began. Stores closed; horses and cars and other vehicles were decorated for the occasion. A public holiday was proclaimed throughout the province. The *Nanaimo Free Press* headlines declared: "WAR IS OVER, KAISER IN FLIGHT"—Germany's unconditional surrender to the Allies' Terms.[17]

For Nanaimo, however, the real celebration came that evening with a torchlight parade through town to Bate Square, led by the Silver Cornet Band and the South Wellington Brass Band.[18] People marched through the streets—no cars were allowed in the procession—to a platform at the foot of Albert Street, to listen to Mayor Henry McKenzie and MLA William Sloan give patriotic speeches. Everyone wore masks, but few were thinking of the influenza epidemic.

A place of honour was reserved for the women of the Canadian Red Cross, Nanaimo Branch, who wore caps and armbands. Also in the parade were the Imperial Order of the Daughters of the Empire, the High School Red Cross Club, and the Returned Soldiers and Next-of-Kin Association, plus other lodges and societies.

All speakers appealed to residents to not forget to raise Nanaimo's contribution to the Victory Loan Program of $450,000. The money was needed to:

> bring the boys home: To maintain them in Europe till peace is firmly established: To maintain our industrial activities and provide new employment for munitions workers, soldiers as they return: To continue our loans to Britain for buying Canadian food: To enable Canadian workers to get their rightful share of orders for rebuilding Belgium and France.
>
> Monday, November 11th will be recorded as the greatest day in British history. We all relaxed and rejoiced and will remember it as long as we live.

Nanaimo officially celebrated the end of the war on July 19, 1919.

Soldiers Return to a Different World

B.C. was not the province that soldiers left behind at the beginning of the war. Somewhere along the way, it had gained a Canadian identity. In the battlefields of Europe and in British hospitals, returning soldiers had become more Canadian. It has been said that the war was the defining moment when Canada became a country. Returning soldiers could take their discharge wherever they pleased, and as their numbers grew, the bonds with other provinces were cemented.

In Nanaimo there was a lot to forget: the Big Strike that had divided the community in the two years prior to the war, and the loss of lives from both the war and the Spanish influenza. Adding to these losses was the tragic mine accident at Protection Island that had claimed more lives. Funerals were a fact of life in Nanaimo, and they had become more frequent.

Economically, the province was still in the doldrums. Premier John Oliver set about putting men back to work, attempting to

Honourable discharge certificate of Private H.E. Tanner, October 30, 1917.

absorb returning soldiers into peacetime occupations without displacing the regular work force that now included women. MLA Mary Ellen Smith now sat in the legislature, and women were running for municipal office in towns and villages around the province. Nanaimo had kept the "home fires burning" with coal production, but the best new opportunities for the future lay in the forest and fishing industries.

Nanaimo could boast of having free mail delivery within the city, a cause the Board of Trade had championed, and airmail service between Vancouver and Nanaimo. The road to Victoria had opened and there was a daily bus to Victoria operated by Thomas Plimley.[19] The stone beacon installed by Richard Nightingale in 1880 beside the CPR wharf was demolished; it had been an impediment to harbour traffic for years .[20]

Sadly, in September 1919, Nanaimo's outstanding historic landmark, the Bastion, was in danger of being sold at auction. The Native Sons of B.C. Post Number 3, who had cared for the building, was in arrears with taxes. When the group took over the stewardship of the building they had 40 members. This number had dwindled, and the burden of upkeep was beyond their means.[21] The Bastion needed a benefactor to save the day.

Royalty Says Thanks

On September 26, 1919, Nanaimo residents put all their troubles on hold for a day to welcome a royal visitor who wanted to thank them for their efforts during the war. His Royal Highness Edward, Prince of Wales, arrived by train and was driven to the courthouse for the formal reception, escorted by a special guard of returned soldiers under the command of Captain Arthur Leighton. A choir of 500 schoolchildren, led by Emry Jones and accompanied by the Silver Cornet Band, sang and played "God Bless the Prince of Wales."

Mayor McKenzie told the prince how readily the city's sons had rallied to the call of the Empire: "Many of our people are from the Mother land, and they very highly prize its institutions and government."[22] He hoped the royal visit would strengthen those ties. The prince thanked Nanaimo for the great effort made during the last four years in the cause of humanity and justice. He said, "Now that the war has been brought to a happy and victorious termination, I feel sure that the same spirit which carried you through those dark days will help you to solve the many problems of reconstruction which lie before us all. The future of your City is I know a bright one ... and I look forward to finding Nanaimo, on the

On September 26, 1919, the Prince of Wales presented medals to First World War veterans.

Street scene in Nanaimo, circa 1920.

occasion of my next visit, even more smiling and prosperous than she is today."[23]

Medals were presented to the following citizens: a Distinguished Conduct Medal to the widow of Sergeant Peter McCorkindale, who was killed in action in March 1917; a Distinguished Conduct Medal and Military Medal to Sergeant Matt Gunness; a Military Medal to Cadet John Dudley and to Corporal J. Gaskill; and a Military Medal, with Bar, to Corporal W.G. Martin.

The prince asked the mayor to grant all the schoolchildren in Nanaimo a holiday. When Mayor McKenzie said they already had a holiday on this day, the Prince added—as a favour to him—they should have another.

Epilogue

Nanaimo was like a chameleon: Somehow it was able to adapt to new situations and opportunities. Until the beginning of the twentieth century it had been a coal-mining community. As the wheels of time passed, it reinvented itself as the "Hub City," an important transportation junction on Vancouver Island with rail passenger service connecting to the mainland ferry service. With the coming of the automobile and new roads opening up to Victoria and northern Vancouver Island communities, this new role took on some importance. Mining remained economically important, but new opportunities were opening up, and the city looked to a future when mining would no longer be viable.

The labour movement in B.C., which began in Nanaimo mines, had reached out across the province, testing political thinking and the consequences of speaking up for injustice in the workplace. It would continue to be a force to be reckoned with in the future. The women's movement had a valuable ally in Mary Ellen Smith, who would prove to all the cynics that women had a place in B.C. politics. The multicultural aspect of life in Nanaimo in the first two decades of the twentieth century only enriched all social aspects of the community.

However, in reflection, there was sadness felt in the four decades from the 1880s to 1920. Too many people had died unnecessarily. The local cemetery was full of unfulfilled dreams, of fathers, brothers, and sons lost in the mines. Added to these were the deaths from the influenza epidemic, which put an added burden on the community already grieving for those killed in the war. Somehow, Nanaimo residents showed their resilience by putting all this sadness behind them and looking forward—with anticipation—to a bright and challenging future.

Mayors and Councils Serving Nanaimo, 1875–1920

1875–Mayor Mark Bate: Council: John Bryden, Richard Brinn, William Raybould, John Dick, Richard Nightingale, John Pawson, John Hirst.

1876–Mayor Mark Bate: Council: Richard Brinn, William E. Webb, Joseph Bevilockway, Samuel Gough, John Hirst, John Sabiston, George Baker.

1877–Mayor Mark Bate: Council: John Bryden, Richard Nightingale, John Hirst, John Sabiston, William Reid, Richard Brinn, William Pringle.

1878–Mayor Mark Bate: Council: John Bryden, George Baker, John Hirst, John Sabiston, Richard Nightingale, Richard Brinn, Robert Brown.

1879–Mayor Mark Bate: Council: William Earl, Richard Nightingale, James Harvey, John Meakin, John Sabiston, Thomas Miller, Thomas Morgan.

1880–Mayor John Pawson: Council: John Hirst, Richard Nightingale, James Harvey, Richard Brinn, Joseph P. Planta, Thomas Miller, William Wilks.

1881–Mayor Mark Bate: Council: John Hirst, John McNeil, Richard Brinn, Thomas Miller, Joseph Curry, Joseph P. Planta.

1882–Mayor Mark Bate: Council: John Whitfield, Henry McAdie, James Akenhead, George Bevilockway, Charles Smith, John Hilbert, George Baker.

1883–Mayor Mark Bate: Council: Henry McAdie, Richard Nightingale, James Akenhead, Michael Manson, George Campbell, George Baker, Joseph Curry.

1884–Mayor Mark Bate: Council: John Dick,* Richard Nightingale, Joseph Webb, James M. Brown, William E. Webb, George Baker, Donald Smith. *Dick resigned February 4, 1884. John Mahrer elected on February 11, 1884.

1885–Mayor Mark Bate: Council: Richard Nightingale, John Mahrer, William E. Webb, Walter Wilson, John Hilbert, James Lewis,* Jonathan Blundell. *Lewis resigned March 23, 1885. Donald Smith was appointed April 13, 1885.

1886–Mayor Mark Bate: Council Adam Grant Horne, Charles Wilson, William E. Webb, Walter R. Wilson, John Hilbert, James Knight, George Bevilockway.

1887–Mayor Richard Gibson: Council: Ralph Craig, John Mahrer, William E. Webb, John Hilbert, Walter R. Wilson, Joseph Randle, Robert Aitken.

1888–Mayor Mark Bate: Aldermen: John Mahrer, Richard Nightingale, John Hilbert, William E. Webb, Joseph Randle Jr., Robert Aitken, George Baker.

1889–Mayor Mark Bate: Aldermen: John Mahrer, Richard Nightingale, James A. Abrams, William E. Webb, Thomas E. Peck, George Baker, William M. Hilbert.

1890–Mayor John Hilbert: Aldermen: Richard Nightingale, Ralph Craig, James A. Abrams, Edward Quennell, William H. Morton, George Baker, William M. Hilbert.

1891–Mayor John Hilbert: Aldermen: William M. Hilbert, Charles McCutcheon, Thomas Dobeson, George Campbell, George Bevilockway, Joseph Ganner, George Baker, Duncan S. McDonald, Gilbert McKinnell.

1892–Mayor Andrew Haslam: Aldermen: Thomas Dobeson, Richard Nightingale, Joseph M. Brown, William M Hilbert, Joseph Ganner, Edward Quennell, George Baker, George Campbell, Gilbert McKinnell.

1893–Mayor Andrew Haslam: Aldermen: Richard Nightingale, Ralph Craig, William Keddy*, Edward Quennell, William M. Hilbert, Joseph Ganner, Gilbert McKinnell, John H. Cocking, John Frame. *Declined to serve term. Thomas Dobeson elected; took his seat February 6.

1894–Mayor Edward Quennell: Aldermen: Thomas Dobeson, Murdoch Morrison, Ralph Craig*, John H. Pleace, Richard Nightingale, Arthur Wilson, John H. Cocking, George Churchill, Thomas Wilks. *Craig died May 22, 1894. Jeremiah A. Callaghan was elected May 28.

1895–Mayor Edward Quennell: Aldermen: Thomas Dobeson, Matthew Sinclair, Albert E. Planta, John H. Pleace, John E.R.

Taggart, Joseph H. Davison, John H. Cocking, Duncan S. McDonald, James Bradley.

1896–Mayor Joseph Davison: Aldermen: Albert E. Planta, Coral N. Westwood, Matthew Sinclair, John D. Foreman, Arthur Wilson, William H. Morton, James Bradley, Duncan S. McDonald, Joshua Martell.

1897–Mayor Joseph Davison: Aldermen: Daniel A. Galbraith, Henry McAdie, Murdoch Morrison, George Campbell, John D. Foreman, William H. Morton, Thomas Brown, James Bradley, Robert Brydon Lamb.

1898–Mayor Mark Bate: Aldermen: William Manson, Albert E. Planta, Henry McAdie, Edward Quennell, James Knarston, Frances LeFeuvre, Thomas Brown, John H. Cocking*, William E. Webb*. *Cocking and Webb appointed by council.

1899–Mayor Mark Bate: Aldermen: William Manson, Albert E. Planta, Richard Kenyon, James Knarston, E.C. Barnes, Frances LeFeuvre*, John H. Cocking, William E. Webb, Henry McAdie. *Resigned June 19, 1899. John K. Hickman was elected July 10.

1900–Mayor Mark Bate: Aldermen: William Manson, Albert E. Planta, Charles Wilson*, Edward C. Barnes, John Hickman, James Knarston, John H. Cocking, Henry McAdie, Gilbert McKinnell*. *Appointed by council.

1901–Mayor William Manson: Aldermen: Albert E. Planta, C. McCutcheon, J. Hodgkinson, J.S. Knarston, John Hickman, Edward C. Barnes, John H. Cocking, Charles Wilson, George Johnson.

1902–Mayor William Manson: Aldermen: Albert E. Planta, J. Hodgkinson, H. McAdie, J.S. Knarston, Edward C. Barnes, Richard Booth, Charles Wilson, Morgan Harris, John W. Graham.

1903–Mayor William Manson: Aldermen: Albert E. Planta, J. Nicholson, Edward C. Barnes, Richard Booth, Charles Wilson, M. Harris, J.W. Graham.

1904–Mayor William Manson: Aldermen: J. Nicholson, Thomas Hodgson, G.D. Barlow, Edward C. Barnes, Morgan Harris, J.A. Macdonald, Charles Wilson, J.W. Graham, J.C. Stewart.

1905–Mayor A.E. Planta: Aldermen: J. Nicholson, Thomas Hodgson, William Kirkham, Edward C. Barnes, William Dick, J.S. Knarston, Charles Wilson, J.W. Graham, John Newton.

1906–Mayor A.E. Planta: Aldermen: Thomas Hodgson, William Kirkham, E.D. Barlow, Edward C. Barnes, William Dick, J.S. Knarston, J.W. Graham, John Newton, James Handlen.

1907–Mayor A.E. Planta: Aldermen: Alex Forrester, Thomas Hodgson, D.G. Dailey, Edward C. Barnes, William Dick, J.S.

Knarston, H. McRae, J. Newton, Charles Wilson.

1908–Mayor A.E. Planta: Aldermen: Thomas Hodgson, Alex. Forrester, D.G. Dailey, Edward C. Barnes, William Dick, J.S. Knarston, John Newton, H. McAdie, Charles Wilson.

1909–Mayor Thomas Hodgson: Aldermen: Albert E. Planta, Alex Forrester, John Shaw, Frederick A. Busby, Richard Booth, H. Shepherd, E.G. Cavalsky, H. McRae, J.W. Graham.

1910–Mayor A.E. Planta: Aldermen: Alex Forrester, John Shaw, C.H. Leicester, Frederick A. Busby, William Bennett, E. Shakespeare, H. McRae, James Young, James Watson.

1911–Mayor A.E. Planta: Aldermen: John Shaw, John Sampson, George Fletcher, H. Shepherd, Frederick A. Busby, J.R. McKinnell, Charles Wilson, E.G. Cavalsky, Benjamin Baker.

1912–Mayor John Shaw: Aldermen: J.R. McKinnell, Alex Forrester, William Grieve, Henry Shepherd, Frederick A. Busby, Henry McKenzie, E.G. Cavalsky, James Young.

1913–Mayor John Shaw: Aldermen: Joseph Booth, J.R. McKinnell, C.G. Stevens, Henry McKenzie, Henry Shepherd, Frederick A. Busby, James Crossan, James Young, W.J. Ferguson.

1914–Mayor A.E. Planta: Aldermen: Alex Forrester, James Crossan, J.R. McKinnell, Henry McKenzie, Frederick A. Busby, P. Killeen, W.J. Ferguson, E.G. Cavalsky, James Young.

1915–Mayor A.E. Planta: Aldermen: James Crossan, John Shaw, J.W. Coburn, Henry McKenzie, Frederick A. Busby, P. Killeen, J. Young, W.J. Ferguson, E.G. Cavalsky.

1916–Mayor Frederick A. Busby: Aldermen: John Shaw, J.R. McKinnell, J.W. Coburn, E.W. Harding, W.H. Morton, Henry McKenzie, James Young, W.J. Ferguson, E.G. Cavalsky.

1917–Mayor Henry McKenzie: Aldermen: J.W. Coburn, Alex Forrester, E.W. Harding, W.H. Morton, W.J. Ferguson, John Sharp.

1918–Mayor Henry McKenzie: Aldermen: Edward C. Barnes, Alex Forrester, Frederick A. Busby, W.H. Morton, W.J. Ferguson, John Sharp.

1919–Mayor Henry McKenzie: Aldermen: Edward C. Barnes, Evan D. Jones, Thomas Matthews, J.E. McGuckie, William Burnip, James Young.

1920–Mayor Henry McKenzie: Aldermen: Thomas Hodgson, James Knight, J.M. McGuckie, William Hart, John Rowan, John Barsby.

Nanaimo Provincial Representatives, 1871–1920

(Including legislation enacted during this period)

1871	John Robson
1874	Chinese and Natives disenfranchised.
1875	John Bryden
1877	David William Gordon
1878	James Atkinson Abrams. Schoolteachers prohibited from voting or campaigning.
1882	Robert Dunsmuir, William Raybould
1886	Robert Dunsmuir, William Raybould
1887	By-election following death of Raybould. George Thomson elected
1889	By-election following death of Dunsmuir. Andrew Haslam acclaimed
1890	Thomas William Forster, Colin Campbell McKenzie, Thomas Keith acclaimed
1894	James McGregor, Nanaimo City; John Bryden, Nanaimo North; William Wymond Walkem, South Nanaimo
1895	Japanese disenfranchised.
1898	Robert Edward McKechnie, Nanaimo City; John Bryden, Nanaimo North; Ralph Smith, South Nanaimo
1900	Ralph Smith, Nanaimo City; William Wallace Burns McInnes, Nanaimo North; James Dunsmuir, South Nanaimo

1900	By-election: Smith resigned to contest Federal election. James Hurst Hawthornthwaite acclaimed, Nanaimo City
1902	By-election: William Wallace Bruce McInnes, Nanaimo North
1903	James Hurst Hawthornthwaite, Nanaimo City; Parker Williams, Newcastle
1903	First provincial election run along federal party lines.
1907	James Hurst Hawthornthwaite, Nanaimo City; Parker Williams, Newcastle
1907	Hindus disenfranchised.
1909	James Hurst Hawthornthwaite, Nanaimo City; Parker Williams, Newcastle
1912	John Thomas Wilmot Place, Nanaimo City; Parker Williams, Newcastle
1916	William Sloan, Nanaimo; Parker Williams, Newcastle
1916	Clergy no longer prohibited from running in a provincial election.
1917	Franchise extended to women.
1918	By-election: James Hurst Hawthornthwaite; Parker Williams resigned; appointed to Workmen's Compensation Board, January 1, 1917.
1918	First woman to run and be elected, Mary Ellen Smith, Vancouver by-election January 24, 1918. First time women voted in a provincial election.
1920	William Sloan, Nanaimo; Samuel Guthrie, Newcastle

Nanaimo Federal Members, 1871–1920

1871   Robert Wallace
1872   Sir Francis Hincks
1874   Arthur Bunster
1878   Arthur Bunster
1882   David William Gordon
1886   David William Gordon
1890   David William Gordon died in office. Andrew Haslam
        acclaimed.
1893   Andrew Haslam
1900   Ralph Smith
1904   Ralph Smith
1908   Ralph Smith
1909   Ralph Smith
1911   Frank H. Shepherd
1917   Frank H. Shepherd
1920   John McIntosh

(In 1904 the name of the riding changed from Vancouver Island to
Nanaimo)

APPENDIX IV

Mining Deaths

The following list comprises miners killed in major accidents before 1920 in Nanaimo and Wellington mines as recorded in Minister of Mines Reports and other related documents.

1879, April 17: Dunsmuir. Wellington Colliery.
   Edward Campbell, Apollis Daney, John Dixon, Ruben Gough, John Hoskins, Lewis Prelee, William Rennie, plus four unidentified Chinese men.

1884, June 30: Dunsmuir. Wellington Colliery No. 3.
   Harry Arnold, Vittoria Verdotti, Lazarro Vettoni, James Condley, Milletto Domionico, James Donohue, John Eno, Daniel Evans, John Frear, John Gill, Christopher Hoskins, John Jones, Ben F. Jose, John Lowry, Martin Lowry, Barney McGinnes, Thomas Pettigrew, Dominico Ricono, Peter Traffo, Roberto Vergino, Rosetti Vergino, Michael Wilkinson, John Winders.

1887, May 3: Vancouver Coal Company, No. 1 Pit, Esplanade, Nanaimo.
   F. Allen, G. Bartolero, Edward Benton, George S. Bertram, Herbert Bevilockway, William Bone, George Bowden, Jonathan Bramley, Robert Buffington, H. Burns, William Burns, James Byres, James Campbell, William Campbell, William L. Cochran, Michael Corcoran, William L. Davis, James Davy, William Davy, Daniel Dawson, Charles Drake, Peter Ducca, Arthur Ellis, David Ellis, Thomas Evans, John C. Fallen, Anderoti Fillippia, Joseph Forest, William Gilbert, Thomas Gorman, William Hagne, James Hoggan, William Hoy, Samuel Hudson, Andrew Hunter, James

Isbister, Edward Johns, Nicholas Johns, John Johnson, Evan Jones, Henry Lee, Hudson Lee, Abraham T. Lewis, John Linn, William Lukey Sr., William Lukey Jr., James Lyons, Michael Lyons, John Malcolm, Thomas Martin, Frederick Mittisson, Alexander McDonald, Roderick McDonald, John McGuffie, Malcolm Mclean, Arthur Meakin, John Meakin, James Milton, David Morgan, John W. Morgan, William Morris, Andrew Morton, John Morton, Andrew Muir, Archibald Muir, Samuel H. Myers, John Myles, George Old, Thomas Perry, Benjamin Popplewell, John Richards, William Ridley, William Scales, George Simmons, Allan Smilley, John Smith, John J. Smith, William Henry Stephenson, John Stevens, John Stove, Robert Stove, James Thomas, John Thompson, Joseph Thompson, Frank Tully, Joseph Watson, Harry Westfieldt, Edward Wilkins, Caton Willis, Copley Woobank, John Woobank, John Zermani. Also killed were 53 unidentified Chinese men.

1888, January 24: Dunsmuir. Wellington Colliery No. 5.
John Barki (Breca), John Belloni, Joseph Chenat (Chano), Elisha Davis, William Dawber, William Finch, Ezra Godfrey, David Gordon, Robert Greenwell, William Horne, James Jones, Jacob Klein, John Marshall, Frank McCoy, Duncan McDonald, John McNeill, James Morrison, John Ness, Leopold Rejard, Xevier Rejard, Robert Robinson, Lance Robson, Alexander McKay Ross, John Stewart, Charles Tillar, Silvio Valerio, Richard Vincent, John Wienkotter, William Wilks, John Williams, Robert Williams.

Chinese: Sing Fom, Bum, Soon, Sing, Fue, Chung, Gin, Jow, Eye, Lock, Wing, Fong, Paden, Fue, Tate, Jim, Ack, Hen, Sam Sug, Al Len, Ah Kee, Ah Foie, I. Yon, Yon, Ton, Fie, Dan, Saul, Ywo. Also killed were seventeen other unidentified Chinese men.

1898, November 12: Vancouver Coal Company No. 1 Mine.
Ed. Edmonds, Peter High, Frederich Hurst, George Lee, William McGregor, James Price, Harry Shepherd.

1909, October 5: Wellington Collieries Company No. 2 West Mine Extension.
Andrew Moffatt, Thomas O'Connell, Jas. Molyneux, Thomas Thomas, Alex Milanich (Milos), Harold Taylor, William Keserich, Geo. Bodovinac, Robert Marshall, Wm. Robinson, Peter Nieland, John Ewart, Charles Scheff, W.A.

Selburn, William Quinn, Alex Keserich, William Davidson, Edward Dunn, Fred Ingham, Winyard Steele, Alex McClellan, Robert White, John Isbister, John Bulish, Mike Gustav, Oscar Nyman, Charles Salo, Thompson Parkin, Todd Rombovia, John Wargo, Mike Danculovich, Herman Petersen.

1915, February 9: South Wellington Colliery, Western Fuel Company
Olaf Lingeran, Glagorris Marvos, Robert Miller, Jim Hornis, William Gilson, William Irving, John Stewart, Peter Fearon, Joseph Fearon, Thomas Watson, Samuel Wardle, John Hunter, William Anderson, Frank Hunter, Joseph Cadr, Frank Marvelle, David Nellist, Joseph Foy, P. Finn.

1915, May 27: Reserve Mine, Western Fuel Company
William Ball, Ephraim Walishvil, Robert McMillan, Robert Kirkbride, Robert Haddow, Alfred Williams, Hiram Guffog, James L. Mazs, Frederick Crew, John Leach, J.W. Davis, Lewis Show, Edmund Beck, James McEwan, William McEwan, Robert Broom, Nick Selek, Fred Leschek, Thomas Harker, Thomas Bewley, Paul Vittar, Thomas Sutter.

1918, September 10: Canadian Western Fuel Company, No. 1 Protection Mine.
M. Eussa, Lionel Barlow, Angelo Sedola, Caleb Price, Joseph Sturma, Robert Kelly, James Bond, Joseph Turner, Augusta Eussa, David Eddy, Rathom Maisuradse, William Blinkhorne, John Rollo, T. Bonaz, John Kernahan, Robert McArthur.

Honour Roll of Those Killed in Action, 1914–1918

John Addison, Peter Aitken
Benjamin Barnes
Douglas Bate
James Bateman
Joseph Beck
Gilbert Blank
Albert Brown
James. Brown
Samuel Brown
Walter Bryant
Archibald Bushfield
J.M. Cairns
James Caldwell
William Campbell
John Chaison
Arthur Charman
Allan Clarke
Harold Cochran
Thomas Collier
Ernest Corbett
Mitchell Caveney
Jas. Crawford
Harold Cunningham
James Cunningham
Arthur Davidson

Desmond Davis
Elwyn Davis
Thomas Davison
Milford Devlin
Albert Dixon
Matthew Dobbin
Richard Drew
Arthur Eastwood
John Edwards
Reginald Emblem
Bert Fenn
R. Fotheringham
Arthur Gavin
John Glen
J.W. Gowland
Samuel Greenaway
Charles Hardy
Edmund Harrison
Robert Hastie
Arthur Hazel
Victor Hazel
H.R. Hickling
Fred Hillier
J.T. Hinds
David Hoggan

Robert Honeyman
George Jack
Thomas Jackson
H.R. Jepson
J.A. Jepson
Duncan Johnston
Edmund Jones
William Juriet
John Knox
J.A. Langlands
John Lucas
Arnold Malpass
Henry Mason
Peter McCorkindale
Robert McCourt
David McGuckie
Alexander McKenzie
Duncan McKenzie
Murdock McLean
Kenneth McLellan
William McLellan
Neil McNiven
Robert McNiven
Joseph Millburn
John Milligan
William Mitchell
James Moore
Charles Morrison
Fred Morrison
John Nicholson
Alfred Patterson
Archie Patterson
James Pender
Arthur Penning
Oswald Peto
James Petre
David Pittendrich
Edward Planta

William Pollard
J.T. Porter
John Quinn
Laurence Randle
James Reath
David Reid
John Reid
Percy Richardson
David Roberts
Frank Rogers
John Ross
John Rowan
J. Scott
Daniel Shields
Frank Silva
Robert Spowart
Thomas Stewart
George Strath
Charlie Swanson
Alex Swanson
Robert Swanson
William Syer
R.J. Thompson
Robert Thomson
W.E.H. Thorne
William Waddington
Thomas Wakelem
Lance Warn
James Watson
John Watson
J.W. Watson
B.J. Wicking-Smith
A. Williamson
Carl Wilson
Rupert Wilson
John Wilkinson
John Young

Coal Companies and Their Mines, 1886–1920

Vancouver Coal Mining and Land Company
Esplanade No. 1 & 2, 1881 to 1903
Southfield No. 1 & 2, 1882 to 1894
Southfield No. 4 & 5, 1888 to 1901
Chase River No. 3, 1886 to 1894
New Vancouver Coal Mining and Land Company
Esplanade/Protection Island, 1890 to 1903
Harewood Mine, 1884 to 1903
Northfield, 1889 to 1895
Western Fuel Company
Esplanade/Protection, 1903 to 1938
Brechin No. 4, 1903 to 1914
Douglas Slope (Chase River), 1911 to 1914
Reserve Mine, 1910 to 1939
Canadian Western Fuel Company
Wakesiah Mine, 1918 to 1930
South Wellington Mines Limited
Fiddick/Richardson, 1907
Pacific Coast Coal Mines (Collieries)
South Wellington, 1907 to 1921
Morden Mine, 1912 to 1921
R. Dunsmuir & Sons
Wellington/ Extension, 1895 to 1931
Alexandra (Alexandria), 1882 to 1902

Canadian Collieries (Dunsmuir) Limited
South Wellington No. 5, 1919 to 1927
Vancouver-Nanaimo Coal Company
Jingle Pot Mine
Owners, H. Maynard & J. Grant, 1907 to 1908
Owner, Alvo von Alvensleben, 1908 to 1917
British Columbia Coal Manufacturing Company
Jingle Pot Mine, 1917 to 1919
Granby Consolidated Mining, Smelting & Power Company
Cassidy, 1917 to 1932

Endnotes

Abbreviations:
NCA–Nanaimo Community Archives
BCA–British Columbia Archives
NHS–Nanaimo Historical Society
NDM–Nanaimo District Museum

Chapter One
1. The Coal Industry of Vancouver Island Brochure, dated 1898, NCA, Mark Bate fonds.
2. Walter J. Meyer Zu Erpen thesis, 31, which cites "Nanaimo, British Columbia, Its Development and Resources: A Sketch of Fifty Years Enterprise and Advancement, 1851–1903."
3. Minister of Mines Report, 1878, 382.
4. Coroner's report and death certificates verify this number.
5. *Nanaimo Free Press,* 8-20 May 1887.
6. Nicholls, vol. 2, Biggs family.
7. Pethick, 86.
8. Ibid., 88.
9. Kerr and Begg, 155.
10. Bowen (1987), 270.
11. NCA Education file, Code 20, Box 3, St. Ann's Convent, Nanaimo District Museum Collection.
12. Stonebanks, "Mine Blasts Took 148 Lives," 4, 5.
13. Letter to James D. Robinson, City Clerk, Victoria, City of Nanaimo: City Clerk Office fonds: Series 3, Letterbook: 51, NCA.
14. Currie.
15. Ibid.
16. Currie.
17. NCA History Box 1, Code 5, NDM.
18. *Harewood: Land of Wakesiah*, NCA Pamphlet file.
19. *Nanaimo Free Press,* 16 May 1893; 20 June 1905.
20. NCA City Directory 1892, 321.
21. From "Robins' Garden," biographical information compiled by C. Gisborne, S.M. Robins family file, NCA.

Chapter Two

1. Greene, 19.
2. Rushton, 12.
3. Ibid., 20.
4. Merilees, 37.
5. Greene, 20.
6. "A Stroll Around Nanaimo in 1874," speech, Mark Bate fonds, NCA.
7. Turner, 25.
8. Greene, 53–4
9. Turner, 92.
10. NCA Family File—Sabiston, Peter, John, and James.
11. John Dunham Tape No. 33 93-006-M, Transcript 6, Nanaimo Historical Society collection, NCA.
12. Norcross (1979), 69.
13. NCA City of Nanaimo Civic Boards and Committees: Board of Health minutes, 26 July, 1897.
14. Graham, 102.
15. Lewis-Harrison, 39.
16. Graham, 102.
17. Ibid., 102.
18. Lewis-Harrison, 196.
19. Mark Bate fonds, NCA.
20. Rushton, 13–4.
21. Ibid., 14.
22. Greene, 106.
23. Ibid.
24. Greene, 152–3.
25. Rushton, 27.
26. Turner, 12.
27. "Nanaimo built Vessel Wrecked on West Coast," n. d., Terry Simpson research.
28. Sage decendants, Nicholls, vol. 4.
29. Ibid.
30. "Music in Nanaimo long ago," speech, Mark Bate fonds, NCA.
31. NCA Transportation file: Shipbuilding.
32. Forbes, "He's Lived a Century—and Enjoyed It," *Nanaimo Free Press,* 23 July 1983.
33. "Capt. Yates' Yacht," *Nanaimo Free Press*, 18 Jan. 1905.

Chapter Three

1. Bowen (1987), 134
2. Barman, 152.

3. Tennant, 45.
4. Ray, 203–5.
5. Fisher, 1809.
6. Ray, 223.
7. Duff, 67-68.
8. Letter from Gilbert Malcolm Sproat, Joint Indian Reserve Commissioner, to Provincial Secretary Hon. A. C. Elliott, dated 20 Dec., 1876, Sproat correspondence GR 0494: B11011, British Columbia Archives: Provincial Secretary records (1876–78).
9. Ibid., 16.

Chapter Four
1. *Colonist*, 8 May 1867.
2. *Resources of British Columbia*, Feb. 1885, vol. 2, No.12, "Celestial."
3. NCA Family file—Mike Manson.
4. NCA Ethnic groups: Chinese #2, NDM.
5. NCA Report on the Royal Commission on Chinese immigration, Dom, sessional papers, vol. XVIII, No. 2, 1885.
6. Report on the Royal Commission on Chinese immigration, Dom, sessional papers, vol XVIII No. 2, 1885.
7. Ibid.
8. Lai, 46.
9. NCA Ethnic groups: Chinese #2, NDM.
10. *Nanaimo Free Press*, 10 Sept. 1884, 1.
11. Zu Erpen, 215, citing Sanitary Inspector's report of 1897.
12. *Nanaimo Free Press*, 5 Nov. 1884, 3.
13. Letter from City Clerk Sam Gough to Provincial Secretary Hon. J. Robson, 18 Dec. 1886, asking for approval of the extension of the city limits, Letterbooks 1885, 1886, and 1887, NCA City Clerk Office fonds. Also letter approving draft proclamation, 11 Jan. 1887, 3.
14. Zu Erpen, 159. See Appendix E, 137. The Lieutenant Governor issued Letters Patent on 13 Jan 1887.
15. NCA Ethnic groups: Chinese, Savory paper, NDM.
16. Daphne Paterson research.
17. *Victoria Colonist*, 12 July 1904, 2.
18. NCA Ethnic groups: Chinese, Savory paper.
19. Ibid., Dick Mah manuscript, see also Chuck Wong's "A History of the Chinese Community in Nanaimo."
20. NCA Ethnic groups: Chinese, Savory paper, also *Nanaimo Free Press*, 9 Mar. 1908.

21. *Nanaimo Free Press*, 1 June 1908.
22. "Chinese" Oath, Magistrate's Office fonds, NCA.
23. Lai, 75.
24. NCA City of Nanaimo Assessment Records, Chinatown.
25. Lai, 77.
26. Daphne Paterson research.
27. Lai, 55, citing Canada, Department of Immigration and Colonization, Annual reports, 1918, 1919.

Chapter Five
1. British Columbia Archives, Nanaimo: file no. C/AA/30.71/N15.
2. Macfie, 49.
3. British Columbia Archives: Franklyn Papers, file GR 1372, B01392.
4. MacDonald, 379.
5. "A Stroll Around Nanaimo in 1874," speech, Mark Bate fonds, NCA.
6. Galloway and Strachan, 2.
7. Boam and Brown, 106.
8. Galloway and Strachan, 2.
9. Ibid., 3.
10. NCA Family file—Edward Quennell.
11. NCA Family file—Stark. See also Peter Murray: *Homesteads and Snug Harbours, 98–100.*
12. Lewis-Harrison, 197.
13. Ibid., see also Ovanin, 39.
14. NCA Martha Kenny file: Hirst, NDM.
15. Gallacher, 108.
16. Bowen, 1989, 7.
17. McGaffey, Ernest, 159–162.
18. Vancouver Island Development League pamphlet, 65–71, B.C. Northwest Collection # 917.1134, Nanaimo branch, Vancouver Island Regional Library.
19. *Nanaimo Free Press*, 6 Oct. 1894, see also *Nanaimo, The Story of a City*, 42.
20. Barman, 115.
21. Underhill, 48.
22. Fisheries report, 1886.
23. NCA Charles Edward Stuart Journal, 22 Aug. 1855.
24. NCA HBC Nanaimo Memoranda 1855–1859, March 17, 1856.
25. Fisheries report, 1877.
26. Rattray, 77.
27. Innis, 46.

28. NCA Family file—McKay.
29. Morton, 12.
30. Olsen, 34.
31. Nicholls, vol. 2, Samuel Gough.
32. Morton, 32.
33. *British Columbia Directory*.
34. Duncan, 143.
35. New Westminster Museum/Archives.
36. NCA Family file—Andrew Haslam.
37. *Nanaimo Free Press*, 7 Nov. 1905.
38. NDM, *Nanaimo: The Story of a City*, 15.
39. Olsen, 94.
40. Allerdale, 213.
41. Boam, 259.
42. NCA Surrounding communities: Nanoose and Red Gap, see also Nicholls' *The History of Nanoose Bay*.

Chapter Six
1. Ministry of Mines Report, 1923.
2. *Colonist*, 29 Oct. 1864, 2.
3. Zu Erpen, 209.
4. Smith, citing J.C. McGregor, "Gaols of Nanaimo," 1.
5. Nicholls, vol. 2, Gough family.
6. British Columbia Archives: Franklyn papers, 12 Aug. 1865, GR1372 BO1392.
7. Minister of Mines Report, 1879.
8. Nicholls, vol. 2, Gough family.
9. *Nanaimo Free Press*, 13 Dec. 1894.
10. NCA Nanaimo Police Commissioners Board, loc. A-04-05.
11. NCA Family file—John Crossan.
12. *St. Andrew's Presbyterian Church 125 Anniversary*, 8.
13. Zu Erpen, 223.
14. Ibid., 81.
15. *Nanaimo Free Press*, 11 Jan. 1898.
16. Ibid., 11 Jan. 1905, 2, NCA Information file: Law Enforcement: Police.
17. Ibid., 20 Feb. 1905, "Editorial," 2.
18. Ibid., 27 Feb. 1905.
19. NCA Information file: Law Enforcement, Chiefs of police.
20. NCA Family file—Henry Wagner. See also Paterson, 33–34 and Mason, 21–22.

Chapter Seven
1. Tom Barnett, "Alberni Riding Member of Parliament."
2. Kerr and Begg, 279.
3. Electoral History of B.C. 1871–1966, Victoria Legislature Library, 1988.
4. Kerr and Begg, 79.
5. Ibid., 172–3.
6. James K. Nesbitt.
7. Ibid.
8. NCA Family file—David William Gordon.
9. Lai, 29. Shakespeare became mayor of Victoria in 1882 and served as Member of Parliament for Victoria in 1887.
10. Reksten, 61.
11. Ibid., 75.
12. Ibid., 74.
13. British Columbia Archives: Macdonald Papers.
14. *Nanaimo Free Press*, 16 Apr. 1889.
15. Reksten, 118–9.
16. *Nanaimo Free Press*, 17 May 1890, 1.
17. Nesbitt.
18. *Weekly Herald*, Nanaimo, Dec. 1903, NCA Family file—Ralph Smith.
19. Norcross, "Not Just Pin Money."
20. *Nanaimo Free Press*, 8 Dec. 1911.
21. Electoral History of B.C., 1871–1986.
22. *Nanaimo Herald*, 17 April 1900.

Chapter Eight
1. NCA Family file—John Meakin.
2. Nicholls, vol. 5, George and Mary Ann Baker.
3. *Nanaimo Free Press*, 11 June 1889, 22 June 1889, and 17 July 1889.
4. Cass, NCA Code 5, Parks file.
5. Letter from Canadian Western Fuel Company to Mayor McKenzie, 10 June 1918, City of Nanaimo: City Clerk's Office fonds, NCA.
6. Letter from Canadian Western Fuel Company to Mayor McKenzie, 28 Apr. 1919, Ibid.
7. Rowan.
8. NCA City Clark Office fonds, Bylaws.
9. Bird, 2.
10. Ibid., 14–16.
11. "Invincible Hornets Made Nanaimo Famous in Sport."

12. Rowan.
13. Garrard memoirs.
14. Turner, 32.
15. *Nanaimo Free Press*, 27, 30 July 1897.
16. NCA Family file—John David Stewart.
17. Barraclough, "Recollections," Ibid.
18. McGregor, "Klondyke Gold Rush."
19. Bowen (1987), 372.
20. Nicholls, vol. 5, Meakin descendants.

Chapter Nine
1. Houle.
2. Edward Drummond Taylor.
3. Obituary from Synod Journal, Pacific Biological Station.
4. Lewis-Harrison, 98.
5. D'Acres and Luxton, 23.
6. Peterson (1996), 23.
7. Lyons, 228.
8. Rev. G.W. Taylor.
9. Edward Drummond Taylor.
10. D'Acres and Luxton, 23.

Chapter Ten
1. NCA Muralt Collection, report from *Nanaimo Free Press*, 15 Oct. 1897.
2. NCA Muralt Collection, *Nanaimo Free Press*, 2 Sept. 1898.
3. Reksten, 135.
4. Reksten, 156.
5. Ormsby, 320.
6. Howay. See also *Colonist*, 2 Mar. 1900.
7. Ibid.
8. Reksten, 161.
9. Electoral History of B.C., Ninth General Election 1900.
10. Jackman, 140.

Chapter Eleven
1. Currie.
2. NCA Canadian Collieries fonds, data collected by S.V. Isaacson.
3. Report of Vancouver Island Coal Mines 1900, Thos. Morgan, Inspector of Vancouver Island Collieries.
4. Lewis-Harrison, 241.

5. Ministry of Mines Report, 1905.
6. Ibid.
7. *Nanaimo Free Press*, 24 Oct. 1907.
8. Lewis-Harrison, 235.

Chapter Twelve
1. City of Nanaimo Directory 1900.
2. *Nanaimo Free Press*, 7 July 1903.
3. Vancouver Island Development League, 65–71.
4. NCA Nanaimo History, Code 5, NDM.
5. *Nanaimo Free Press*, January 4, 1891.
6. Barraclough, "Early days of Wharf and Front Streets," NCA Building file: 17 Church Street."
7. NCA Building file: Church Street 17: Canadian Bank of Commerce.
8. Royal Bank of Canada Archives.
9. *Nanaimo Free Press*, 25 Apr. 1918.
10. "Stannard name active locally since year 1882," *Nanaimo Free Press*, Jubilee Edition, 1948.
11. Information from Jill Stannard.
12. NCA Retailing file, NDM.
13. *Nanaimo Free Press*, 16 Dec. 1916.
14. Norcross (1979), 119.
15. Hamlyn.
16. NCA Family file—Charles F. Bryant. See also buildings file: Victoria Cres.
17. NCA Family file—Mr. and Mrs. Rummings and family.
18. Loyal Order of Moose, Nanaimo Lodge No. 1052 newsletter, Vol. 5 No. 1, "The founder of Nanaimo Lodge No. 1052," Dec.–Jan., 1990–1991.
19. NCA Code 22, Box 11, file 37: Nicholson, Dr. Wilfred, NDM.
20. Peterson (1992), 219.
21. *Nanaimo Free Press*, 17 July 1916.
22. NCA Nanaimo history file: Theatres of Nanaimo. See also NCA Buildings file, 22 Commercial Street.
23. *Nanaimo Free Press*, 26 Dec. 1918.
24. Mah, 15.
25. NCA Information file: Communications, telephone.
26. Mar (1993), 5, 6.
27. NCA Information file: Communications, telephone.
28. NCA Darryl E. Muralt Collection, Wellington Enterprise, 66.
29. NCA Information file: Communications, telephone, *Daily Free*

Press, 23 Mar. 1967, Centennial Edition, "Grows from 37 sets in 1890 to 11,289." See also *Nanaimo Free Press*, 12 Dec. 1901.

30. *Nanaimo Free Press*, 17 Feb. 1905.
31. Bennett.
32. Ibid.
33. *Nanaimo Free Press*, 9, 10 Sept. 1903.
34. Christine Meutzner, NCA manager, speech to Nanaimo Historical Society meeting, April 1998.

Chapter Thirteen
1. Mar, 2000.
2. NCA Nanaimo Regional Hospital Society fonds: Series 6, file 2.
3. NCA Public Service, Code 4, Box 1, NDM.
4. NCA Mrs. W. McGirr, Junior Red Cross. Tape No. 1, Side B, Nanaimo Historical Society fonds, Series 2.
5. Nicholls, vol. 2, Amanda Theresa Norris.
6. *Nanaimo Free Press*, 14 Sept. 1907.
7. "History of Convent Bound Up With City."
8. *Nanaimo Free Press*, 12 July 1910.
9. NCA City of Nanaimo Finance Dept. fonds, Series 8. Statements 1910.

Chapter Fourteen
1. Lawrance.
2. Norcross (1979), 97.
3. "Felice Cavallotti Society, 100 Years of Community Service," *Nanaimo News Bulletin*, 26 Oct. 2000 Feature.
4. Juricic, "Croatians enlivened mining towns," NCA Information file: Ethnic, Croatians.
5. Interview: Zelimir B.Juricic with Tom Kulai, NCA Information file: Ethnic, Croatians.
6. Report of the Minister of Mines 1910, 209–210.
7. "Extension miner killed on Monday."
8. Report of the Minister of Mines 1910, 210.
9. *Nanaimo Free Press*, 5 Oct. 1909.
10. *Victoria Daily Times*, 6 Oct. 1909.
11. *Nanaimo Free Press*, 6 Oct. 1909.
12. *Victoria Daily Times*, 7 Oct. 1909.

Chapter Fifteen
1. NCA Mark Bate fonds.
2. *British Columbia Biographical*, 304–6.

3. NCA City of Nanaimo Finance Dept. fonds, statement of 1910, 7.
4. Letter from WFC manager Stockett to Mayor Planta, 16 Sept. 1911, NCA City Clerks Office fonds, file 6-1.
5. NCA Family file—Thomas Hodgson.
6. *Nanaimo Free Press*, 15 Apr. 1912.
7. Ibid., 20 Jan. 1908.
8. NCA Family file—John Shaw.
9. NCA Family file—Frederick A. Busby.
10. *Nanaimo Free Press*, 5 Feb. 1920.
11. NCA Family file—Alexander Forrester.
12. NCA Family file—Edward George Cavalsky.
13. See advertisement for "A Candy and Cigar Stand Just Opened On the Crescent. Proprietor George Cavalsky," *Nanaimo Free Press*, 31 Dec. 1887.
14. *The Daily Herald*, 15 Jan. 1913.
15. Ibid., 16 Jan. 1913.

Chapter Sixteen
1. *Nanaimo Free Press*, 8 Mar. 1907.
2. NCA Industry: Information file: Fishing.
3. *Nanaimo Free Press*, 14 Mar. 1905.
4. Ibid., 17 Oct. 1906.
5. Department of Fisheries annual report, 1905–07, 46.
6. *Nanaimo Free Press*, 5 Nov. 1908.
7. Merilees, 86.
8. Sutherland.
9. *British Columbia Magazine*, May 1911, 235–237.
10. *Nanaimo Free Press*, 21 July 1910.
11. Ibid., 23 Sept. 1910.
12. Ibid., 12 Nov. 1910.
13. Canada: Marine and Fisheries report, 1911–12.
14. Boam, 237.
15. Trower, 93–98.
16. Peterson (1999), 112.
17. Henderson, 3, NCA.
18. Webb, 187.

Chapter Seventeen
1. "Dunsmuir Mansion Turned into Hostel," NCA Code 27, Box 1, Surrounding Communities: Departure Bay, NDM.
2. Reksten, 183.
3. Ibid., 184.
4. *Colonist*, 9 Mar. 1902.

Chapter Eighteen
1. Report of the Minister of Mines 1903.
2. *Province*, 11, 13 Mar. 1903.
3. Wargo, 56.
4. *Colonist*, 7, 14 Apr. 1903.
5. Wargo, 55.
6. *Nanaimo Free Press*, 20 May 1903.
7. Steeves, 12.
8. Ormsby, 337.
9. Miner Jimmy Phillipson quote, Wargo, 53.
10. Electoral History of British Columbia 187–1986.
11. NCA Parker William fonds.

Chapter Nineteen
1. *Province*, 28 March 28, 1905, Reksten, 216.
2. Ibid., 6 Jan. 1908.
3. Ibid., 3 Feb. 1908.
4. Reksten, 224.
5. NCA Canadian Collieries fonds: Transactions.
6. *Victoria Times*, 14 Sept. 1911.
7. Reksten, 221.
8. *Nanaimo Free Press*, 14 Mar. 1911.
9. Turner, 36–37.
10. Greene, 113–119.
11. *Nanaimo Free Press*, 9 Oct. 1911.
12. Turner, 35.
13. *Nanaimo Free Press*, 11 May 1912.
14. Turner, 59.

Chapter Twenty
1. Norcross (1979), 144–5.
2. McClughan.
3. *Nanaimo Free Press*, 7 Feb. 1903.
4. Bowen (1982), 108.
5. *Nanaimo Free Press*, 19 May 1910.
6. Mah, 16.
7. *Nanaimo Free Press*, 15 Jan. 1913.
8. The names of the crew come from Rogers, 53.
9. "Incidents of the Explosion," *Nanaimo Free Press*, 16 Jan. 1913.
10. Norcross, "Birthday Tapes Tell Story of Nanaimo." The taped interview was recorded July 17, 1966, on William Lewis's 99th birthday. William Barraclough had his tape recorder handy, as

Lewis recalled early Nanaimo. Lewis died at age 103 in 1968.

11. Rogers, 54.
12. *Nanaimo Free Press*, 16 Jan. 1913.
13. Ibid., 20 Jan. 1913.
14. Norcross (1979), 146.
15. Weir and Smith, 178.
16. Juricic, "Croatians Killed in Ladysmith Mine Blast."
17. Kavanaugh.
18. Steeves, 19.
19. Hinde.
20. Strike pay is cited from report of the Royal Commissioner on Coal Mining Disputes on Vancouver Island, *B.C. Federationist*, 14 Aug. 1913, 46.
21. Steeves, 17.
22. *B.C. Federationist*, 14 Aug. 1913. See also Ormsby, 367.
23. B.C. Miners' Liberation League brochure, NCA Parker William fonds.
24. Ibid., 13.
25. Usukawa.
26. NCA Parker William fonds.
27. Annual report June 30, 1913, NCA Canadian Collieries (Dunsmuir) Ltd. Fonds.
28. *Nanaimo Free Press*, 19 Aug 1913.
29. Financial reports. Report of Chief of Police, 1913, NCA City of Nanaimo Finance Department fonds.
30. NCA Nanaimo Historical Society fonds: William Barraclough.
31. NCA, *B.C. Federationist*, 28 Aug. 1914.
32. Inspector of Mines Annual report 1913, K340.

Chapter Twenty-One

1. Hannon, 30.
2. *Nanaimo Free Press*, 9 Aug. 1914.
3. Ibid., 11 Dec. 1915.
4. NCA Military file: Historical Notes on Nanaimo Military Camp, by Major (Ret'd) A.G.M. MacIsaac, Royal Canadian Artillery, March 1980. NDM.
5. Campbell, NCA Code 21, Box 1, file 2: German Prisoners, NDM, *PHSC Journal* 58, 28–9, June 1989.
6. Juricic, "Internment."
7. NCA Code 21, Box 1, file 2. Internment Operations, 1914–1920. Report by Major General Sir William Otter (1921), as cited by Campbell. NDM.
8. *Nanaimo Free Press*, 22 Sept. 1914.

9. NCA Canadian Collieries fonds, annual report 1915.

10. Jackman, 167–176.

11. NCA Philip H. Morris, The Canadian Patriotic Fund, from 1914 to 1919.

12. NCA Family file—Rudd, John.

13. *Nanaimo Free Press*, 30 Aug. 1916.

14. *Alberni Pioneer News*, 30 Jan. 1909.

15. *Nanaimo Free Press*, 26 Aug. 1916.

16. Electoral History of B.C. 1871–1986.

17. Ibid., Plebiscites and referenda: Temperance plebiscite 1920.

18. Ibid., Women's Suffrage Referendum 1916, The Provincial Election Act Amendment Act, SBC 1917, c.23. passed in April 1917. Act repealed the Women's Suffrage Act of 1916.

19. *Nanaimo Free Press*, 2 Sept. 1916.

20. Ibid., 20 Dec. 1916.

21. NCA Family file—Leighton, Arthur (Anne Royle Research).

22. NCA Arthur and Alice Leighton fonds, diary and correspondence.

23. NCA City Clerk Office fonds, Dominion Government file 6-5.

24. "Woman Wins in Nanaimo School Trustee Contest," *Vancouver Sun*, 14 Jan. 1922.

25. Colombo, 502.

26. NCA Pamphlet file: "Born to Kill," by Allan Hynd, *Liberty*, 25 May 1940, 6-9.

27. *Nanaimo Free Press*, 24 Apr. 1918.

28. Ibid., 29 Sept. 1919.

29. Ibid., 6 Oct. 1919.

30. Report of Minister of Mines 1918, K 350.

31. *Nanaimo Free Press*, 10 Sept. 1918. Some of the victims' names differ from that of the Minister of Mines report.

32. Report of Minister of Mines 1918, K351.

Chapter Twenty-Two

1. NCA, City of Nanaimo, City Clerk's Office fonds, correspondence, file C4.

2. Ibid.

3. NCA City of Nanaimo: Civic Boards and Committees, Nanaimo Board of Health fonds, Oct. 1918.

4. *Nanaimo Free Press*, 19 Oct. 1918.

5. Ibid.

6. McGirr.

7. NCA City of Nanaimo: Civic Boards and Committees: Nanaimo Board of Health fonds, October 20, 1918.

8. Mah ms. Mah was the grandson of Bing Kee.
9. NCA City of Nanaimo, City Clerk's Office fonds, correspondence, file C4.
10. *Nanaimo Free Press*, 26 Oct. 1918.
11. Article from *The Daily Herald*, November 26, 1918, NCA Family file—Ketchin.
12. *Nanaimo Free Press*, 29 Oct. 1918.
13. Ibid., 26 Oct. 1918.
14. Ibid., 16 Nov. 1918.
15. NCA City of Nanaimo Finance Dept. fonds, Statements 1918, 8, 9.
16. Pethick, 180–190.
17. *Nanaimo Free Press*, 11 Nov. 1918.
18. Ibid., 11, 12 Nov. 1918.
19. Ibid., 2 Jun. 1919.
20. Ibid., 9 Aug. 1919.
21. Ibid., 19 Sept. 1919.
22. NCA City of Nanaimo, City Clerk Office fonds: Royal visit file 14, address by Mayor McKenzie.
23. Ibid., speech by His Royal Highness Prince Edward.

Sidebar Endnotes
1. "A Stroll Around Nanaimo in 1874" speech, Mark Bate fonds, NCA.
2. Barman, 157.
3. Hodding, 24.
4. Bowen (1987), 361.
5. Fisheries report, 1886.
6. NCA HBC Memoranda, 1855-1857: August 25, 1855.
7. *Nanaimo Free Press*, 25 April 1883.
8. Norcross (1979), 137.
9. *Nanaimo Free Press*, 10 Dec.1906.
10. Rowan. All information about the early wrestlers comes from this source.
11. Ibid.
12. NCA, Natives, Code 16. NDM.
13. Greene, 109.
14. Rushton, 37–8.
15. NCA Information file: Nanaimo Fire protection.
16. Wm Barraclough interview with William R. Manson, 15 Mar., 1966. Nanaimo Historical Society fonds. Series 2, NCA.
17. NCA Family File—Manson family.
18. *British Columbia Magazine*, May 1911, 235–237.

222

2222222

19. Howay, 525.
20. Ormsby, 336.
21. *Nanaimo Free Press*, 15 July 1903.
22. Canada, Royal Commissions, Report of the Royal Commission on Industrial Disputes in British Columbia, 1903, 13.
23. Reksten, 217.
24. *Nanaimo Free Press*, 2 Mar. 1907.
25. Greene, 247.
26. Norcross, *Nanaimo Retrospective*, 145.
27. *Nanaimo Free Press*, 1 Jan. 1913.
28. Gogo.
29. Carroll.
30. Berton, 135.

Bibliography

Books, Articles, and Pamphlets

Barman, Jean. *The West Beyond the West: A History of British Columbia*. Toronto: University of Toronto Press, 1991.

Barraclough, William. "Early Days of Wharf & Front Streets." [NCA.]

——. "Recollections of Nanaimo people." [NCA.]

Barnett, Tom. "Alberni Riding Member of Parliament." *Twin Cities Times* 25 Oct. 1967: n. pag.

Bate, Mark. "Music in Nanaimo Long Ago." Speech. [Mark Bate fonds, NCA.]

——. "A Stroll Aound Nanaimo in 1874." Speech. [Mark Bate fonds, NCA.]

Bennett, R.B. "Laying a Cable to the Island." *British Columbia Magazine* 19 Jul. 1913: 384-390.

Berton, Pierre. *Vimy*. Toronto: McClelland & Stewart Limited, 1986.

Bird, George. *Tse-Wees-Tah, One Man in a Boat*. Port Alberni, BC: Alberni District Museum and Historical Society, 1971 (1972).

——. "Early B.C. Sawmills." *West Coast Advocate* 24 May 1944: n. pag.

Boam, Henry J., and Ashley G. Brown, eds. *British Columbia, Its History, People, Commerce, Industries and Resources*. London: Sells Ltd., 1912.

Bowen, Lynne. *Boss Whistle*. Lantzville: Oolichan Books, 1982

——. *The Dunsmuirs of Nanaimo*. Nanaimo Festival, 1989. [NCA.]

——. *Three Dollar Dreams*. Lantzville: Oolichan Books, 1987.

"Capt. Yates' Yacht. Nanaimo Man Purchases Vessel in Victoria." *Nanaimo Free Press* 18 Jan. 1905.

British Columbia Biographical. Vol. 4. Vancouver: S.J. Clarke Publishing Co., 1914.

Campbell, J. Colin. "WWI Internment at Nanaimo, and a Scarce Censor Mark." *Photographic Historical Society of Canada* [PHSC] 58 (1989): 28–29.

Carroll, H. *History of Nanaimo Pioneers, 1849–1935*. [NCA.]

Cass, John. *The History of Nanaimo City Parks*. 1967. [NCA.]

"Celestial." 2.12. *Resources of British Columbia*. Feb. 1885. [NCA.]

Coal Industry of Vancouver Island, 1898, The. [Mark Bate fonds, NCA.]

Colombo, John Robert. *Colombo's Canadian References*. Toronto: Oxford University Press, 1976.

Currie, A.W. "The Vancouver Coal Mining Company: A Source For Galsworthy's Strife." *Queen's Quarterly* 70.1 (1963): n. pag.

D'Acres, Lilia, and Donald Luxton. *Lions Gate*. Burnaby: Talonbooks, 1999.

Duff, Wilson. *The Indian History of British Columbia*. Vol. 1. *The Impact of the White Man*. Memoir 5. Anthropology in British Columbia, 1964. [Provincial Museum of British Columbia, Victoria.]

Duncan, Eric. *From Shetland to Vancouver Island: Recollections of Seventy-Five Years*. Edinburgh: Oliver and Boyd Ltd., 1937.

"Dunsmuir Mansion Turned into Hostel." *Nanaimo Free Press* 2 Dec. 1978: n. pag.

"Extension Miner Killed on Monday." *Ladysmith Chronicle* 27 Dec. 1929: n. pag.

Fisher, Robin. *Contact and Conflict: Indian-European Relations in British Columbia, 1774–1890*. Vancouver: UBC Press, 1977.

Forbes, David. "He's lived a century—and enjoyed it." *Nanaimo Free Press* 23 Jul. 1983: n. pag.

Friesan J., and H. K. Ralston, eds. *Historical Essays on British Columbia*. Toronto: McClelland and Stewart, 1976.

Gallacher, Daniel Thomas. "Coal Management in British Columbia, 1864-1889." M.A. Thesis. University of Victoria, 1970.

Galloway, Mrs. Allan, and Robert Strachan, eds. *A History of the Cedar, Bright, Cranberry and Oyster Districts on Vancouver Island, B.C. 1858–1958*. Cedar Centennial Committee, 1950. [Vancouver Island Regional Library, Northwest Collection 971-1.]

Garrard, Frank C. *Memoirs*. [Alberni District Historical Society Archives, Port Alberni, BC.]

Gogo, Dodie. *History of St. Peter's Church*. [NCA.]

Graham, Donald. *Keepers of the Light*. Madeira Park: Harbour Publishing, 1985.

Grainger, M. Allerdale. *Woodsman of the West*. Victoria: Horsdal & Schubart, 1994.

Greene, Ruth. *Personality Ships of British Columbia*. Vancouver: Marine Tapestry Publications, 1969.

Hamlyn, Chris. "The End of a Legacy." *Nanaimo News Bulletin* 6 Jan. 2000: n. pag.

Hannon, Leslie F. *Canada at War: The Record of a Fighting People*. Canadian Illustrated Library. Toronto: McClelland and Stewart, 1968.

Harewood—Land of Wakesiah. Nanaimo Centennial Committee, 1966–67. [NCA.]

Henderson, Vi. *Piper's Lagoon*. Nanaimo: Quadra Graphics, 1984.

Hinde, John R. "Stout Ladies and Amazons: Women in the British Columbia Coal-Mining Community of Ladysmith, 1912-1914." *B.C. Studies: The British Columbia Quarterly* 114 (Summer 1997): 33–57.

"History of Convent Bound Up Wth City." *Nanaimo Free Press* 15 Mar. 1962: 7.

Hodding, Bruce Alan. *North Cowichan: A History in Photographs*. Duncan: The Corporation of the District of North Cowichan, 1998.

Houle, Valerie. "Upon the Shoulders of Giants: Taylor's Marine Legacy." *Gabriola Sounder* 30 Nov. 1993: 11-12.

Howay, F.W., and E.O.S. Scholefield. *British Columbia From the Earliest Times to the Present*. 4 Vols. Vancouver: S.J. Clarke Publishing Co., 1914.

——. "The Settlement and Progress of B.C. 1871-1914." *Historical Essays on British Columbia*. Ed. J. Friesan and H.K. Ralston. Toronto: McClelland & Stewart, 1976.

Innis, H.A., ed. *The Japanese Canadians*. Toronto: University of Toronto Press: 1938.

"Invincible Hornets Made Nanaimo Famous in Sport." *Nanaimo Free Press*, Golden Jubilee Edition 1874–1924.

Jackman, S.W. *Portraits of the Premiers: An Informal History of British Columbia*. Sidney, BC: Gray's Publishing Ltd., 1969.

Juricic, Selimir B. "Croatians Enlivened Mining Towns." *British Columbia Historical News* 3 (Summer 1994): 22–25.

——. "Croatians Killed in Ladysmith Mine Blast." *British Columbia Historical News* 4 (Winter 1992–93): 20–23.

——. "Internment." *Times Colonist, Islander* 24 Aug. 1997: C8.

Kavanaugh, J. The Vancouver Island Strike. B.C. Miners' Liberation League, 1914. [NCA.]

Kerr and Begg. *Biographical Dictionary of Well-Known British Columbians*. Vancouver: Kerr & Begg, 1890.

Lai, David Chuenyan. *Chinatowns: Towns Within Cities In Canada*. Vancouver: UBC Press, 1988.

Lawrance, Scott. "Sointula: Saltfish and Spuds Utopia." *Raincoast Chronicles First Five*. Ed. Howard White. Madeira Park, BC: Harbour Publishing, 1976: 164–168.

Lewis-Harrison, June. *The People of Gabriola*. Cloverdale, BC: D.W. Friesen, 1982.

Lyons, Cicely. *Salmon: Our Heritage*. Vancouver: B.C. Packers, Mitchell Press, 1969.

MacDonald, Duncan George Forbes. *British Columbia and Vancouver Island*. London: Longman, Green, et al, 1862.

Mah, Dick. "History of Mah Bing Kee 1847-1942." Ms. 1988. [NCA.]

Mar, Pamela. *The Light of Many Candles: One Hundred Years of Caring Service*. Nanaimo Auxiliary to NRGH, 2000.

——. "A Long Distance Line to the Past." *British Columbia Historical News* (Spring 1993): 5–6.

Mason, Elda Copley. *Lasqueti Island, History & Memory*. Lantzville, BC: Byron Mason, n.d.

McClughan, Aileen. "Powder Making In Nanaimo." *British Columbia Magazine* Oct. 1911: 1059–1062.

McGaffey, Ernest. "Progressive Community Publicity—The Vancouver Island Development League." *Westward Ho!* (Mar. 1910): 159-162.

McGirr, Mrs. W. *Junior Red Cross*. Paper. [NCA.]

McGregor, Jack Charles. "The Klondyke Gold Rush." Ms. N.d. [NCA.]

——. "The Gaols of Nanaimo." Paper. 1954. [NCA.]

Merilees, Bill. *Newcastle Island: A Place of Discovery*. Surrey, BC: Heritage House, 1998.

Morris, Philip H. *The Canadian Patriotic Fund From 1914 to 1919*. [NCA.]

Morton, James. *The Enterprising Mr. Moody: The Bumptious Captain Stamp*. North Vancouver: J.J. Douglas Ltd., 1977.

Murray, Peter. *Homesteads and Snug Harbours*. Ganges, BC: Horsdal and Schubart, 1991.

Nanaimo and District Museum Society. *Nanaimo: The Story of a City*. 1983.

"Nanaimo and the Herring Industry." *British Columbia Magazine* 7.3 1911: 235-237.

Nanaimo Community Heritage Commission. *Columns, Cornices & Coal*. City of Nanaimo, 1999.

Nesbitt, James K. "He Did Well at Nanaimo." *Daily Colonist* 22 Jan. 1956: 4–5.

Nicholls, Peggy. *From the Black Country to Nanaimo 1854*. Vols.1–5. Nanaimo Historical Society and Peggy Nicholls, 1991 to 1995.

——. *The History of Nanoose Bay*. 1958. [NCA.]

Norcross, Elizabeth Blanche. "Birthday Tapes Tell Story of Nanaimo." *Daily Colonist* 4 Feb. 1979: n. pag.

——. "Not Just Pin Money." Essay. Camosun College, 1984. [NCA.]

——., ed. *Nanaimo Retrospective: The First Century*. Nanaimo Historical Society, 1979.

Olsen, W.H. *Water Over the Wheel*. Chemainus, BC: Schultz Industries, 1963 (1981).

Ormsby, Margaret A. *British Columbia: A History*. Toronto: Macmillan, 1958.

Ovanin, Thomas K. *Island Heritage Buildings*. Islands Trust, 1984 (1987).

Paterson, T.W. *Ghost Towns & Mining Camps of British Columbia*. Vol. 1. Langley: Stagecoach Publishing, 1979.

Peterson, Jan. *The Albernis, 1860-1922*. Lantzville: Oolichan Books, 1992.

——. *Cathedral Grove, MacMillan Park*. Ibid., 1996.

——. *Journeys Down The Alberni Canal to Barkley Sound*. Ibid., 1999.

Pethick, Derek. *British Columbia Disasters*. Langley, BC: Stagecoach Publishing, 1978.

Province of British Columbia. *Electorial History of British Columbia 1871–1986*. Legislative Library, Victoria, B.C., 1988.

Rattray, Alexander. *Vancouver Island & British Columbia*. Edinburgh: Smith, Elder & Co., Cornhill, M.DCCC.LXII [1862]. [Vancouver Island Regional Library, Northwest Collection, Nanaimo. NN917:11 RAT.]

Ray, Arthur J. *I Have Lived Here Since the World Began: An Illustrated History of Canada's Native People*. Toronto: Lester Publishing and Key Porter Books, 1996.

Reksten, Terry. *The Dunsmuir Saga*. Vancouver: Douglas & McIntyre, 1991.

Rogers, Fred. *More Shipwrecks of British Columbia*. Vancouver: Douglas & McIntyre, 1992.

Rowan, A.H. "Club Housed Some Great Ones." *Times*, 12 Nov. 1983: 9A.

Rushton, Gerald A. *Whistle up the Inlet: The Union Steamship Story*. Vancouver: Douglas & McIntyre, 1974.

Savory, Kathleen M. "Nanaimo's Chinese Community." Paper. N.d. [NCA.]

Smith, Brian Ray Douglas. "A Social History of Early Nanaimo." M.A. Thesis. University of British Columbia, 1956.

St. Andrews' Presbyterian Church 125 Anniversary: 1865–1990. [NCA.]

Steeves, Dorothy G. *The Compassionate Rebel*. Vancouver: J.J. Douglas, 1960.

Stonebanks, Roger. "Mine Blasts Took 148 Lives." *Times Colonist, Islander* 2 May 1999: 2, 5.

Sutherland, C.A. "The 'Hub' of Vancouver Island." *Westward Ho!* (Jun. 1908): 55–59.

Taylor, Edward Drummond. *A Very Gentle Man*. Ms. Pacific Biological Station, 1990.

Taylor, Rev. G.W. "A Plea for a Biological Station on the Pacific Coast."
Paper. Royal Society of Canada, 1907.

Tennant, Paul. *Aboriginal Peoples and Politics*. Vancouver: UBC Press,
1990.

Trower, Peter. "B.C.Whaling, The White Men." *Raincoast Chronicles First
Five*. Ed. Howard White. Madeira Park, BC: Harbour Publishing, 1976.
93–98.

Turner, Robert D. *The Pacific Princesses*. Victoria: Sono Nis Press, 1977.

——. *Those Beautiful Coastal Liners*. Ibid., 2001.

Underhill, Ruth. *A Place to Prosper, or Just Survive? Motivations for the
Emigration of Scottish Labourers to Vancouver Island 1848–1852*.
M.Litt. Thesis. University of St. Andrews, Scotland, 1997.

Usukawa, Saeko, ed. *Sound Heritage: Voices from British Columbia*.
Vancouver: Douglas & McIntyre. 1984.

Vancouver Island Development League. *Nanaimo District*. [Vancouver
Island Regional Library, Northwest Collection, Library 917.1134.]

Wargo, Alan John. "The Great Coal Strike, The Vancouver Island Coal
Miners' Strike, 1912-1914." B.A. Thesis. University of British Columbia,
1962.

Webb, Robert Lloyd. *On the Northwest: Commercial Whaling in the
Pacific Northwest 1790–1967*. Vancouver: UBC Press, 1988.

Weir, Patricia, and Howie Smith. "Down in the Coal Mines: The Big Strike
of 1912." *Sound Heritage: Voices from British Columbia*. Ed. Saeko
Usukawa. Vancouver: Douglas & McIntyre. 1984.

White, Howard, ed. *Raincoast Chronicles First Five*. Madeira Park:
Harbour Publishing, 1976.

"Woman Wins in Nanaimo School Trustee Contest." *Vancouver Sun* 14
Jan. 1922: n. pag.

Wong, Chuck. "A History of the Chinese Community in Nanaimo."
[NCA.]

Zu Erpen, Walter J. Meyer. "Towards an Understanding of the Municipal
Archives of Nineteenth Century British Columbia: A Case Study of the
Archives of the Corporation of the City of Nanaimo, 1875–1904." M.A.
Thesis. University of British Columbia, 1985.

Newspapers, Periodicals, and Magazines

Alberni Pioneer News [Port Alberni, BC]
British Columbia Historical News [Cranbrook, BC]
British Columbia Magazine [Vancouver, BC]
British Columbia.Federationist [Vancouver, BC]
Colonist [Victoria, BC]
Daily British Colonist [Victoria, BC]
Daily Colonist, [Victoria, BC]
Daily/Weekly Herald [Nanaimo, BC]
Gabriola Sounder [Gabriola Island, BC]
Ladysmith Chronicle [Ladysmith, BC]
Nanaimo Free Press [Nanaimo, BC]
Nanaimo News Bulletin [Nanaimo, BC]
Photographic Historical Society of Canada (PHSC), [Toronto, ON]
The Province [Vancouver, BC]
Queen's Quarterly [Kingston, ON]

Times [Nanaimo, BC]
Times Colonist, The Islander [Victoria, BC]
Twin City Times [Port Alberni]
Vancouver Sun [Vancouver, BC]
Victoria Colonist [Victoria, BC]
Victoria Times [Victoria, BC]
Wellington Enterprise [Wellington, BC]
West Coast Advocate [Port Alberni, BC]
Westward Ho! [Vancouver, BC]

Audiotapes, Letters, Interviews, Minute Books, Journals, Notes, and Research

Charles Edward Stuart Journal, 1855. [NCA.]
Barraclough, William. Interview of William R. Manson. 15 Mar. 1966. [NCA.]
Dunham, John. Audio tape. Tape No. 33 93-006-M. [NCA.]
Franklyn, William Hales. Papers. BCA.
Gilbert Malcolm Sproat, Joint Indian Reserve Comm. "To Hon. A. C. Elliott, Provincial Secretary." 20 Dec. 1876 Letter. BCA.
HBC Nanaimo Memoranda 1855–1859. [NCA.]
Hudson's Bay Company Daybook. [NCA.]
Paterson, Daphne. Research on Nanaimo's Chinese community.

Government Records

Canada: Department of Immigration & Colonization. Annual Reports 1918, 1919.
Canada: Marine and Fisheries Report 1911–12.
City Clerk Office fonds—letter books.
City of Nanaimo Annual Financial Statements, 1901–1915.
City of Nanaimo Assessment Records, Chinatown.
Department of Fisheries Annual Report 1905–07.
Inspector of Fisheries Reports 1877, 1886.
Ministry of Mines Reports 1875–1923.
Nanaimo Board of Health fonds.
Nanaimo City Directory.
Nanaimo Police Commissioners Board Minute Book.
Royal Commission on Chinese Immigration. Sessional papers. 1885.
Royal Commission on Indian Affairs for the Province of British Columbia. Extract.

Photo Credits

Alberni Valley Museum: p. 103 (PN 98)

Nanaimo Community Archives: p. 19 (989.29 B5/135); p. 20 (1993-028-A-P8); p. 31 (989.29 B5/135); p. 35 (2003-004-A-P3); p. 52 Kin Jung Lee photo (1996-024-A-P4); p. 71; p. 79 (989.29 B5/135); p. 108 (989.29.B5/135); p. 129 top; p. 144 (989.29 B5/135); p. 150 (1996-034-A-296); p. 163 (1995-021-A-PC 10); p. 165 (2003-011-A-P1); p. 172 (1993-031-M-PC2); p. 200 (2000-012-A-PC3); p. 207 (2003-016-M-92); p. 212 (2003-005-A-P1); p. 222 (1998-007-A-P1); p. 223 (1993-034-M-P22)

Nanaimo District Museum: p. 22 (I3-16); p. 26 (Q3-156); p. 27 (H2-3); p. 36 I1-255); p. 41 (A-80); p. 49 (I2-244); p. 50 (I2-48); p. 53 (K1-20); p. 56 (U3-20); p. 58 (C3-52); p. 68 (C4-53) Stanley C. Dakin photo; p. 70 (U1-55); p. 72 (I3-20); p. 73 (U1-60); p. 78 (M1-31); p. 81 (J1-2); p. 84 (I2-71); p. 99 top (G1-88) and bottom (G1-71); p. 102 (G1-12); p. 104 (G1-74); p. 105 (I2-142); p. 107 (L-13); p. 111 The Elite Studio, Nanaimo (G1-15); p. 129 bottom (Q2-3); p. 133 (C3-19); p. 135 Peter Schwarze (B1-10); p. 136 (C3-32); p. 137 (U3-16); p. 138 (C3-28); p. 146 R.L. Pocock photo (I3-37); p. 147 (I3-57); p. 148 (M1-3); p. 151 (C1-2); p. 153 (F1-19); p. 161 (C3-55); p. 162 (J-4); p. 173 (U2-9); p. 174 (U2-12); p. 177 (I2-107); p. 185 (I2-55); p. 198 top W. Coughlan (U3-25) and bottom (U3-1); p. 208 (M1-38); p. 229 (M1-7); p. 241 (M1-1); p. 243 top (2-59) and bottom (B1-6)

New Westminster Archives: p. 68 inset

Pacific Biological Station: pp. 115, 117

Peter Schwarze, Schwarze Photographers, Nanaimo: p. 127

Parker Williams family: p. 187

Stannard family: p. 134

Front cover: Paul Grignon, "Harbour City," acrylic, 24" x 36", 1984

Back cover: Jan Peterson

Index

HUB CITY

HUB CITY

Peck, Thomas E., 26
Pendleton, Frank, 71
People's Steam Navigation Co., 32
Phillipps-Wolley, Clive, 46
Pimbury, Edwin W., 104, 135, 141
Pittendrigh, G.E.T., 142
Place, Jack, MLA, 187, 204, 206, 210
Planta, Albert Edward, son of Joseph,
wife Amy (Gordon), children, 35,
49; mayor, 81-83, 104, 149, 161-63,
217-18
Planta, Joseph Phrys, 77, 89
Policing, 74-83; jail, 210-12; 76
Population, 74
Port Alberni, 25, 103, 192
Portrey, Isaac, 203
Post office, 61, 76, 131, 166; Big
Frank, 201
Praeger, Dr. Emil Arnold, 141
Princess Royal pioneers, 55, 107, 132
Prior, Edward G., 11, 15, 124-25, 179,
184
Pritchard, James, 182
Prohibition, 216-19
Protection Island, Gallows Point, 28,
33, 83, 194; mine, *see* Vancouver
Coal Company/Western Fuel
Company; Mine Cage Disaster, 233-
34; *Oscar* incident, 199-202

Quennell, Edward, wife (1) Julie
(Wilcox), (2) Maria (Biggs),
Quennell & Sons, 57-58, 90, 141,
185

Randle, Joseph, WFC, 181
Raybould, William, wife Phoebe
(Shakespeare), 90, 92-93
Red Cross Club, (Canadian Red
Cross), 148-50, 236, 240
Red Fir Lumber Company, 70, 171
Red Gap, 71-73
Robins, Samuel Matthew, wife Maria,
10, 11, 17, 21-23, 101, 116, 181;
attitude toward Chinese, 44-45
Robson, John, wife Susan, 87-88
Royal Commission on Chinese
Immigration, 44-45
Royal visit, 242-44
Rudd, John M., 174, 217
Rummings Bottling Works, 136-37
Russell, Thomas, WFC, 181

Sabiston, John, 26; Enas, 33; Peter,
88, 141

Schools, Central/John Shaw, 164,
200; Crace Street, 15; Middle Ward,
200; North Cedar, 58; Thomas
Hodgson, 163; Quennell, 200
Scotch Bakery, Evans Brothers,
Jerome Wilson, George Leask, 134-
35
Seaforth Highlanders, 206-7, 220, 226
Shakespeare, Noah, 91
Shaw, John, 143, 164, 195, 217; calls
for military, 206
Shepherd, Frank (Harry), MP, 158,
185, 201, 204-5
Shepherd, Henry, 167
Ships, 106, 112, 130, 142; *Alcedo*,
35; *Alpha*, 33-34, 75; *Amelia*, 32,
166; *Beaver*, 24-26; *Cadboro*,
62; *Cariboo Fly*, 26; *Charmer*,
194; *City of Nanaimo*, 31-32,
130, 189, 193; *Cutch*, 29-32, 105,
107; *Estelle*, 34; *Isabel*, 93, 105;
Islander, 106; Joan, 31-32, 106,
151, 189, 193-94; *Kootenay*, 34;
Maude, 25-26; *Nanaimo*, 33-34;
Otter, 25, 175; *Pekin*, 12; *Princess
Mary*, 193-94; *Princess Patricia*,
195; *Princess Victoria*, 143-44,
193; *Quadra*, 194-95; *Rainbow*,
105; *Robert Dunsmuir (Dirty
Bob)*, 29-30, 130; *R.P. Rithet*, 32;
Tynemouth, 89; tugs *Czar*, 130-31,
189; *Nanoose*, 189. *See also* the
Oscar
Shipyards, 32-34
Silver Cornet Band/Nanaimo Brass
Band, 33, 90, 106, 166, 240, 242.
Sisters of St. Ann Convent church,
school, 16, 150-52
Sloan, William, wife Flora (McGregor
Glaholm), son Gordon, Sloan and
Scott, MLA, MP, 108-9, 112, 224,
233, 240
Smith, Ralph, wife Mary Ellen
(Spear), 95-96, 144-45, 184-85,
242; death, 220
Snuneymuxw, 37-41, 88, 149; mining,
16; logging, 65-66; longshoremen,
37; Indian Act, 38; schooling, 40;
fishing, 62-64, 168; flu, 236
Social Democratic Party, 167
South Wellington, 48, 112, 155, 204,
210, 240
Sports, 97-105, 139, 166
Stannard, Francis John, F.J. Stannard
flour and grain store. *See also*

286

The Author

Jan Peterson was born in Scotland; she immigrated with her family to Kingston, Ontario, in 1957. In 1972 she moved to the Alberni Valley with her husband Ray and their three children. She is recognized for her many years of involvement in the arts and in community service, for her skill as an artist, and for her interest in history. Jan is the author of five books: *The Albernis: 1860-1922; Twin Cities: Alberni-Port Alberni; Cathedral Grove: MacMillan Park; Journeys down the Alberni Canal to Barkley Sound; and Black Diamond City: Nanaimo—The Victorian Era.*